DR LACHLAN GRANT OF BALLACHULISH,
1871–1945

DR LACHLAN GRANT
OF BALLACHULISH,
1871–1945

Edited by
Ewen A. Cameron
and
Annie Tindley

First published in 2015 by
John Donald, an imprint of Birlinn Ltd

West Newington House
10 Newington Road
Edinburgh
EH9 1QS
www.birlinn.co.uk

ISBN: 978 1 906566 74 6

The publishers gratefully acknowledge the support
of the Wellcome Trust and the Carnegie Trust
for the Universities of Scotland
towards the publication of this book

British Library Cataloguing-in-Publication Data
A catalogue record for this book is available on request
from the British Library

Typeset in Garamond by
Koinonia, Manchester
Printed and bound in Britain by
Bell and Bain Ltd, Glasgow

Contents

PART II   A Selection of the Writing and Speeches
of Dr Lachlan Grant

Acknowledgements

The editors would like to gratefully acknowledge the financial support received in support of the research for and publication of this volume from the Wellcome Trust (Research expenses grant WT095208MA) and the Carnegie Trust for the Universities of Scotland (Publication grant). The editors would also like to thank the various archives and libraries from which the transcribed material has been selected, including the Trustees and staff of the National Library of Scotland, the *Lancet*, the *British Medical Journal*, the Working Class Movement Library, Salford and The National Archives. Copyright material from the Ramsay MacDonald papers is reproduced by permission of the granddaughter of the Late Malcolm MacDonald.

List of Contributors

Ewen A. Cameron
Sir William Fraser Professor of Scottish History at the University of Edinburgh

Annie Tindley
Senior Lecturer in History at the University of Dundee

Roderick MacLeod
Retired General Practitioner, Ballachulish

Allan I. Macinnes
Professor of Early Modern History, University of Strathclyde

Patricia Whatley
University Archivist, University of Dundee

John Stewart
Professor Emeritus, Glasgow Caledonian University

Neville Kirk
Professor Emeritus, Manchester Metropolitan University

Marjory Harper
Professor of History, University of Aberdeen

Andrew Perchard
Senior Research Fellow, Centre for Business in Society, Coventry University

Introduction

EWEN A. CAMERON AND ANNIE TINDLEY

This book is a consideration and evaluation of the life and work of Dr Lachlan Grant (1871–1945), general practitioner, medical researcher, social and political campaigner in the western Highlands. Grant has received some attention from historians, including a recent biography, but this book is the first major attempt to evaluate his contributions across a wide variety of fields and to present him in his own words.[1] This volume takes a dual approach, therefore; firstly, it presents the reader with a series of essays covering the important aspects of Grant's thinking and his contributions to social, economic and political debates of his time. Secondly, a selection of his writings, speeches, reports and correspondence is presented, organised thematically to support the structure and content of the essays.

Before turning to introduce the essays in more detail it is important to make some comments on the source material relating to Dr Grant. We are fortunate, indeed, to have a 'Lachlan Grant Collection' at the National Library of Scotland.[2] This is a fascinating body of material organised by Grant and his family into a series of volumes replete with newspaper clippings of articles penned by Dr Grant and relating to his activities. Although there is not a vast body of correspondence which could give us an insight into his private thoughts or behind-the-scenes politicking there are some interesting letters between Grant and his eminent friend J. Ramsay MacDonald. There are also some letters from his co-agitator in the Highland Development League, Rev. Thomas Murchison. There is also a good selection of photographs of the Grant family and material relating to the highly successful Gaelic-singing career of Mrs Grant as well as evidence for aspects of the local

---

1 R. MacLeod, *Talent and Tenacity: Dr Lachlan Grant of Ballachulish, his Life and Times* (Colonsay, 2013), 20–1.
2 Edinburgh, National Library of Scotland, Acc. 12187.

history of Ballachulish and the surrounding area. All of the essays in
this volume have made use of this collection and it clearly represents
a key source for the life and times of Dr Grant and provides evidence
for a range of wider topics, not least the associational culture of Gaels
in lowland Scotland, there being myriad cuttings relating to ceilidhs
and other gatherings in Glasgow, Paisley and elsewhere in the Scottish
lowlands. Grant also figures prominently in the manuscript collection
of J. Ramsay MacDonald held at the National Archives of the United
Kingdom in London. In some ways this collection is as valuable for the
student of Grant as his own collection in Edinburgh. Grant was in the
habit of sending to MacDonald copies of his journalism, offprints of his
many essays on diverse subjects and the other side of his correspondence can be found here.[3] MacDonald was a very controversial figure.
His biography, from his illegitimate birth in Lossiemouth in 1866 to
his occupancy of Downing Street as the first Labour prime minister in
the government of 1924, is well-known and has been frequently told.[4]
MacDonald headed the second minority Labour government in 1929
but ensured his lasting obloquy in the Labour tradition by agreeing to
remain in office as premier of a 'National government' from 1931 to
1935. Both he and his son, Malcolm MacDonald, lost their seats at the
general election of 1935 and a famous cartoon plays on the massacre of
Glencoe by depicting them in a Highland landscape, wearing kilts and
thumbing a lift from a car marked 'National government'. Father and
son made their way back to Parliament at by-elections in 1936 and 1937.[5]
MacDonald's friendship with Grant has not been noted by any of his
major biographers but it was clearly warm at a personal level, although
the correspondence lays bare their political disagreements on a range of
topics, not least the economic development of the Scottish Highlands.
The friendship might be considered of more than passing interest in a
wider sense because of the strand of writing which emphasises Ramsay
MacDonald's liking for hob-nobbing with the landed aristocracy and
leading socialites, as opposed to the land reformers and leading socialists

---

3 London, The National Archives of the UK, James Ramsay MacDonald Mss,
   PRO30/69/1518.
4 D. Marquand, *Ramsay MacDonald* (London, 1977) is authoritative as a
   biography and a chronicle of the shifting attitudes to MacDonald.
5 E. A. Cameron, 'Rival Foundlings: The Ross and Cromarty By-election of
   February 1936', *Historical Research*, 81 (2008), 507–30.

from earlier circles of acquaintance. His most controversial friendship was with the marchioness of Londonderry, herself the granddaughter of the 3rd duke of Sutherland, and among their mutual interests was the folklore of the Scottish Highlands.[6] The friendship with Grant, himself outside the mainstream of Scottish left-wing activity, might be seen as an important line of continuity through the various personal and political vicissitudes that punctuated MacDonald's career.

As the second section of this book is designed to show, Grant was a voluminous writer in many registers. He wrote frequently and at length for the *Northern Times*, an advanced Liberal newspaper published in Golspie. By the 1920s and 1930s there were fewer Highland outlets for the campaigning journalism of a figure like Grant. The important titles which had sustained the various radical Highland causes of the late nineteenth century, such as the *Oban Times* or the *Highland News*, were pale shadows of their former selves and no longer carried much political news or radical opinion.

The essays presented in the first section deal with Grant's thinking on issues as diverse as medical provision in the rural Highlands and Islands, emigration, land reform and economic development. For Grant, as should become apparent, these were interlinked in a holistic manner. This can be seen in the range of material he published across a long public career which encompassed a period of fast-paced change. The second section of the book, showcasing his most important written and spoken contributions, aims to demonstrate this.

The volume starts with two biographical pieces on Grant, so the reader can see the range of his life and work. The first is provided by his biographer, Roddy MacLeod, in the form of an appreciation. Dr MacLeod was one of Dr Grant's successors as the GP at Ballachulish, and brings both a medical and social perspective to Grant. This is followed by a biographical sketch of both Grant and Ballachulish by Allan Macinnes who brings intimate knowledge of the community in which he grew up in the years after Grant's death.

The rest of the essays in section one address a specific aspect of Grant's career and thinking, although they should not be seen in isolation. As each contributor makes clear, these issues were interlinked in Grant's mind, and his holistic approach to the challenges facing the people

6 Marquand, *MacDonald*, 687–92.

and economy of the Highlands and Islands constitutes one of his most powerful influences.

Grant trained as a doctor, and excelled as a medical student and researcher at the University of Edinburgh, in the late nineteenth century.[7] Section one opens with two chapters addressing this facet of his life. Firstly, Patricia Whatley discusses Grant's major contributions to the debate surrounding the provision of medical care in the Highlands and Islands from the early twentieth century. Medical care was supported during this period to some extent by the Scottish Poor Law, but very few general practitioners or nurses were working across the region. Difficulties with transport, communications, housing, working conditions and pay meant that many people living in the region simply went without medical attention. Grant was one who campaigned for this to change, as can be seen in his evidence to the Dewar Committee, set up in 1912 to investigate issues around medical provision in the region, and reproduced in section two of this volume.

Secondly, John Stewart uncovers the fluid nature of medical research and bio-medicine in Scotland during Grant's lifetime.[8] It was against this background that Grant pursued his own medical career, firstly in Edinburgh, but later among the people of the western Highlands and Islands, to the medical care of whom he was deeply committed.[9] This can be seen in his establishment of a laboratory in Ballachulish to support his own practice and that of many doctors in the region, and also by his many contributions to the medical press, some of which are reproduced in section two of this book.

Medicine was the basis of Grant's education and career, but his contributions spread out in many directions, some arising from his various passions, but others by local circumstances. Neville Kirk's essay takes one of the latter in his discussion of the Ballachulish-slate-quarry dispute in the first decade of the twentieth century.[10] As described in the essay, Grant found himself at the centre of a dispute between the Ballachulish

7 MacLeod, *Talent and Tenacity*, 23.
8 A. Crowther and M. Dupree, *Medical Lives in the Age of Surgical Revolution*, (Cambridge, 2007).
9 J. Stewart, 'Sickness and Health', in L. Abrams and C. Brown (eds), *A History of Everyday Life in Twentieth Century Scotland* (Edinburgh, 2010), 228–53.
10 N. Kirk, *Custom and Conflict in the 'Land of the Gael': Ballachulish, 1900–1910* (Monmouth, 2007).

Slate Quarry Company and its employees over which had the right to appoint or dismiss Grant as medical officer to the quarrymen. The case highlighted the often unfair contractual conditions faced by general practitioners in rural Scotland, and was taken as far as the Court of Session. It also convinced Grant of the importance of the trade-union movement, something he would transfer to other aspects of his outlook, such as land reform.

Grant was a man of broad views, as the two essays by Marjory Harper and Annie Tindley demonstrate. Grant regarded the population of the Highlands and Islands as its greatest resource, and wrote in increasingly strident terms about the dangers to the 'race' represented by the large-scale emigration from the region in the 1920s and 1930s.[11] Marjory Harper's essay puts these views into their historical context and considers the experiences of the migrants themselves, alongside an analysis of Grant's views on this pressing issue.[12] Land was the other great resource represented in the region. Land – what it represented economically, but also socially, culturally and historically – was central to Grant's views and in this he was in line with most thinking on the Highlands and Islands, since the late 1870s in particular.[13] Grant was an advocate of economic diversification but he also recognised that much of the economy would necessarily have to be based on innovative approaches to land use. As such, he argued that land tenure and the ways in which the economic proceeds from land were distributed would have to change, and these views are teased out in the essay by Tindley.

Economic diversification of another type is discussed in detail by Andrew Perchard in his essay on Grant's role and experience as medical officer for the British Aluminium Company's operations in the western Highlands from the 1920s. This was exactly the kind of large-scale, industrial development that Grant had been calling for in the Highlands, and he was a fierce supporter of the Company as a major employer, and aluminium as a product, promoting its use for domestic and medical

---

11 M. Harper, *Emigration from Scotland Between the Wars: Opportunity or Exile?* (Manchester, 1998), 202, 209–10.

12 M. Harper, *Scotland No More? The Scots Who Left Scotland in the Twentieth Century* (Edinburgh, 2012), 77–8.

13 J. Hunter, *The Making of the Crofting Community* (Edinburgh, 1976); E. A. Cameron, *Land for the People? The British Government and the Scottish Highlands, c. 1880–c. 1925* (East Linton, 1996).

instruments and tools. As Perchard discusses, this may have led Grant to refrain from outright criticism of the Company's safety and environmental record.[14]

In his later career Grant's commitment to the cause of Highland development, discussed in Ewen Cameron's essay, came to the forefront of his concerns. In many ways this adherence was nothing new to Grant; he had been espousing ideas of economic development and diversification for decades, but in the 1930s these found an organisational focus and touched a nerve in public and political opinion.[15] Grant, compiling the many strands of his thinking, called for root and branch reform in the political and economic approach to the needs of the people of the Highlands and Islands, and utilised his personal connection with the leading politician J. Ramsay MacDonald, to further this aim.

Taken together, these essays present a rounded view of a man who campaigned on many different fronts across a long and productive career. We will end this introduction by asking some broader questions about his relevance and importance in twentieth-century Scottish history.

Firstly, what does his career tell us about political and social leadership in Highland society over the first half of the twentieth century? Grant was able to make a contribution to many important debates on policy direction and development for the region by occupying a position of social (and economic) authority.[16] He was one of a very small cadre of middle-class, educated professionals living and working in the rural Highlands. Alongside men such as ministers, teachers and estate managers, doctors like Grant, by virtue of their urban education, links to literary and newspaper circles and inevitable membership of a range of clubs, societies and organisations, held an influential position in Highland society. Grant was certainly prepared to use this position to the best of his ability. While Grant advocated positions which could be placed in a tradition of Highland activism, he was also an unrepresentative and non-representative figure in the debate about the Highlands.

14 A. Perchard, *Aluminiumville: Government, Global Business and the Scottish Highlands* (Lancaster, 2012).

15 E. A. Cameron, *Impaled upon a Thistle: Scotland since 1880* (Edinburgh, 2010), 50, 162.

16 See, for example, A. Tindley, "'They sow the wind, they reap the whirlwind!' Estate Management in the Post-clearance Highlands, *c.* 1815–*c.* 1900', *Northern Scotland*, 3 (2010), 66–85.

His positions were individualist and he was a self-conscious leader unburdened with the need to engage in much consultation with those whom he sought to represent. An unkind view of Grant would be that he was highly confident that, as far as the interests of the Highlands and its population were concerned, he knew best. A more favourable view would be that he had a coherent view of the kind of policy which would best bring about a transformation of the region and he was determined to articulate it at every possible opportunity. That this vision was extremely 'top down' and dependent on major industrial interests merely meant that he was in the mainstream of progressive opinion about the means of economic development and social transformation in the 1930s.

Given the advantages of this position, what was his overall impact on the changing economic and social landscape of the Highlands; that is, did he live to see the reforms and developments he had campaigned for take root in the region? The picture here is mixed. The arrival of the British Aluminium Company in the western Highlands certainly met his views of the dire necessity for economic diversification in a region still dominated by agriculture and fishing in a period when neither was doing particularly well. It would only be after Grant's death in 1945, however, when the first hydro-power schemes were laid down, a policy for which Grant had long campaigned as making the most of the Highland's rich natural resources. Land reform, in the form of land settlement schemes, was all but over in the Highlands by 1930 and emigration, although slowing to a trickle in the 1930s, would remain a central challenge to government and Highland society, as would rapid depopulation well into the 1970s. Overall though, the kind of holistic vision or programme of interlinked and complementary investment and reform that Grant envisaged never came to pass. While Grant would have been pleased to have seen the establishment of the Highlands and Islands Development Board in 1965 (while pointing out that it was at least thirty years too late), the depressing limitations of the party political system and changing priorities after the Second World War would perhaps have disillusioned him.[17] National priorities would overtake the claims and demands of regions, especially those as sparsely populated as the Highlands and Islands. Grant might be said to provide a bridge between the radicals

17 J. Burnett, *The Making of the Modern Scottish Highlands, 1939–1965: Withstanding the 'Colossus of Advancing Materialism'* (Dublin, 2011).

of the 1880s who helped to bring to prominence issues relating to the Scottish Highlands and post-1945 activists who focused their activities on lobbying government. In pointing out that there were ambiguities, at the very least, in Grant's career is not to differentiate him from either his predecessors or successors in Highland activism. This was true of Crofter MPs such as Charles Fraser MacKintosh and Donald Horne MacFarlane who were both accused at various times of trimming their views to suit the circumstances in the way that Grant might be said to have done in his playing down of health and safety issues in aluminium smelters in the 1930s. An interesting comparison might be pursued between Grant and Roderick MacFarquhar. MacFarquhar, born in Inverness in 1908, was involved in radical Labour activity in the Highlands but was drawn to Scottish nationalism later in life, partly from his disappointment at Labour's ineffectiveness on Highland affairs. Although not so strident a supporter of industrial development, MacFarquhar was a persistent advocate of the notion of a Highland Development Authority and he became a vocal critic of the HIDB as, in his view, it failed to tackle vested interests and was insufficiently radical on questions relating to land and crofting.[18]

Lastly, what does Grant's contribution tell us about the period covered by his life as a whole, from a Highland and wider Scottish perspective? It is an obvious point to make, but clearly, Scottish society, particularly in the Highlands and Islands, changed rapidly and fundamentally between the 1870s and 1945. In the Highlands there was a marked change as the population began to decline; the state legislated successively in 1886, 1911 and 1919 to manage and negotiate land holding, and started its long road to becoming a significant landowner in its own right. In Grant's own field of medical science great leaps were made with the introduction of bio-medicine, the advancement of surgical techniques and the discovery of penicillin in the 1920s; what was within the realms of possibility for a rural general practitioner to achieve changed almost beyond recognition. Lastly, Britain's political system embraced the full electoral franchise of men and women and, as we can see in the efforts Grant made to encourage or expedite change, the ways and means of influencing the political system changed. For Grant, this did not always equate to change

18 J. N. McRorie, *The Highland Cause: The Life and Times of Roderick MacFar-quhar* (Regina, 2001), 177–220.

for the better, and he supported self-government in Scotland as the best available means to achieve meaningful reform.

Grant's life and career therefore illuminates many of the key issues facing Scottish society –urban and rural – in the first half of the twentieth century. It illustrates the diversity of thinking on governance, administration and political economy in Scotland during these decades, and as such has warranted this volume on his life, writings and times.

Dr Lachlan Grant (1871–1945)
An Appreciation

RODERICK MACLEOD

Lachlan Grant was born in Johnstone, Renfrewshire, in 1871. He spent his early years in that Scottish industrial town. Both his parents were native to the town, and his paternal grandfather had lived there for some years, though originally a native of Dingwall in Ross-shire. This in effect gave the boy a Highland ancestry. However, Lachlan Grant may never have set foot in Ballachulish, or come to spend his days there, had it not been for the catastrophic collapse of the City of Glasgow Bank in 1878, which bankrupted his father and wiped out the family's carpentry and saw-milling business. From that state of penury the family were rescued by Lachlan's aunt, Annie Barr (nee Grant), who relocated *en famille* to North Lorn where she took lease of the local stores in Ballachulish, and set up in business as Barr & Coy, General Grocers, Drapery and Ironmongery Stores, in the slate-mining village. The year was 1880, and young Lachlan was then nine years of age. In Ballachulish the 'immigrant' family reframed their lives and worked up the business, to prosper once more. In those bygone days North Lorn and the whole County of Argyll was very much a stronghold of the Gaelic language and culture, home to the National Mod, and a cradle to shinty. That indeed was the milieu in which the whole Grant family were marinated.

Overall, the family integrated well socially and culturally into this west Highland community, and Lachlan, like his siblings, was educated at the local public school. Though his schooling was over at the age of 14 years, his intelligence was spotted and fully recognised. His headmaster and the local United Free (UF) minister, who were both notable classicists, coached and tutored him for a time, then passed him on to a private tutor in Glasgow, whereby he gained his university entrance qualification. At Edinburgh University medical school he was a star student, who graduated with distinction in 1894 at the age of 23 years. Through ongoing study Grant accumulated a galaxy of higher medical degrees and awards.

As a result he was talent-spotted by two eminent Edinburgh consultants who made him their protégé, with a view to creating academic succession. No account of Lachlan Grant would ever be complete without reference to his academic qualifications in medicine and an examination of the maternal side of his family. With regard to his medical degrees, he had gained just about all the recognised degrees that a general practitioner of his time could qualify to sit. In 1894 he graduated from medical school with an MB CM (with distinction), followed by an MD (with Commendation) in 1896. In 1911 he added the DPH, the RCPS Edin. and the RFPS Glasg., leading to his award of the FRFPS Glasg., in 1921. Early on in his medical career, in 1906, he was appointed a Justice of the Peace for the County of Argyll, and so added the appellation to his name. These awards speak well of his academic achievements and prowess. He seemed destined for a glittering career in either ophthalmology or psychiatry. Yet it was at this point that Grant made clear his own career plan, and his wish to honour an earlier promise (made to himself) to return to the Highlands to 'practise medicine among his own people'. Thus Dr Grant made good his escape from the ivory towers of Edinburgh, heading first for Oban, but in the same year (1895) his appointment as the medical officer at Gesto Hospital took him further north to Skye. Gesto was a 12-bedded care unit that was funded from the legacy of an island benefactor who had made his fortune as an indigo planter in India. Opened in 1876, it was the only hospital then in the whole of Skye, and the only such facility on the island to provide clinic-type care, inpatient and dispensary services. As medical officer, Grant was single-handed throughout his four to five years in post, assisted only by a matron and minimal ancillary staff. The set-up was the complete antithesis of what had been his experience in Edinburgh. It was physically and professionally demanding work, with little back-up support. Besides, the grim social surroundings and the grinding poverty on view must have been emotionally draining for him. Indeed, the evidence is that the nearly five years he spent on Skye were to greatly influence him, and recalibrate his political thinking. The island at the time was in the immediate aftermath of the land war of the 1880s, with land reform top of the agenda. There a lasting impression was forged that undoubtedly focused his own mind on the future reforms for which he craved.

A return home to Ballachulish on appointment as medical officer to the Ballachulish Slate Quarries Company in 1900 was looked upon as the ideal scenario until, within two years, Grant was dismissed from his post by the quarry management. This led to the now infamous episode in Highland history, the 'Ballachulish Lock Out', a dispute that lasted 18 months, with recourse to the law courts and an appeal to the House of Lords. The stress of that period could well have broken Dr Grant were it not for the fact that his great and good friend, his future brother-in-law, Angus Clark, proved to be such a capable leader of men. The loyal support he received from the quarrymen (to a man) throughout the 18-month-long dispute also proved crucial to the final successful outcome: Dr Grant's reinstatement as medical officer to the quarries' company, the quarrymen and their families, and the north Lorn neighbourhood.

Once the quarry disputes were resolved, Dr Grant emerged unscathed and went on to champion the causes dear to his heart – the crofters and cottars, local transport improvement, fostering new local industry such as the building of the Blackwater Dam, the pipe-line, the Power House, the factory and the new village of Kinlochleven. Incredibly, Dr Grant had overall medical responsibility for up to 3,000 men, at various times in the construction phase. The new industry of aluminium smelting, powered by hydro-electricity, and the transformation of the head of Loch Leven from two sparse hamlets, divided by a river, into the dynamic, populated place Kinlochleven village became, gave Dr Grant huge satisfaction. The 'City among the Hills' he lovingly christened it, and the project from beginning to end could not have had a more doughty champion. In the words of his daughter Mrs Sheena Roddan, 'I can't remember a time when father was not actively involved in pursuing the means by which to promote jobs for Highland people.'

The state of medical health care throughout the Highlands and Islands greatly concerned Grant, so it was with huge relief on his part he saw the government set up the Dewar Committee, to examine the deficiencies that racked the service. When it came to Dr Grant's turn to present his evidence before the committee in Oban on 28 October 1912, he was well prepared. Grant concentrated on solutions to the problems presenting. Therefore, he must have felt fully vindicated, and delighted, when, through the Dewar Committee, the government accepted these recommendations in full, and set up the Highlands and Islands Medical Service in 1913 to put the measures into effect. Such a health care and social reform seemed almost beyond one's wildest dreams, but Lachlan Grant viewed them in a philosophical and phlegmatic manner. It just had to happen.

A new direction had to be paved. What is revealing, though, is that Dr Grant had all along been advocating the creation of a national medical service that covered the entire country and every citizen within it. In this matter he was well ahead of his time and his peers. For such vision Grant deserves much greater credit than has hitherto been paid to him. But at least it was the one campaign he fronted that brought the greatest good to the greatest number of people. And to be counted a success.

While the Great War cut across everyone's aims and plans, Dr Grant kept up campaigning without pause on land issues, land resettlement, protection for the west coast inshore fishermen (the Sea League), the need for new industry and the development of hydro-electric power, with Foyers, Fort William and Kinlochleven providing examples. This ultimately brought Grant to national notice in the 1930s, when he published his pamphlet *A New Deal for the Highlands*. In this plan he was ably assisted by many like-minded colleagues, especially the Rev. Tom Murchison of Skye, Glenelg and Govan, and the veteran Liberal politician, Johnnie Bannerman (the late Lord Bannerman of Kildonan). On all these noble aims and political matters Grant also formed a close and beneficial relationship with Tom Johnston, the remarkable Secretary of State for Scotland. At the end of the day the question of delivery by a southern-based parliament and government caused proponents, like Grant, much anguish and no little despair. Besides, a gathering world war, and engagement in it, served to sap their strength and dash all hope.

Dr Grant enjoyed an exquisite friendship with Ramsay MacDonald, the prime minister, which takes most people by surprise. Many among the public knew there was a bond between the two men, but the depth and intimacy of that friendship is what is not appreciated, and is revealed in personal letters, holiday postcards and personal gifts, exchanged between them (and family members). True, on journeys north or south the prime minister would arrange his pit-stop at Craigleven (the Grant family home), visit the Grants, have a meal or a dram, and toast himself before the roaring open fireplace! Likewise, Dr and Mrs Grant would receive their invitation to luncheon at Number 10 with the PM and, usually, his daughter Ishbel, who often acted as her father's host. In 1932 it was Dr and Mrs Grant who welcomed, and bid adieu to, the PM when he visited the National Gaelic Mod at Fort William. This, incidentally, was the year following Mrs Grant's tie in the Mod Gold Medal competition; MacDonald always showed great interest in her singing success.

One intriguing question which inevitably hangs over Grant, in view of his lifelong interest in campaigning for reform on social matters, and the 'rights of man', is why he himself did not transfer to politics and set his sights on Parliament? He had every chance to do this, and one particular opportunity in 1936, in the Ross and Cromarty by-election. But in spite of all the advantages he harboured, over others, it did not happen.

The combination of such character and intellect admirably equipped Lachlan Grant for the role of single-handed general practitioner in a remote and rural setting; physically isolated from professional colleagues. He embodied a confidence that was well-placed, and never shaken. From within his medical practice he gave clinical lead, and brought enhanced medical services, as a benefit, to his own people, for example, in public health improvements, personal health education and social medicine in its accepted sense. Indeed, preventive medicine was very much his agenda – the value of good nourishment, physical exercise, activity and sport, personal hygiene and public vaccination, he always emphasised.

Furthermore, the value of early accurate diagnosis in the context of best outcome for the patient, prompted him in 1930 to provide his own bacteriological laboratory service, which he extended to other GP colleagues at the time in north Argyll and south Lochaber. His recognised interest and expertise in ophthalmology enabled him to offer such a service to his patients, and extend the provision of spectacle lenses to them, an innovation in itself.

To Dr Grant, it would appear that necessity was indeed the mother of invention, for it stimulated him to create his own solutions to some of the clinical problems of the day. Cross infection and puerperal infection were of major medical concern then (as now), with an often fatal result to the patient. To address the issue Grant devised a portable reservoir with wash spray, to enable doctor or nurse to 'scrub up' under fresh flowing water, and not recycle bacteria. His additional creation, by use of the 'new metal', aluminium, to fashion an improved throat swab, had hygienic advantage over the historic iron and copper ones, and conferred greater diagnostic value and accuracy in the swabbing of tissue for bacterial analysis. As a tool in use for making early and specific diagnosis, the invention won professional recognition. These two examples are typical illustrations of Grant's probing mind.

All in all, Dr Grant's fifty years in medicine was a remarkable record in itself, and his very many and varied interests show how extensive and deep his hinterland was. He enjoyed music, played the piano, provided musical accompaniment, in private and public, for his wife's Gaelic singing, played golf, enjoyed photography, wrote and published countless pamphlets, read extensively, and staunchly supported the ancient game of shinty, being president of the Ballachulish Shinty Club for over forty years. Indeed, his life, as he lived it, was not about 'all work and no play'. Lachlan Grant retired from medicine in 1945, and died shortly after. He ended his days peacefully at home in Craigleven on 31 May 1945, and three days later his funeral service at home and at the Appin graveside was conducted by his local pastor and his great and good friend, the fellow veteran campaigner, the Rev. Thomas Moffat Murchison.

Dr Lachlan Grant
A Qualified Appreciation

ALLAN I. MACINNES

For the forty-five years prior to his death in 1945, Dr Lachlan Grant was medical officer for Ballachulish and vicinity in the North Lorn district of Argyllshire. Not only was he a conscientious general practitioner, but he was also a medical researcher who developed his own laboratories to provide best practice for his patients. He was much more than a highly respected GP, however. He was a steadfast supporter of Gaelic culture and a visionary promoter of Highland development by land and sea. Above all, he proved himself a heroic figure in the dispute between management and workers in 1902–3, when his removal as medical officer to the slate quarriers led first to a lock-out and then a strike. This industrial dispute, which was marked by local violence against scab labour imported from Glasgow to remove slates, won the support of the Labour movement from Keir Hardie to the Scottish Trade Union Congress. Grant, who in no way condoned the violence, showed immense personal fortitude in publicising the case against the grasping opportunists who ran the Ballachulish Slate Quarry Co. Ltd, whom he fought all the way to the Court of Session and its appellate jurisdiction. A settlement was eventually reached which restored Grant as the medical officer to the East and West Laroch quarries before the case came before the House of Lords.

Grant, a debonair character and pioneer motorist who initially favoured the Argyle car, went on to become a leading promoter of open health services in the Highlands from 1913, which, it has been argued, presaged the creation of the National Health Service after his own death. In the interim, he proved himself a resolute political activist and formidable polemicist for the purposeful development of indigenous and industrial resources in the Highlands. He was particularly active in this respect during the 1930s, a decade of unremitting hardship in the Highlands. Amongst his affiliations were the Sea League (1933), the Highland Development League (1936) and the Skye Crofters Association (1938). In this context, he can be viewed as a significant contributor to the Scottish Renaissance in politics and literature during this depressing decade. Along with his close collaborator, The Rev. Dr Thomas Murchison, he even faced charges of parliamentary contempt in propagating his radical ideas. His ultimate legacy to the Highlands, albeit not instituted until 1965, was the Highlands and Islands Development Board, which sought to diversify the Highland economy while conserving the crofting communities in north-western Gaeldom.

Although I was born four years after the death of Dr Grant, I was very conscious of his legacy, his influence and his friendship to my own and many other families in Ballachulish. He was indeed viewed as a heroic figure for his role in the lock-out/strike of 1902–3, for his staunch support of shinty and other aspects of Gaelic culture, such as individual and choral singing, in which the village excelled. It was not only in medicine, industrial relations and cultural activities that the Grant family impacted on the villagers of Ballachulish, Glencoe and Kinlochleven. Grant's parents, aunt and brothers ran Barr's Stores, the major supplier of provisions until the advent of the Co-operative Stores in the 1950s. For a time they also ran the passenger shipping to the aluminium works at Kinlochleven, until squeezed out by MacBraynes. Their dominance of provisioning was relatively benign and analogous neither to a parasitic truck system nor to the malevolent monopoly of supplies that John MacDougall Hay excoriated in his novel *Gillespie* (1914), based on Tarbert, Mid-Argyll.

As literature no less than history bears out, however, heroic figures are not best served by hagiography which transcends time and stretches if not suspends belief. Growing up in Ballachulish in the 1950s, the pillars of village life since the late seventeenth century – Episcopalianism, Gaelic culture and slate quarrying – were in marked, indeed critical, decline. We have to evaluate Dr Grant's life and achievements set against this local triangulation. As a member of the United Free Church (which declined to merge with the Church of Scotland in 1929), he was not directly connected to Episcopalianism, the confessional mainstream for slate quarriers, which was running out of Gaelic-speaking clerics. Although the United Frees were predominantly urban bourgeoisie, their adherents in Ballachulish included some of the more radical slate quarriers, including Grant's brother-in-law Angus Clark, who were to the fore in the lock-out/strike of 1902–3. Clark went on to make his fortune in London as a financier in shipping, operating through the

East India Docks, before returning to Scotland (to Stirling) as a major developer of extractive industries. Grant and Clark, like most other Highlanders, were also caught up in the tide of Anglicisation which saw English not Gaelic as the language of progress in the twentieth century, a view certainly shared by my own parents, as Gaelic culture was being undermined by education, preaching and broadcasting in English. Grant was undoubtedly part of this process in his polemical writings, albeit this is easily justified in the attempt to gain the widest possible currency for prospective Highland developments. Grant was particularly open to American social and economic ideas. His and Dr Murchison's promotion of a Highland Development Board was based on the Tennessee Valley Authority promoted by President Franklin D. Roosevelt to bring the Unites States out of depression in the 1930s. His development ideas, which were treated with supercilious condescension by civil servants in the Scottish Office, had one major omission: there was no place for slate quarrying. When the Ballachulish quarries closed ten years after Dr Grant's death, what had once been a trickle became a flood, as families of quarriers emigrated to Australia, New Zealand, Canada and the United States.

His role with regard to slate quarrying leaves Dr Grant most open to criticism. A few specific points can be instanced. Firstly, Grant showed undoubted fortitude in 1902–3 in standing up against a ruthless capitalist enterprise. Nevertheless, he did not have to endure the dire sufferings and hardships of workers who either had to relocate to quarries in Luss on Loch Lomond, Luing and Easdale on the Argyllshire Slate Islands or to undertake daily walks of over twelve miles in the hills to create a trout loch for a sympathetic local landowner, Major Bullough. Grant certainly mobilised public sympathy for the plight of the quarriers, but he did not endure the mountain travails of my own grandfather, Paul Macinnes, as a blacksmith-cum-navvy. Secondly, poor industrial relations in Ballachulish did not end in 1903. There were strikes and other significant unrest in 1905, 1911, 1923 and 1937. On these occasions, Dr Grant was a peripheral figure at best, notwithstanding his strong personal connections to such politicians as Ramsay MacDonald, John M. Bannerman, Angus Sinclair and Tom Johnston. Thirdly, in the reconstruction of the balance between capital and labour in the quarries (the most productive in Scotland from the mid-nineteenth century) in 1907, 1918, 1922 and 1937, Grant was again a shadowy figure, even when a workers' co-operative was operating as a Friendly Society in association with the local Haldane landowners between 1922 and 1937. Likewise, he seems to have played no significant role when Angus Grant sought to develop alternative slate and quartzite quarries in 1934. When the Haldanes, with their Liberal Party associates, Charles Tennant and Co., the petro-chemical aggregate, seized control of the quarries in 1937 and gradually phased out worker participation in management over the next ten years, Grant's presence was minimal. Fourthly, although Grant assiduously promoted better medical conditions for those under his charge, these cannot be divorced from living wages and sound housing. It was not until the 1950s that Argyll County Council, not the quarry owners or the medical officer, transformed the housing stock with the removal of the quarriers' rows that characterised East and West Laroch – just before the quarries closed permanently in 1955.

In conclusion, Dr Lachlan Grant was indisputably an upstanding man of his time. Beyond his uncontested medical achievements, this well connected and visionary professional sought to improve the condition of the Gael and promote industrial diversification in the Highlands. He was a steadfast supporter of the aluminium works at Kinlochleven and of the potential of hydro power. He apparently accepted, however, that slate quarrying had run its course well before his death. Grant over-stretched his commitments to regional development, albeit his frustration with central government's mismanagement of the Scottish Highlands led him reluctantly to espouse the cause of Home Rule. Perhaps this makes him a figure for the present as well as his own time!

PART I

Interpretation

CHAPTER 1

'A full State medical service'
The Development of Medical Services in the Highlands and Islands, 1845–1936

PATRICIA WHATLEY

In his evidence to the Highlands and Islands Medical Service Committee on 28 October 1912, Dr Lachlan Grant suggested 'a new departure', recommending that a 'full State medical service' should be established within the Highlands and Islands.[1] His words were prophetic: in 1913, a centralised and unique Highlands and Islands Medical Service (HIMS) was established which embraced many of the issues he had raised in his evidence. This chapter will examine the background to the new service in the Highlands, primarily the role and the impact of the Medical Service Committee, known as the Dewar Committee, to gather information on the adequacy of the medical service in the Highlands and Islands and to make recommendations on how it might be improved.[2] It will also consider and assess the development and impact of the HIMS.

By the mid-nineteenth century Scotland's economy and infrastructure were adjusting to the stresses placed on it by rapid industrialisation and urbanisation. Within the Highland counties large areas of the north and west were still reliant on a subsistence economy, which influenced the nature, scale and effectiveness of medical assistance available in each region. The impact of that tension within society and the economy resulted in mounting levels of pauperisation, as the Poor Law struggled to cope with increasing levels of poverty. Consequently, following a two year enquiry, the Poor Law (Scotland) Act 1845 created a new central administrative body, the Board of Supervision, which had oversight of newly formed local Parochial

---

1 *Minutes of Evidence of the Highlands and Islands Medical Service Committee*, vol. 2, Cd 6920, 1913, Q. 19,719, p. 394.
2 The Highlands and Islands Medical Service Committee was referred to as the Dewar Committee, after the chair, Sir John A Dewar, MP for Inverness-shire. *Report of the Highlands and Islands Medical Service Committee*, vol. 1, Cd 6559, Minute of Appointment, 11 Jul. 1912.

Boards, which had the power to raise funds at the local level by assessment. In 1847 a Medical Relief Grant (MRG) was established which required that all participating parishes should appoint quali-fied medical officers, with fixed salaries, to attend the registered poor with the intention of increasing the efficiency of medical relief to that specific section of the population.[3] A few years later the Physi-cians' Enquiry Report of 1851 demonstrated for the first time the difficulties of providing medical services to the population of the Highlands and Islands, within the constraints of remoteness, difficult terrain and lack of medical personnel.[4] Few doctors were resident in the Highlands and ministers and other lay individuals carried out medical procedures or assisted the doctors. Many of the doctors were older, with little or no up-to-date medical knowledge. Salaries were low and doctors were reliant on the fee as parish doctor. General fees for treatment of the non-pauper population were often not paid. Working conditions were hard and the distances covered were long and arduous. The factors which resulted in poor medical services were, therefore, both geographical and economic.

By 1880 some limited progress in the provision of a medical service had been made and within the c. 160 Highland parishes only six did not employ a doctor.[5] Increasing numbers of doctors did not, however, neces-sarily lead to improvements in the medical service and general health of the population; physical conditions resulted in long waits for the doctor, while insanitary dwellings, a poor diet and the continuation of local customs and folk medicine militated against any improvement made in medical provision.[6] For those doctors employed in the Highlands life was not easy: they had no security of tenure, long working hours and extensive travel within their practice, lived in poor housing or lodgings, had no pension provision or holidays, often did not receive their fees

---

3　The Medical Relief Grant was established by Parliament during the financial year 1847–8 as part of John Peel's scheme to relieve local rates, *Local Govern-ment Board Report on Poor Law Medical Relief,* vol. 1, Part 3/5, 1904, p. 6.

4　Royal College of Physicians of Edinburgh (RCPE), CK4, 11, Physicians' Enquiry, 1852.

5　*Parish Medical Officers (Scotland),* HMSO, London, 1905. The return to the Physicians Enquiry in 1852 had stated, 'The people of Gigha feel the want of medical aid much; and complain of such want as a great deprivation.' Little had changed since 1850.

6　Dewar, *Report,* 7–13.

from an impoverished population and were professionally isolated.[7]

Medical provision for those insured under the National Insurance Act, who were located in the Highlands, was not guaranteed. The debates leading to the National Insurance Act in 1911 intensified the prevailing view, discussed at length in Parliament, that poverty in the Highlands would prevent the new legislation being implemented.[8] This, together with economic depression, land wars, increasing destitution in the western Highlands and a radical, modernising Liberal government, was undoubtedly a key factor in the establishment of the Highlands and Islands Medical Services Committee in 1911.

The Dewar Committee, having among their members three prominent medical experts who provided specialised knowledge on aspects of social welfare and practical experience of working in the Highlands, was an impressive body of professional knowledge and expertise, with significant personal experience of economic and social conditions of the Highlands and Islands.[9] Evidence was collected by enquiry schedules requesting information from doctors and other professional and local individuals, and during a programme of visits to localities in the Highlands and Islands. The areas under examination were the counties of Argyll, Caithness, Inverness, Ross and Cromarty, Sutherland, Orkney and Shetland, and other localities in the Highland District of Perthshire. The enquiry sought information on all groups of Highland society, especially on the class which was ineligible to participate in the National Insurance Scheme, but not poor enough to be entitled to poor relief. The report, which provides a comprehensive account of life in the Highlands during 1911 was published on Christmas Eve 1912, five months after the Committee was established. The Minutes of Evidence were published seven months later in mid-1913, containing an impressive 23,558 questions and responses and a 159-page index.[10]

The Report set out the general factors hindering the efficiency of the medical provision in the Highlands and Islands. The circumstances

7 Dewar, *Report*, 13–16.
8 *House of Commons Debates*, 18 March 1912, vol. 35, cc1519–21.
9 The medical expertise came from Dr W. Leslie MacKenzie, medical member for the Local Government Board for Scotland; Dr John Christie McVail, deputy chairman of the National Health Insurance Commission for Scotland and Dr Alex Cameron Miller, a general practitioner in Argyll.
10 Dewar, *Report*, 2–3.

of the people was a major factor. Many of them were unable to pay doctors' fees; insanitary dwellings led to disease and compromised the effectiveness of medical treatment; primitive customs and habits prolonged the use of traditional cures at the expense of professional medical treatment. An inferior diet, both from inadequate availability of nutritious wholesome food and the increasing consumption of tea and white bread in place of milk and porridge was also a problem.[11] The increasing burden of local rates was viewed as a major factor preventing parishes improving medical provision. For example, in Uig parish (Lewis) the rates rose from 10s 1⅓d to 23s 3¾d in 1912, which was echoed in other parishes of the Western Isles and, to a lesser extent, other western seaboard parishes. The cost of retaining a doctor, there-fore, represented 'a heavy charge on an otherwise overburdened rate'.[12] The final general point raised was the partial operation of the Insur-ance Act in the non-industrial Highland counties where employment was often seasonal and temporary, placing most workers outside the compulsory terms of the Act and unable to afford to pay voluntary contributions.

Within that general context the Committee concluded that medical provision was unlikely to be adequate, not as a result of too few doctors practising in the Highlands, as doctors often did not have a high consultation rate, but due to uneven distribution of them throughout the Highland counties. Conditions affecting the adequacy of medical services included the lack of motor-cars: doctors used a variety of means to carry out their work, many having no alter-native but to walk. Few doctors had their own means of transport, except perhaps a bicycle, and were often forced to hire a horse and cart, often with a considerable walk over rough ground to reach the patient. The benefits of having a telephone service between doctors' homes and post offices were clear in the evidence to the Committee. The potential advantage of being able to speak to patients before a visit, allowing doctors to take the correct appliances and drugs, was stressed.

11 This point was also made by the duchess of Atholl in *Working Partnership*, where she recalled the evidence given by a doctor in Barra, 71. Katherine Marjory Murray, duchess of Atholl, *Working Partnership: Being the Lives of John George, 8th duke of Atholl and his wife Katherine Marjory Ramsay* (London, 1958).

12 Dewar, *Report*, 12.

It had been anticipated by the enquiry that doctors' incomes would be low but the evidence collected showed that many doctors were earning levels 'well below the level of income tax'. From that they had to pay their living expenses and many were also supporting a family. The 'Return of Information from Medical Practitioners' showed that of 47 doctors who provided the information, 28 were earning an average gross income of £200, which left, after rent and travelling expenses had been deducted, a net annual income of £120. This put the average net income of the 47 doctors just over the tax limit. The lowest figure given was £100 gross income, which gave the doctor a net weekly wage of between a pound and thirty shillings.[13] This can be contrasted with doctors' incomes of £800 to £1000 a year in Lancashire and Yorkshire.[14] Doctors' salaries were dependent on parish salaries and fees from private practice. A consequence of low, insecure incomes was that doctors were unable to save or provide for old age or retirement, lengthening the working life of a doctor practising in the Highlands and Islands. Consequently doctors continued working long into retirement.[15]

The recurring question of security of tenure for doctors, a major issue raised by Lachlan Grant, remained unchanged throughout the nineteenth century and first decade of the twentieth century. It was believed to prevent 'good' medical men from accepting posts in the Highlands. Doctors were thus vulnerable to the actions of Parish Councils who had the power to remove them from office and had no right of appeal available to them.

Another important issue which was reported throughout the enquiry was the persistent lack of provision and poor quality of housing for doctors. Despite the fact that parish councils were very keen to keep their doctors, and were legally bound to provide medical care for the registered poor, little effort was made to ensure adequate accommodation. The burden of the rates on Parish Councils was heavy and if little local support was available or forthcoming, then there was not much they could do. In many instances doctors were forced to provide their own houses and surgeries, sometimes by building them.[16]

13 Dewar, *Report*, 14.
14 Dewar, *Evidence*, Q. 7,228.
15 Dewar, *Report*, 14.
16 Dewar, *Evidence*, Q. 19,498.

Doctors in the Highlands were seldom able to take a holiday; their income did not permit the cost of a locum, if one could be obtained, which was by no means certain. This was considered a serious problem. Firstly, doctors could not relieve the strain, both physical and mental, of arduous Highland practices and, secondly, they were unable to take post-graduate courses to keep abreast of new developments in medicine. It was considered that a doctor who had been unable to attend post-graduate courses for ten years would be lacking in up-to-date medical knowledge and unless he was able to keep abreast of new developments at home 'would not even know the terminology of disease'.[17] The implications for the adequacy of medical provisions are clear.

The Committee concluded therefore that inadequate salaries, pensions and holidays and insecurity of tenure, together with the difficulties of communication and finding an acceptable house to live in, all affected the general effectiveness of the medical services provided. The Report also demonstrated the inadequate nature of medical attendance by citing high numbers of uncertified deaths and illnesses not attended, as disclosed by school medical inspection and in the continuing use of patent medicines and traditional cures.

Nursing provision was found by the enquiry to be one of the most vital factors affecting the effectiveness of medical provision. Both doctors and non-medical witnesses were unanimous 'that no matter affecting the welfare of the people of the Highlands and Islands is more urgent than the provision of an adequate supply of trained nurses'.[18] Lord Lovat, when questioned on the role of nursing, was even more adamant stating 'The medical salvation of the Highlands lies [. . .] in organised nursing'.[19] In 1900, when Lachlan Grant took up office in Ballachulish there were 225 trained Jubilee nurses working in Scotland, only 32 of them located in the Highlands. Of the 32, seven nurses were located in the burghs of Tobermory, Campbeltown, Inverary, Oban, Stornoway and Lerwick, leaving only 25 in the rural parishes.[20] By 1912 there were 232 Jubilee nurses in Scotland, 49 were working in the Highlands, 13 of whom worked in the burghs. Only 36, therefore, were located in

17 Dewar, *Evidence*, Q. 1,725.
18 Dewar, *Report*, 20.
19 Dewar, *Evidence*, Q. 2,312.
20 *Queen's Nurses in Scotland, Twelfth Annual Report of the Council of the Scottish Branch of the Queen Victoria's Jubilee Institute for Nurses*, 1900.

the rural parishes, an increase of only 11 trained nurses in 12 years. The provision of skilled nursing in the Highlands, as in the rest of Scotland, also relied on County- and Parish-Council funding and the voluntary effort of individual benefactors and philanthropic agencies (although the Argyllshire Nursing Association funded 31 nurses throughout the county).[21] In the Highlands some landowners also organised nursing services to tenants, such as those delivered by Mrs Mackintosh of Mackintosh, who initially provided nurses during a diphtheria epidemic in Lochaber and subsequently provided two cottage nurses and a trained Jubilee nurse in Lochaber and in Strathdearn.[22] Nurses, of course, whoever employed or funded them, faced the same conditions as doctors, including long journeys to patients and poor housing.[23]

Hospital provision was also regarded as 'particularly vital to the adequacy of medical provision in the Highlands and Islands'.[24] In 1912 only 20 hospitals existed in the Highlands and Islands. The largest hospital was the Northern Infirmary in Inverness, with 68 beds. The Gilbert Bain hospital in Lerwick was opened in 1902, near the site of the original isolation hospital, which was itself opened in 1841. The 19 others had an average of 11 beds. Many areas were without even basic hospital provision. Together with the lack of hospitals, dispensaries and druggists were rare. The provision of drugs in the Highlands and Islands fell largely on the medical practitioners due to the lack of dispensing chemists in many localities. Medical graduates of Scottish universities were qualified pharmacists and thus authorised to supply drugs.[25] A Lewis doctor claimed: 'It is one of the biggest expenses to me in this island. It is an awful drain on my purse.'[26] By not receiving payment for medical attendance therefore, doctors were not only poorly remunerated for their time expended but also for drugs prescribed.

The findings of the Dewar Enquiry echoed those of the Physicians' Enquiry almost 50 years earlier.[27] While improvements to the

21 Dewar, *Evidence*, Q. 252.
22 Dewar, *Evidence*, Q. 2,238–42.
23 Dewar, *Report*, 24.
24 Dewar, *Report*, 25.
25 Dewar, *Evidence*, Q. 11,674.
26 Dewar, *Evidence*, Q. 11,521.
27 Dewar, *Report*; Physicians' Enquiry, Royal College of Physicians of Edinburgh (RCPE), 1852.

infrastructure of the Highlands eased communication and travel to a certain extent and Imperial grants and public health developments assisted the treatment of infectious diseases, this also placed a heavy burden on parish rates.[28] There was most certainly a greater awareness of the conditions, but structurally, the ability of the rural medical practitioners to work and live in those areas had remained very similar since the Poor Law Act of 1845 and those improvements which did occur were positioned within virtually the same administrative structures which had been established over 60 years earlier. To increase administrative efficiency Leslie Mackenzie recommended a scheme for the consolidation of the various medical services, within a dual structure of local committees and an overarching central committee, made up of the Local Government Board, the National Insurance Commission, the General Board of Lunacy and the Scotch Education Department, which would allocate the Imperial Grant.[29]

The conditions that Lachlan Grant reported to the Dewar Committee were therefore validated by the findings of the enquiry. The general recommendation of the Dewar Committee was unambiguous:

> It is clear that having regard to the economic conditions prevailing in the Highlands and Islands, the extent to which the foregoing services are at present subsidised from Imperial funds is quite inadequate, and that as local resources are in many parishes already well-nigh, if not wholly, exhausted, any general amelioration of the existing medical service cannot be achieved without a further and more substantial subsidy.[30]

It recommended that an additional Imperial grant should help develop the medical and nursing services and their administration and provide a 'more satisfactory financial basis for general medical practice'. The improvements were also intended to incorporate nursing and hospital provision and a specialist service. The recommendations contained in the Report were debated at length in Parliament and were unanimously accepted by the government. The Highlands and Islands (Medical Service) Grant Act was passed in August 1913, less than a year after the Dewar Committee presented its report to Parliament.

28 Dewar, *Report*, 34.
29 Mackenzie's scheme is in Appendix 1 of the Dewar Report, 49–50.
30 Dewar, *Report*, 41.

The Dewar Enquiry had recommended a sum of £42,000 for the new grant, the estimates 'largely speculative but the result of a good deal of discussion'.[31] The grant was to provide for a number of schemes designed to cover adequate medical attendance, nursing provision, hospital provision, special maternity grants, payment of telephone rents and administration costs.

The Dewar Enquiry and the visits of the Committee to the localities had raised public awareness of the issues surrounding the provision of medical service in the Highlands and the conditions to be found there.[32] It had thus generated goodwill for the potential for change. When the HIMS was established and its Board appointed there was, therefore, an anticipation of rapid improvement, for both the conditions and salaries of doctors and nurses and for medical care for those living in the Highlands and Islands. However, early progress was considerably delayed and that goodwill was initially dissipated. The delays were partly the responsibility of the Board. The circulation of the Circular Letter to all doctors was significantly weakened by the Board not placing a financial limit on the responses. By doing so it received suggestions for improvements which far overran the available grant of £42,000. It had the effect of raising local expectations and at the same time confirmed the magnitude of what needed to be achieved in each area to secure an effective medical service. The visits to the localities by the HIMS Board, so soon after the Dewar Committee also became a source of discontent, with a perception of the Board wasting time and resources.

However, the main issue that caused delays was the need to reformulate the schemes following a late decision of the Treasury not to have a two-tier system within the HIMS, such as had been recommended by Mackenzie in the Dewar Report. The decision to place the administration solely in the hands of the Board and not have local administrative committees required the complete reworking of schemes, which delayed their approval till August 1915, almost two years after the HIMS was established. Dissatisfaction of doctors also arose from the administrative burdens of the grants and the increase

31 Edinburgh, National Records of Scotland (NRS), HH65/74, Correspondence from L. Mackenzie to Sir James Dodds, 13 January 1913. That sum was to prove inadequate to fund the HIMS schemes.
32 NRS, HH65/5, Highlands and Islands Medical Service, general papers, 1914.

in their workload. A further issue leading to dispute was the cost of attendance on insured persons. The grant of £42,000 included the sum of £10,000 (approved prior to the publication of the Dewar Report) connected with the attendance on insured persons in the Highlands and Islands, which was administered by the Insurance Commissioners. The corresponding grant for the Lowlands was £16,000, a disparity between the Highland and Lowland Insurance payments which was an increasing source of dissent between the doctors, the British Medical Association and the Board.[33]

The publication of the first report was also delayed and questions were asked in Parliament and in the *British Medical Journal*. By that point war had broken out and the finances of the Service were frozen. Although the unspent funds accumulated each year the lack of substantial progress was damaging to the reputation of the HIMS. Post-war inflation prevented any progress in the schemes apart from the Medical Service, and that was limited in the early years to travelling costs. The Board, therefore, lost goodwill during the early years and from that point the British Medical Association was intent on protecting its doctors from any reduction in their conditions of work or salaries.

The war was to have serious repercussions on the newly founded Medical Service, both in terms of the availability of funds during the war and the subsequent rise in post-war costs. Payment of the Medical Service Fund was suspended and, as a result, short-term ad hoc measures had to replace solid long-term planning for structural change. At the inception of the Service the supply of doctors and nurses fell as the armed forces enlisted medical personnel, 'tempted by the new opportunities'.[34] The *British Medical Journal* also attributed the fall in supply of doctors to the increasing numbers of young men 'whose attention was directed to science' choosing alternative careers as engineers and in the chemical industries, and the poor conditions in the Highlands faced by doctors. That included 'the faulty administration of the Parish Councils and the overbearing attitude assumed

---

33 The new grant therefore was effectively £32,000; the estimates of £42,000 thus immediately represented a shortfall in the estimated costs of the Dewar Committee.

34 'The Prospects of Young Doctors', *BMJ*, 2:2766 (3 Jan. 1914), 51.

in some districts by the representatives of the landowners'.[35] The Board worked in cooperation with the Scottish Medical Emergency Committee to try and fill posts left vacant as a result of the war.[36]

The need to amend and seek approval for the revised schemes following the slow decision of the Treasury and Scottish Office not to have local administrative committees, was cumulatively responsible for affecting public opinion and diminishing the level of confidence in the potential of the Service. Therefore, those who have written uncritically of the HIMS do so from limited knowledge of how the Service operated and developed in practice.[37] The HIMS struggled to establish the schemes after the war and through the 1920s. It was simply under-resourced.

A report of the Consultative Council for Medical Services in the Highlands and Islands in 1927 was a crucial point in the development of the HIMS.[38] The report documented clearly that although some progress had been made in the Medical and Nursing Services, there were still weaknesses in the numbers and distribution of nurses, and that housing for both doctors and nurses were limited to refurbishment of older houses which were few in number. The Consultative Council recommended a sizeable increase in the grant, and although the Treasury refused to increase the grant, they did agree to a variable amount which could be voted for each year. It was only after 1929, when additional funding was made available and the HIMS was incorporated by the Department for Health for Scotland, that real progress was made. The Local Government Act 1929, in expanding the functions of the County Councils and increasing their resources, made it possible for equitable partnerships to be established. By the 1940s the dissent from doctors had disappeared and the HIMS was acceptably established.

35 Ibid.
36 *Scotsman*, 9 July 1915, 8.
37 M. McCrae, *The National Health Service in Scotland* (East Linton, 2003). McCrae begins his book on the National Health Service in Scotland with a chapter on the HIMS. It has limitations in its analysis and is factually incorrect in several areas, including the initial administrative structures of the HIMS and in the level of progress made. Lacking effective primary research it documents general and unmitigated progress; examination of the Treasury and Scottish Board of Health (SBH) files contradicts this picture.
38 The National Archives of the UK (TNA), T161/1304, S2433/2, Report of the Consultative Council on the Highlands and Islands, 1927.

Therefore, what did the HIMS achieve and how successful was it? In 1851, 75 GPs were employed in the Highlands. By 1912 there were 170 doctors, many of whom had insecure incomes, poor working conditions and no job security. There were very few fully trained nurses. By 1935, 153 doctors had arrangements with the HIMS and seven were employed directly by the Service at a cost of £47,500, and 198 nurses were employed by 30 grant-aided nursing organisations at a cost of £18,500.

Though the numbers of doctors (entering into agreements with the Medical Service) remained fairly static, the Dewar Committee were correct in stating that few additional doctors were required. The quality of doctors working in the Highlands, however, was perceived as having improved, with younger doctors attracted by better working conditions and salaries, though salaries still lagged behind those in the more populous areas. However, it was a more secure minimum income, together with improved housing and access to locums. Specialist services were established, including orthopaedics and gynaecology and a full-time surgeon was employed at Lewis hospital in 1924. A proposed new hospital in Lerwick costing £45,000 was subsidised by the HIMS by £36,000 and the general hospital in Inverness was developing into a hub for Highland surgery.[39]

The HIMS was most successful in the very remote areas where doctors' incomes were guaranteed and where the employment of trained nurses removed some of the burden from them. Improvements in the telegraph and telephone made it easier to communicate with patients and nurses, and the air ambulance service provided a vital means of transporting doctors to sick patients and in removing patients to hospital. The employment of an experienced doctor employed directly by the Board to act as a locum, Dr Shearer, who enabled doctors to have holidays and professional development, was a liberation for those who could benefit from his and other locums' attendance.[40] In addition, fully trained nurses could ease the workload of a doctor. The requirement of the HIMS for nurses to be under the supervision of doctors at all times and, on the other hand, be placed in districts – such as islands – where no doctor was available, or in remote areas not close to the

39 A. Shearer, 'The Highlands and Islands Medical Service, What It Is and What It Has done', *Transactions of the Edinburgh Medico-Chirurgical Society*, 1938.
40 Shearer, 'Highlands and Islands Medical Service', 101.

doctor was a paradox which was dealt with by adhering to the rule if it was possible and ignoring it if it was not. That demonstrates pragmatism in the actual running of the HIMS: flexibility was essential.

Was the HIMS a 'complete State system' as Lachlan Grant had envisaged, and a precursor to the National Health Service (NHS)? The items in Grant's model of a State service – adequate salary, housing, the need for holidays and post-graduate classes, specialist services, increasing mobility of doctors and an efficient nursing service – were all included in the HIMS model. His vision was the product of his medical education and his drive to raise the calibre of medical provision in the Highlands, as well as his early travel and post-graduate education in Canada and the US, where he would have experienced remote areas similar to the Highlands. He argued in the *Edinburgh Medical Journal*, 'for a separate independent, governmental department' and 'a nationalisation of the whole medical service and the 'reorganisation and coordination of all medical and Public Health activities'.[41] The HIMS attempted to do all of those things. Just as it has been argued that the Liberal reforms laid the foundations for the creation of the welfare state some forty years later, the HIMS has been cited as also being an important step in that direction. It was unique in providing low-cost care to the poor, but those entitled to reduced fees were clearly delineated as the non-registered poor, the crofter and cottar classes and the dependents of insured individuals. It was not a free service to all and those who, before 1913, had paid the standard fee of the doctor, continued to do so. It was, rather, an example of the modification of the Victorian self-help ethic within the context of a publicly-funded subsidised service for a particularly vulnerable section of society.

The principle of local contribution was paramount and was applied with ruthless effectiveness by the Treasury, which clearly did not understand the circumstances of the Highlands: poverty, lack of employment, in some areas few cash incomes, and the relentless pressure on the rates. The ambiguities of the poor-law principles, sitting side-by-side with the new social welfare reforms were encompassed within the HIMS, self-help and government intervention,

---

41 R. Macleod, *Dr Lachlan Grant of Ballachulish: His Life and Times* (Colonsay, 2013); N. Kirk, *Custom and Conflict in the 'Land of the Gael': Ballachulish 1900–1910* (Monmouth, 2007); quotations from *Edinburgh Medical Journal* from NLS, Lachlan Grant Collection, Acc. 121187/1.

with no means testing. In 1948 William Beveridge wrote *Voluntary Action*, acclaiming the voluntary sector at a time when the state was significantly increasing its role. The State was required, through its own actions, to forge a course between national and local provision, with the 'weight assigned to statutory and voluntary agencies'.[42]

The factors of remoteness, inclement climate and island communities were (and still are) obstacles to reaching the sick and disincentives to encouraging doctors to move to Highland practices. Doctors in remote areas require greater 'medical initiative and self-reliance' than in more populated areas, where specialised services are more readily available. From the practitioners' viewpoint the HIMS, for some, provided a real element of security and income. However, from the outset doctors complained to the central authorities about the time-consuming administrative burden associated with HIMS grants. Reactions to the announcement of the schemes were built upon long-standing dissatisfaction with the administration required of doctors. The dissatisfaction was not short-lived. From 1915, following the announcement of the full range of the Board's schemes, significant discontent felt by many Highland doctors was voiced in the *British Medical Journal*. Though the preparation and announcement of the schemes was one of the Board's main achievements since its inception in 1913, their reception was at best lukewarm and in some areas actively hostile. The schemes were considered 'radical, sweeping and subversive', and were compared to problems experienced at the onset of the National Insurance Act 'marred by many of the same faults'. 'A feeling almost bordering upon dismay' was the reaction to the grant scheme.[43]

While the HIMS was unique in providing medical services to all for a minimum fee, it was not an unmitigated success. It was, however, an important factor in the development of the NHS in Scotland and facilitated amendments to the structure when the tri-partite model was not successful in some rural areas. A clear conclusion is that, regardless of the processes which are put in place, any system for the provision of medical services in rural and remote areas will be affected by the difficulties of access and the challenges of attracting professionals to those areas.

42 A. Digby and J. Stewart (eds), 'Welfare in Context', *Gender, Health and Welfare* (London, 1996), 2, 8.
43 NRS, HH65/6, Reported in Allocation Fund, general file.

CHAPTER 2

Medicine and Healthcare Provision in Scotland in the First Half of the Twentieth Century

JOHN STEWART

This essay addresses three issues. First, we examine trends in medicine and health from the late nineteenth century to the middle of the twentieth century, which is the era in which Dr Grant lived and worked. We shall also note the rather alarming mismatch between Scotland's role in advancing medical science and its own actual health outcomes. Second, and more briefly, we describe in general terms the organisation of health care services in Scotland in the same period, focusing in particular on what has long been seen as the problem of supplying health care in geographically remote and challenging areas, such as that in which Lachlan Grant worked. And third, and again briefly, we say something about how the particularity of Scottish health services and health outcomes led to the creation of a separate National Health Service (NHS) for Scotland under the terms of the National Health Service (Scotland) Act 1947.

First, then, changes in medical science and technology. The latter part of the nineteenth century saw huge breakthroughs in medical science, including the establishment of germ theory. What this showed beyond doubt was that certain micro-organisms, germs, were responsible for the spread of certain diseases. These kinds of scientific breakthroughs ushered in the era of what is now described as biomedicine, a form of medical science which argues that cures for disease can be found primarily through scientific, often laboratory-based, means. Another important aspect of biomedicine was that it tended to focus on the individual rather than on the broader population. We return to this below for, as we shall see, there are other ways of analysing and addressing health problems. One implication of germ theory, though, was that if you could destroy such organisms or prevent their presence the spread of disease or infection might be halted. And of course one of the great proponents of anti-sepsis was Joseph Lister who was Professor of Surgery at both Glasgow and Edinburgh Universities in the mid-nineteenth century, posts which were not only clinical but also had important teaching functions.[1]

There are two important points for our story here. First, Lister's work in Scotland highlights the fact that Scottish medicine and medical education were among the best in the world. Not only were important breakthroughs such as anti-sepsis being pioneered in Scottish hospitals, Scottish medical schools were so highly thought of that they attracted students from beyond the country's borders and indeed were net exporters of doctors throughout the nineteenth century and beyond. It is no exaggeration to say, for example, that the medical services of the Empire on which the sun never set were largely staffed by graduates of Scottish universities. Our second point is that it was in this environment that Lachlan Grant was educated. He took his medical degree at Edinburgh in the late nineteenth century and so would have been acutely conscious of Lister's impact upon medical theory and practice. Against such a background it is thus revealing that one of Grant's professional responsibilities was as bacteriologist to Argyll County Council, a role in which he would have been required to analyse disease phenomena from a biomedical perspective.

So, for example, in an article in the *British Medical Journal* published during the First World War and dealing with the early diagnosis of pulmonary tuberculosis (TB) Grant wrote of the need to carry out a 'complete bacteriological and cytological [that is, analysis of the cells] examination of the sputum [...] at the earliest opportunity at the nearest laboratory'.[2] He was thus bringing the scientific knowledge he had acquired at Edinburgh University and subsequently to bear on a health issue, tuberculosis, which was highly problematic in the Highlands and Islands. It is therefore unsurprising to find that, in his evidence to the Dewar Committee, Grant acknowledged the significant place in his own work for bacteriological examination; that he did such work for other doctors; and that in so doing he sought to 'diagnose and treat patients by the latest modern methods'. He was thus 'convinced that for many diseases *laboratory methods* are nowadays absolutely necessary as an adjunct to clinical work'.[3]

---

1   A. Crowther and M. Dupree, *Medical Lives in the Age of Surgical Revolution* (Cambridge, 2007).

2   L. Grant, 'How is the Early Diagnosis of Pulmonary Tuberculosis to be Made?', *BMJ*, 1:2969 (24 Nov. 1917), 777.

3   British Parliamentary Papers, 1913, 'Highlands and Islands Medical Service

But tuberculosis is also a condition which alerts us to alternative explanations for ill-health and disease and again this is an area in which Scottish scientists played a prominent role. And this alternative explanation revolved around the idea that environment, broadly construed and so including not only physical environment but also matters such as personal hygiene, was at the very least an important contributor to individual and social health. Before discussing this, though, what can be said of the actual health of Scots in this period? There is no doubt that the health of the Scottish people significantly improved over the first half of the twentieth century. So, for example, the infant mortality rate, an extremely sensitive health indicator in any society, dropped from 128 in 1900 to 39 in 1950. Similarly, female life expectancy at birth in 1900 was 48 years whereas in 1950 it was 69.[4] Nonetheless, Scotland, then as now, compared badly with other parts of the United Kingdom and with other parts of Western Europe. One of the implications of this, and recognised at the time, was that purely biomedical explanations of ill-health and disease might be inadequate since they did not appear to explain, for instance, the significant differences in health outcomes by place, by class, by age and by gender. In other words, social and individual environment might be equally important in determining social and individual health.

So what we find in Scotland in the first half of the twentieth century are a number of investigations into the social and environmental causes of ill-health. Perhaps unsurprisingly, most attention was focused on the problems of urban Scotland, and especially Glasgow. But attention was also paid, directly or indirectly, to the Highlands and Islands. One of the most famous of these investigators was Sir John Boyd Orr, later to win the Nobel Prize for his research on nutrition. Boyd Orr, in a piece published in 1937, made particular note of what he considered the poor and deteriorating Scottish diet, and sought to address this in part by the regeneration of the Highlands and Islands. He noted the adverse impact

Committee. Minutes of Evidence Taken Before the Committee to Enquire Into the Provision of Medical Attendance in the Highlands and Islands of Scotland, with Index to Evidence. vol. II', Cd. 6920, Q. 19,669–19,671, 19,719. Emphasis in the original.

4 John Stewart, 'Sickness and Health', in L. Abrams and C. Brown (eds), *A History of Everyday Life in Twentieth Century Scotland* (Edinburgh, 2010), 228–53, at 231, table 9.1. The infant mortality rate is the number of child deaths under the age of one year per thousand live births.

of the outflow of population from the region and suggested the possibility of greater exploitation of its land to increase food supply. This, in turn, would help address the nutritional deficiencies generated by the social and individual environment in which urban Scots especially lived. Intriguingly, Boyd Orr appeared to agree with the proposition that if, for example, the rural to urban population shift of the nineteenth century was not reversed then 'the present economic system will collapse'.[5] It is revealing to see such arguments in the light of Lachlan Grant's then recently-published *New Deal for the Highlands.*[6] The broader context, of course, is the New Deal in the United States, much of which involved rural redevelopment.

More specifically, though, on the actual environmental conditions in the Highlands and Islands it is important to note, first, that, at least early in the twentieth century, in certain respects there appeared to be cause for optimism. A 1913 government report on the health of schoolchildren observed that for both the county of Inverness and the Island District and Western Seaboard very low levels of defective nutrition had been recorded. This was attributable, as one surveyor put it, to the 'almost universal use of porridge'. Oatmeal was a particularly healthy constituent of the Scottish diet and its decline was, at this point, much more evident in urban than in rural areas. On the issue of cleanliness, meanwhile, the same surveyor noted of Inverness county that 'much has been written and said about the dirt and proneness to contagious skin diseases of the Highlander'. It was therefore, and contrary to expectations, 'with great pleasure that one records that the very opposite is found to be the case'.[7] Here, then, were instances of environment, in the form of diet and personal hygiene, playing a positive role in Highlands and Islands health outcomes.

But the situation was more complex than this might suggest and here we consider one piece of evidence to the Dewar Committee which

5   Sir J. Boyd Orr, 'Scotland As It Might Be', in A. Maclehose, *The Scotland of Our Sons* (London, 1937), ch. 6.

6   L. Grant, *A New Deal for the Highlands etc.* (Oban, 1935).

7   W. L. Mackenzie, *First Report on the Medical Inspection of School Children in Scotland* (London, 1913), 54, 66. On the Scottish diet see D. J. Oddy, ''The Paradox of Diet and Health: England and Scotland in the Nineteenth and Twentieth Centuries', in A. Fenton (ed.), *Order and Disorder: The Health Implications of Eating and Drinking in the Nineteenth and Twentieth Centuries* (East Linton, 2000), 45–63.

brings us back to one of the scourges of the region in the first half of the twentieth century, tuberculosis. At almost exactly the same time as Highlands and Islands children were being commended for their health, the District Medical Officer of Health for Lewis reported that the island's poor, insanitary housing made it difficult to isolate TB patients. To make matters worse, patient habits such as spitting 'on the floor, and the floor of churches and meeting houses' scattered the tubercle bacilli everywhere and in such conditions it was impossible to expect anything other than 'a widespread prevalence of the disease'.[8] Here then was an acknowledgement that particular organisms, the tubercle bacilli, were the ultimate cause of a widespread disease alongside the argument that environmental conditions contributed to its spread. The obvious implication of this was, improve the environment and the incidence of tuberculosis will be reduced.

But what of Lachlan Grant? It was suggested earlier that he can be seen, by way of his role as a bacteriologist, as very much part of the newly-emerging biomedicine; and that biomedicine tended to prioritise the individual. But again the situation was rather more complicated. Grant gained his Diploma in Public Health in 1911, strongly implying that his medical interests lay not just in the laboratory but in preventive measures aimed at larger populations. Certainly, his laboratory science was going to help in his public health. Just to give one example from his own writings, in 1930 Grant published an article in the *Lancet* on how to prevent common infections such as boils and other forms of skin inflammation and infection. Such uncomfortable, embarrassing ailments are, of course, easily dealt with today but Grant was writing in an era which pre-dated the discovery of drugs such as antibiotics and when, in consequence, such infections could lead to blood-poisoning and possibly even death. Grant duly acknowledged the underlying cause of such conditions, namely various forms of pathogenic organisms such as streptococcus. As to prevention this lay, he suggested, in high levels of personal hygiene and in properly designed wash basins which incorporated taps with a downward flow which would thereby allow water to flush away harmful organisms rather than leaving them to reside, dangerously, within the sink.[9]

8 Cited in Stewart, 'Sickness and Health', 241.
9 L. Grant, 'A Note on Septic Carriers', *Lancet*, 216:5585 (13 Sept. 1930), 579–80.

Again at a much broader level, we find Grant telling the Dewar Committee that the system of health care provision he was advocating – a number of key aspects of which were to be found subsequently in the Highlands and Islands Medical Service – was 'really a system of police against disease'. It was then, and in the best traditions of public health, preventive in nature.[10] And Grant also engaged with a further aspect of the environment, that in which individuals worked. In a letter to the *Lancet* in the early 1930s he argued that the aluminium workers for whom he was responsible enjoyed good health because of the purity of the material and its products with which they worked. In the course of his twenty years of service, he claimed, he had 'never observed the slightest signs of ill-health, temporary or chronic, which could be attributed to the inhalation of alumina'.[11] Here, then, in Grant's view, was a healthy modern industry with a healthy modern workforce. Grant thus embodied two important strands in modern medicine, namely concerns with the findings and analyses of the laboratory combined with environmental approaches to preventive medicine.

But, as suggested earlier, environment is something we need to see in its broadest context and what we turn to now is a brief account of how Scottish health services were organised in the first half of the twentieth century. From around the time of the First World War those experiencing most types of ill-health or disease could receive treatment in two particular ways. The first of these was primary care, and for present purposes we focus on the general practitioner (GP) although other forms of primary care, such as dentistry, were also important. Access to a GP would depend on an individual's economic status, age, gender, whether or not they were covered by the National Insurance scheme introduced in 1911, and so on. This was all complex enough, even if you lived in an urban area, and the net effect was that working-class women in particular often missed out on this form of primary care. But such complexity was further compounded in remote and topographically challenging areas like the Scottish Highlands and Islands, where population was scant and widely dispersed and significant urban settlements relatively few. It could therefore be extremely difficult for patients to get to GPs, even if they in principle had access, and vice versa. Place, or what is still sometimes

10 'Highlands and Islands Medical Service Committee. Minutes of Evidence', Q. 19,719.

11 Letter, 'Aluminium and Health', *Lancet*, 218:5638 (19 Sept. 1931), 662.

called the 'distance effect', therefore became another determinant of the individual's access to primary care and we know from evidence to the Dewar Committee, for example, that in certain circumstances this could have fatal outcomes.

But suppose an individual had to be hospitalised? Again, the situation was complex but for present purposes there were two principal forms of hospital provision. The first of these were the voluntary hospitals, charitable institutions supported by various forms of voluntary donation. The most prestigious voluntary hospitals were the great teaching hospitals attached to university medical departments and to take the example of Lachlan Grant, his clinical training would have taken place at the Edinburgh Royal Infirmary. At the other end of the spectrum were small, local hospitals staffed by general practitioners. The problem with voluntary hospitals was that they were unevenly distributed across Scotland and, in any event, were almost exclusively urban institutions. The other form of hospital was that provided by the Poor Law, and later by local authorities. These were much more comprehensive in their coverage but, nonetheless, partly because of the dispersed population of the Highlands and Islands, their penetration in that region remained relatively poor. So as with access to GPs, place, or the distance effect, was again important.

And it was, at least in part, just such problems that the Dewar Report, and subsequently the Highlands and Islands Medical Service, sought to address. The latter is sometimes seen as a direct precursor of the NHS. This is something of an exaggeration. Nonetheless, the Service was a form of socialised health care which sought to address the particular problems of a remote part of the United Kingdom.[12] And the recognition of such problems had longer-term implications, and this is our final and concluding point. Discussions about the formation of the NHS in the 1940s largely revolved around the perceived need to do away with inequalities of access; and in many cases the need to pay for medical services. In the famous phrase of the time, health care should be universal, comprehensive and free. In other words, everyone should have access to health care as a right of citizenship; all aspects of health care should be included; and there should be no charge at the point of consumption. It

12 J. Jenkinson, *Scotland's Health, 1919–1948* (Bern, 2002); and the essay by Patricia Whatley in this volume.

is worth noting there that at least at the outset items such as spectacles and prescriptions attracted no cost to the patient.

But another aspect of health service reform in the 1940s was the agreement that Scotland should be treated separately. There was a range of justifications for this, but these included the physical geography of Scotland, by which was primarily meant the particular characteristics of the Highlands and Islands. Such peculiarities, so the argument went, were best dealt with by Scottish ministers rather than by the Ministry of Health in Whitehall.[13] And it was for similar reasons that the Scottish Parliament was given control of the health service as part of the devolution settlement of the late 1990s. More than this, though, the mechanism through which the Scottish health services, before and after devolution, is funded is the so-called Barnett Formula. In strictly financial terms, this disproportionately favours the Scots. But, once again, this has been justified by Scottish supporters of the mechanism on the grounds that, among other things, it remains extremely difficult to provide adequate health services to geographically challenging areas.[14]

So an individual such as Lachlan Grant gave evidence to the Dewar Committee in the specific context of his own medical views and his own medical training. But in seeking a particular solution to Highlands and Islands problems he and his colleagues were to highlight the health care challenges of the region and thereby to feed into a series of health care and political reforms whose ramifications remain with us to the present day.

13 John Stewart, 'The National Health Service in Scotland, 1947–1974: Scottish or British?', *Historical Research*, 76 (2003), 389–410.
14 John Stewart, *Taking Stock: Scottish Social Welfare after Devolution* (Bristol: The Policy Press, 2004), ch. 5.

CHAPTER 3

Lachlan Grant and 'A State of War' in 'The Valley of Glencoe'

NEVILLE KIRK

Introduction

Between 1902 and 1905 Ballachulish, described by contemporaries as a 'peaceful village', 'romantically situated' and 'embosomed by mountains', was shaken to its core by two major, protracted and unprecedented industrial and social conflicts.[1] The first, stretching from July 1902 to December 1903, and involving a twelve months' lockout, revolved around the Ballachulish Slate Quarries Company's dismissal of Dr Grant from his medical duties in both the Ballachulish quarries and the Parish Council district of Ballachulish. The second conflict, which had simmered throughout the previous winter and summer months, came to the boil in the summer of 1905. It was essentially an industrial relations dispute involving issues of hours, conditions, wages, employment and trade-union recognition in the quarries. Yet it also involved a physical attack on the house in Ballachulish of the unpopular quarry manager, Archibald MacColl. The latter had had been Grant's main local adversary during the first conflict. The aims of this chapter are to describe and explain these important, but much neglected, conflicts, and to draw out their wider historical and sociological significance.[2] To fully understand the conflicts, however, it is first necessary to place them in the contexts of the community and the workplace in which they arose.

---

1 The phrase, 'A State of War' in 'The Valley of Glencoe', was first used by 'Gavroche', the pseudonym of William Stewart, a member of Keir Hardie's Independent Labour Party, in the party's weekly organ, the *Labour Leader*, 17 Jan 1903.
2 For this neglect see N. Kirk, *Custom and Conflict in the 'Land of the Gael': Ballachulish 1900–1910* (Pontypool, 2009), 4–11. This book was first published by the Merlin Press (Monmouth) in hardback in 2007. All page references are to the 2009 paperback edition.

The Community and the Workplace

On most counts Ballachulish in 1900 was characterised by its homogeneity, harmony, cohesion and a very strong attachment to shared notions of local place, interest and purpose. These characteristics developed out of a combination of socio-economic, cultural and political factors.

In terms of socio-economic influences, it is useful to start with demography and geography. Ballachulish and its much smaller neighbour, Glencoe, had a combined population of around 1,500 in the 1890s, rising to 1,800 during the following decade. By the third quarter of the nineteenth century residential stability and very limited geographical mobility prevailed. As reflected in the census returns and the valuation rolls, the vast majority of Ballachulish's residents by the 1890s had been born and brought up mainly in Ballachulish itself or nearby parts of Argyllshire. Their parents were also locals rather than 'incomers'. The turbulent era of mass migration from the Highlands and Islands and Ireland, at least in terms of the experience of Ballachulish, had long passed. There also prevailed a very high degree of residential stability, with the inhabitants living, for the most part, either in the same house or on the same street for most of their lives. This settled and powerful physical attachment to the village and the locality constituted an important foundation upon which the villagers would build impressive support for the quarry workers and Grant and their opposition to the 'outside' company.[3]

The dominance of quarrying promoted homogeneity. By the end of the nineteenth century Ballachulish was 'more or less dependent' upon the slate industry for paid employment. The quarries, situated at east and west Laroch, dated back to 1693 and 1694. By the 1880s they had overtaken the 'Slate Islands' of the west as Scotland's 'foremost quarrying location' and employed in the region of 580 workers. Buoyed by the intensive demand created by urbanisation and industrialisation, Ballachulish exported roofing slates to markets not only in Scotland, but also in England, Ireland, America and other overseas destinations. Between 1895 and 1914, however, unsteady and generally falling demand, increased

---

3 Kirk, *Custom and Conflict*, 15, 19, 28–31; B. Fairweather, *A Short History of Ballachulish Slate Quarry* (Glencoe, 1974), 2; for similar residential stability in the slate quarrying communities of north Wales see R. Merfyn Jones, *The North Wales Quarrymen, 1874–1922* (Cardiff, 1983), 21–5, chs 3, 4.

competition, government inaction and the vulnerability of the industry to 'takeovers by city-based conglomerates seeking immediate return for their shareholders' led, in Ballachulish and elsewhere in Britain, to a period of catastrophic decline for the industry.[4]

The Ballachulish Slate Quarries Company Limited, which acquired a 27-year lease on the village's quarries in 1894, constituted an example of a city-based conglomerate. Based in Edinburgh, and chaired by Colonel Edward Donald Malcolm of Poltalloch, a Conservative and one of the foremost landowners in Argyllshire, the company made a conscious effort, from 1900 onwards, to jettison the paternalism generally practised by previous owners and lessees, most notably the Stewart lairds of Ballachulish. Employer paternalism constituted an integral part of a wider system of 'industrial moral economy'. This was based upon the deep-seated and widespread belief among the quarrymen and villagers that 'fairness', 'honourable behaviour', reciprocity and mutuality should inform relations between masters and men or, increasingly, employers and workers. In practice, this state of affairs did not always exist or prevail, but this qualification does not invalidate the importance of 'time-honoured' 'moral-economic' values, norms and expectations among the population of Ballachulish. Furthermore, in direct opposition to this value system, the new company sought 'rationally', single-mindedly and inflexibly, to maximise profits, cut costs and assert its power and control over the workforce.[5] As we will see below, in so doing it was widely perceived to be importing unwelcome 'outside' practices into the community and to be riding roughshod over local rights and traditions.

Common, but gendered, occupational and work experiences informed the villagers' lives. The highly skilled and independent-minded rockmen, splitters and dressers, the 'quarrymen proper', made up about half of the quarrying workforce of around 400 in total by 1902. In theory they were well paid, receiving between 25s and 30s per week, although their wages fluctuated according to market conditions and were subject to deductions for the price of powder and other essential work-based materials. There were a few other skilled workers present in the quarries, such as carpenters and smiths. Labourers and mainly younger male helpers

4 A. Macinnes, 'Good Days, Bad Days: The Story of Scottish Slate', *Sunday Mail Magazine, The Story of Scotland*, vol. 42 (1989), 1146–8; Kirk, *Custom and Conflict*, 34–6.
5 Kirk, *Custom and Conflict*, 2–3, 36–8, 62–5.

and other ancillary workers made up the remainder of the workforce. Many of the helpers would eventually move into their fathers' or other relatives' positions as skilled quarrymen. Familial patterns of recruit-ment and promotion thus prevailed in the quarries and strongly encour-aged family members to display the qualities of loyalty and mutuality. These qualities, along with attachments to the wider workforce and the community, would help to build and sustain impressive popular support and solidarity during the first conflict.[6]

At the same time paid employment opportunities for women and girls in quarrying and other occupations in the village and the surrounding area were extremely scarce. Quarrying was an overwhelmingly male occupation, although the *Oban Times* maintained in 1903 that around 50 'women and children' were usually employed in the Ballachulish quarries. If this indeed was the case, they would have been helpers or other ancillary workers. Unlike urban centres such as Edinburgh and Glasgow, the small size of the local middle class, moreover, meant that few women became domestic servants. Their main responsibility, both in the home and community, was to provide and care for their families on an unpaid basis and for the few local notables who employed them as servants or housekeepers. Yet I have come across no evidence to suggest that the women of Ballachulish questioned their subordinate and secondary status and sought greater individual and collective independ-ence and equality. In truth, shared, but unequal, family and household roles, relationships and values predominated in the community.[7] Both men and women, furthermore, viewed the fortunes of the quarry workers and the quarries as being synonymous with the fate of the village. As we will see in due course, threats to the employment and security of the quarry workers were seen to be to the detriment of the welfare of the community as a whole.

Many people in Ballachulish enjoyed shared patterns of leisure, culture and politics. For example, Lachlan Grant, his fellow middle-class progressives and his numerous working-class allies and supporters prized commitments to respectability, restraint, self-respect and self-improvement. They fought for crofter and worker rights in the face of rapacious 'landlordism' and employer 'tyranny', for Highland socio-

6 Ibid., 19–23, 25–8.
7 Ibid., 24–5.

economic development and improved medical and social-welfare provi-sion.[8] They were extremely proud of their Highland and Celtic heritage and promoted Gaelic customs and habits. With members of the United Free Church to the fore, they held musical and literary 'Gaelic evenings' and supported Ballachulish's very successful shinty team, the Mechanics' Institute, the Public School, the local branch of the Rechabite temperance society and the Volunteers. They took the lead in making Ballachulish a radical Gaelic place, with the vast majority of the villagers speaking Gaelic as well as English. In contrast to Glasgow, there was an absence of deep sectarian divisions and conflicts within the community. In sum, this was a close-knit, relatively homogeneous and generally united village, not only socially and economically, but also culturally and politically.[9]

The Conflicts, 1902–5

The company brought about the first conflict by dismissing Grant from his medical duties in the quarries and in the district in July 1902. This decision was sudden and unexpected, because since its arrival in 1894 the new company had generally abided by established traditions and practices. For example, quarrying crews were allowed to continue their past practice of negotiating contracts, while, in keeping with the custom dating back 'over forty years', the Medical Committee, comprising 'the master and seven workmen', continued to exercise control over 'all matters pertaining to the medical arrangements'. These included the appointment of the medical officer of the quarries and the payment of his salary by means of voluntary deductions from the quarry workers' wages.

Rumours did circulate that the company had effectively forced Dr Farquharson, Grant's predecessor, to resign his position at the quarries in June 1900 because of his criticisms of its inadequate housing and sanitary provisions for its mainly quarrying tenants. Yet in August of the same year Grant's appointment met with the unanimous approval of the Medical Committee. Although a native of Johnstone, Renfrews-hire, Grant was widely accepted and liked as an excellent young doctor and a 'local', a 'true Highlander', well schooled in 'all things Gaelic'. He had been brought up in Ballachulish from the age of nine, attended

8   See Chapter 1 in this volume.
9   Kirk, *Custom and Conflict*, 31–4, 79–81.

Ballachulish Public School, and on leaving school at the age of fourteen worked temporarily as a clerk in the quarry offices of Dr Campbell, the well respected lessee of the slate quarries. After studying medicine with distinction at the universities of Glasgow and Edinburgh, Grant had become medical officer at the Gesto hospital on the Isle of Skye. He returned to Ballachulish to take up his new position and to care for his recently widowed mother.[10]

Eminently well qualified as both a local and a medical practitioner, Grant, nevertheless, was suddenly sacked by the company from his positions in the quarries and the district, with one month's notice and 'without any reason being alleged or any explanation given', just under two years after becoming the medical officer. His incredulity was matched by that of the quarrier members of the Medical Committee who had not been consulted, the quarrying workforce and the entire village. The company's subsequent claims that Grant had not performed his duties well enough and that some workers had complained about him, were exposed as being without foundation. In truth, Colonel Malcolm and his appointee as quarry manager, Archibald MacColl – a native of Balla- chulish and the quarrymaster at Port Mary, Easdale – saw Grant, much like they had Farquharson, as far too much of an independently-minded and radical spirit, a potentially oppositional and disruptive force in the quarries. For Grant was a firm supporter of the quarrymen's demands for good wages, working conditions and decent housing. He was thus seen as a necessary obstacle to be removed in order to enable the company to achieve more or less total control over the lives of their workers and tenants.

In the eyes of the company the means to realise this objective lay in a rapid transformation from traditional to new market-based and managerial practices, norms and values. As seen in the document, *Terms and Conditions of Employment*, issued by the company in January 1903, relations between the company and the workers were to be placed upon a more individual, as opposed to a collective, basis. For example, no 'third-party' (namely, trade-union) 'interference' in the workplace was to be tolerated; the manager would acquire total control over hiring and firing. Many working practices and deductions from the quarry workers'

10 Kirk, *Custom and Conflict*, 39; R. MacLeod, *Talent and Tenacity: Dr Lachlan Grant of Ballachulish. His Life and Times* (Colonsay, 2013).

wages to fund the medical officer's salary would become compulsory and the 'necessary' amount unilaterally deducted by the company.[11]

Meanwhile, general incredulity had given way to widespread anger and protest against the company's 'highhandedness' and 'tyranny'. Mass meetings were held in Ballachulish and petitions drawn up in support of Grant and in opposition to the company's (unsuccessful) attempts to bring in a new doctor 'under more strict terms' and its application to the Court of Session to have Grant 'interdicted from practising in the district, or from attending on the men and their families'. A reconstituted Medical Committee, which excluded 'the master', refused to accept Grant's dismissal and reappointed him. Following a large meeting addressed by Keir Hardie in September 1903, the decision was taken to form a trade union which would embrace all the workers employed in the Ballachulish quarries. There were also mounting grievances among the workers and tenants concerning the company's 'overpricing' of tools, coals, parish and county assessments, its poor housing and sanitary provision and the growing number of sackings and evictions it carried out against labour activists. The locals were also encouraged by the depth and extent of support for Grant and the quarrymen in 1902 and 1903 from the 'whole district', including many religious leaders and medical practitioners, some 'honourable' employers, the *Oban Times* and the *Highland News*. In terms of Scotland and England as a whole, the *Lancet*, the *Edinburgh Medical Journal*, the *British Medical Journal*, the Independent Labour Party's *Labour Leader*, the Glasgow Trades Council, the Scottish Trades Union Congress and the Amalgamated Society of Engineers in London provided strong backing for their cause.[12]

Yet this was to no avail. Despite some signs in October that it might soften its position, the company became even more obdurate. With the 'hardliners', Malcolm and his 'puppet', MacColl, to the fore, it announced in late December that it would not reconsider its position on Grant and that the workers would be obliged to sign the *Terms and Conditions of Employment* document referred to earlier. This meant in practice that the workers would lose much of their customary control and influence over workplace matters, including those of the Medical Committee, and that no concessions were to be made by the company whether in relation to

11 Kirk, *Custom and Conflict*, 44–7.
12 Ibid., 42–4, 50–2, 61–3.

worker and tenant grievances or the demand for union recognition. In refusing to sign the document virtually the entire quarrying workforce was locked out by the company in January following the Christmas break.[13]

During 1903 the 'State of War in the Valley of Glencoe' became even more bitter and prolonged. The lock-out lasted twelve months, during which time the quarries were brought to an entire standstill. The company's application to have Grant interdicted and its attempt to bring in a new doctor were successful. Grant was forced to give up his medical practice in Ballachulish. Fortunately, many of the locked out men found employment, at higher rates of pay, in the quarries of the 'Slate Islands', but their prolonged absences rendered Ballachulish something of a ghost town. Protests continued and appeals for moral and financial support met with a generous response. Yet the company remained seemingly unbowed and confident.

A remarkable change of fortunes occurred at this point. Faced with growing internal divisions around unyielding and unaccommodating strategies, mounting losses, the failure to bring in 'scab' labour, the continuing solidarity of the quarry workers and their numerous supporters and, perhaps most crucially, the continuing availability of well-paid work elsewhere, the company suddenly capitulated in mid-December. Grant was reinstated to both his posts, the full rights of the Medical Committee were restored and work was scheduled to resume in the New Year. The quarry workers, furthermore, were to receive an increase in pay, their union recognised, and new workers' cottages were to be built by the company and a Conciliation Board set up. From being for so long despondent, the workers, the community and Grant were now ecstatic. Impressive worker and community solidarity and outside support had carried the day. The *Labour Leader* rightly described this first conflict as 'one of the most important [. . .] fought by labour and the workers in the north of Scotland'.[14]

Despite these gains, stability and harmony did not last for long. Faced with deteriorating market conditions, the company cut hours and wages and increased layoffs during the winter and spring months of 1904 and 1905. Mass protests ensued but they were unsuccessful. In mid-June 1905 the desperate company closed the quarries 'for a time'. The closure

13 Ibid., 44–9.
14 Ibid., 49–54; *Labour Leader*, 16 Jan. 1904.

was still in force on 15 July when between 200 and 300 people attacked MacColl's house and forced his written resignation. They were seeking their revenge for MacColl's hostility to themselves and Grant during the first conflict and his attempt in 1905 to give preferential treatment to the company's tenants in terms of employment in the quarries. Following the attack MacColl left Ballachulish, but twelve local quarrymen, including three union committee members, appeared in court in Oban on charges of 'mobbing and rioting'. Three were found not guilty, eight received modest fines and the charge against the other was withdrawn. In two other dramatic twists to this remarkable story, the belligerent Colonel Malcolm resigned and was replaced by the far more conciliatory Major Black of Greenock, while the widely respected senior foreman at the quarries, Hugh MacColl, was made the local manager.

In August an agreement was reached for the eventual resumption of work at the quarries, but continuing economic difficulties prevented this happening until the end of the year. Furthermore, for the first time since the conflicts began, a significant division now appeared in the ranks of the workers. Faced with a rapidly deteriorating economic situation, they voted narrowly in favour of full hours and reduced wages for the company's tenants within their ranks rather than reduced wages and hours for all. The results, therefore, were very mixed. Union recognition and collective bargaining had been gained from a far more accommo-dating and conciliatory company keen to restore customary harmony in the workplace and the community. Yet a significant number of workers, the 120 or so who were not tenants of the company, faced immediate unemployment. United for so long, the village was now bitterly divided.

As a postscript, during 1906 and 1907 there were continuing fluctua-tions in employment opportunities, hours and wages against the general background of the industry's continuing decline. Some unemployed quarriers found work at British Aluminium's plant in nearby Kinlochleven, but in August 1907 there came the devastating news that the quarries were to be 'closed indefinitely'. The beginning of 1908, however, brought renewed hope when a new company, the Ballachulish Quarries Limited, met with the men's representatives and 'amicably' agreed terms and conditions of work. The quarries once again became operative.[15]

15   For the second conflict and its aftermath see Kirk, *Custom and Conflict*, 55–60, 69–70.

Wider Significance

The specific conflicts at Ballachulish both raise important questions about and shed new light – albeit in the limited way of a single case study – upon wider historical and sociological issues and debates. For example, as noted by the *Labour Leader* at the time, the fact that two serious disputes took place leads us to question easy generalisations about worker 'backwardness', 'docility', 'instinctive deference' and indifference or hostility towards trade unionism in the Scottish Highlands, as contrasted with the supposedly more 'militant' and 'advanced' consciousness of workers on the Clyde and elsewhere in industrial Scotland. The disputes at Ballachulish demonstrate that given the right conditions industrial workers in a 'traditional' and remote, but far from economically backward Highland location (with its extensive markets at home and abroad), who were strongly wedded to customary, 'moral-economic' traditions and values, could very quickly move to adopt 'modern' ways and means. Thus, while seeking to justify their actions by resort to tradition, the quarry workers at Ballachulish readily embraced the forward-looking instruments of trade unionism, institutionalised collective bargaining and progressive politics. We have also seen that up to the end of 1905 they demonstrated remarkable solidarity and received widespread support. Their leaders, furthermore, exhibited the same personal and leadership qualities – of self-education, of reason, of independence and self-respect, of a capacity for clear tactical and strategic thinking and action and for making alliances with middle-class Liberals and socialist-leaning progressives of the Grant type – as their urban counterparts in Glasgow, Edinburgh and nationally.[16]

In sum, the Ballachulish case strongly lends itself to the argument that we urgently require further research, especially of a comparative nature, into a variety of communities and localities in the Highlands, Lowlands and Borders before we can draw definitive conclusions about Highland 'backwardness', 'docility' and 'deference'. The case also demonstrates the misleading nature of those parts of the general sociological and historical literature that draw an absolute and fixed distinction between

16   Ibid., 74, 82–3; R. Johnstone, *Clydeside Capital 1870–1920* (East Linton, 2000); E. F. Biagini and A. J. Reid (eds), *Currents of Radicalism: Popular Radicalism, Organised Labour and Party Politics in Britain 1850–1914* (Cambridge, 1991); W. Knox, *Industrial Nation: Work, Culture and Society in Scotland 1800–Present* (Edinburgh, 1999), chs 12, 18.

'customary' and 'modern' social movements. To do so is to underestimate their many-sidedness, the overlaps often existing between them and the speed with which 'traditionalists' could and did become 'modernists'.[17]

In terms of employer thought and behaviour, the case of the Ballachulish Slate Quarries Company Limited is instructive in two ways. First, the actions of Malcolm and his supporters add weight to the influential historiographical viewpoint that Scottish employers were generally more autocratic and anti-union than in much of the rest of Britain. Second, this viewpoint must be qualified in two ways. As demonstrated in the infamous and widely publicised contemporary case of Lord Penrhyn and his slate quarries in north Wales, autocratic, determined and protracted employer anti-unionism and obsessions with total power and control were by no means confined to Ballachulish and Scotland. Yet, companies could also pragmatically modify and transform their strategies and tactics. As seen in the Ballachulish case, changing circumstances could persuade companies to adopt more accommodating and conciliatory policies.[18]

Finally, the Ballachulish example fully supports those historians, geographers and sociologists who maintain that the patterns of identity and attachments adopted by individuals and social groups are complex, multiple and often shifting rather than uniform, singular and fixed in character. Thus, the Ballachulish workers, Grant and their supporters expressed, for example, attachments to custom, the local community, the Highlands, Gaelic, Scotland and the wider British nation. They variously described themselves as respectable, independent and 'sturdy' Highlanders, 'modern freemen' in the Scottish tradition of 'Bruce and Wallace' and 'free-born Britons' who celebrated the coronation of King Edward VII and warmly welcomed him on his subsequent visit to Loch Leven. There also rapidly developed strong forms of radical labour and class consciousness among Ballachulish's 'customary' residents and quarry workers, while gendered expectations, norms, values and practices pervaded, albeit in largely unspoken ways, the workplace, the household and the community.[19]

17 Ibid., 71–4.
18 Ibid., 83–4; Jones, *North Wales Quarrymen*, ch. 8; W. Kenefick and A. J. McIvor (eds), *Roots of Red Clydeside 1910–1914: Labour Unrest and Industrial Relations in West Scotland* (Edinburgh, 1996).
19 Kirk, *Custom and Conflict*, 76–81.

Conclusion

The start of operations by the new company in January 1908 brought renewed hope for the works, the quarry workers and the village. Yet the further decline of the industry, mounting international competition, the disruption caused by the First World War and the 1930s depression meant that the succeeding decades were generally very difficult for all concerned. Quarrying at Ballachulish came to an end in 1955. Grant had died ten years earlier. In addition to his district medical duties, he had worked for several years as medical officer for British Aluminium's plant at Kinlochleven.[20] In contrast to treatment at the Ballachulish quarries between 1902 and the end of 1903, Grant was well served by British Aluminium and was full of praise for its 'welfarism' and its commitment to Highland development. Despite being something of an apologist for the company's unsatisfactory heath and welfare provisions,[21] Grant died with his reforming credentials largely intact.[22]

20 See Chapter 7 in this volume.
21 For Grant's work at British Aluminium, see Andrew Perchard, *Aluminium-ville: Government Global Business and the Scottish Highlands* (Lancaster, 2012), 207–8, 242, 245, 248, 250, 252, 272, 285.
22 MacLeod, *Talent and Tenacity*, chs 6, 7.

CHAPTER 4

'The havoc played by an irrational land system'
Dr Lachlan Grant and the Land Question in the Western Highlands, c. 1880–1945

ANNIE TINDLEY

This sad change [the end of the clan system] culminated in the wicked and unpatriotic clearances, which I dare say you know all about; and, at the present day, the havoc played by an irrational land system may be easily seen all over the Highlands. In many parts of the western Highlands the crofters are longing for land, and from what I know of them, I believe they would make the best possible use of further additions to their holdings, should they be able to obtain the same on suitable terms.[1]

What place does a discussion about land reform have in a volume about a medical doctor? Perhaps this field is the one least associated with Dr Lachlan Grant; however, the land reform debate, particularly in the early twentieth century, encompassed many of the themes that he actively campaigned on for many years: emigration and depopulation, Highland economic development and diversification and the social and political 'confidence' of the west Highland population.[2] His experiences during his early career in Skye, and later, during the Ballachulish slate quarry dispute, convinced Dr Grant that when it came to the land question, 'Unity is strength.'[3] He supported, and was deeply involved in, the establishment in 1906 of the Highland Crofters' and Cottars' Association, which was modelled directly on trade union structures and goals, and he wrote on the land question throughout his career.[4]

1 *Oban Times*, 3 Dec. 1904.
2 See for instance, Grant, *A New Deal for the Highlands* (1935), 6, 10–11, 21–3.
3 *Oban Times*, 16 May 1906; for a study of the Ballachulish slate quarriers' strike, see N. Kirk, *Custom and Conflict in the 'Land of the Gael: Ballachulish, 1900–1910* (Monmouth, 2007); for more on his experiences on Skye see R. Macleod, *Talent and Tenacity: Dr Lachlan Grant of Ballachulish, His Life and Times* (Colonsay, 2013), 20–1.
4 *Oban Times*, 16 May 1906; *Oban Times*, 18 May 1906.

In many ways, this should not come as a surprise. The land question
had been and remained the dominant political, social and economic
issue in the Scottish Highlands and Islands for the span of Grant's career
in the region, and as such was impossible to ignore.[5] Likewise, his cures
for these problems shared a common focus: the role of the state. In
his own words: 'They [the crofters and cottars] demanded justice; and
nothing short of the acquisition of large tracts of the country by the
nation, to be let out at reasonable rents to those who could till the soil,
would satisfy those who best understood the question.'[6] What Dr Grant
had in mind was land nationalisation on a large scale: effectively seeing
the State buying out Highland landowners and becoming the majority
landowner in the region. Land was one of a raft of responsibilities that
Dr Grant wanted to see transferred from private to government hands:
health services, promotion of the Gaelic language and industry.[7] For Dr
Grant, the core solution to all of the symptoms of the Highland problem
lay with the government and extension of state responsibilities, and this
included land reform.

Land was clearly a subject that interested him deeply; firstly because
he believed that it was at the root of many of the 'Highland problems'
he diagnosed and campaigned on; and secondly, because he was introduced to the sharp end of the land question in his first Highland post,
at the Gesto hospital, Edinbane on Skye.[8] This essay will examine his
diagnosis, campaigns and cures for the land question, within the context
of his other campaigning.

---

5 See J. Hunter, *The Making of the Crofting Community* (Edinburgh, 1976) and
    E. A. Cameron, *Land for the People? The British Government and the Scottish
    Highlands, c. 1880–c. 1925* (East Linton, 1996) for two surveys on the land
    question in the modern Highlands and Islands.

6 NLS, Lachlan Grant Collection, Acc. 12187, from *Oban Weekly News*, 16 May
    1906.

7 See Grant, *A New Deal*, 11–12, for a mature overall vision, and Grant's evidence
    to the Committee on Medical Services in the Highlands (the Dewar Commis-
    sion) in 1912 for an earlier expression: PP 1913 [Cd. 6920] *Evidence of the
    Highlands and Islands Medical Service Committee* [hereafter *Dewar Committee
    Evidence*], 395–6.

8 MacLeod, *Talent and Tenacity*, 20.

'Freeing the Land': Dr Grant and Land Reform in the Highlands and Islands, 1890–1945[9]

Of course, Dr Grant was not campaigning in a vacuum, and in fact, was treading a path well worn since the mid-nineteenth century. In 1886, the Liberal government had passed a benchmark piece of legislation, as the first state attempt to deal with what had come to be defined loosely as the 'Highland Question': the Crofters Holdings (Scotland) Act. This protected crofters from eviction at short notice and set up a government appointed Land Court, the Crofters Commission, which set crofters' rents and arbitrated on crofter applications for limited extensions of land.[10] By the end of the 1890s, when Grant took up his first Highland posts (first at Oban, then Gesto on Skye, and then, of course, Ballachulish), the land reform debate had moved forward to encompass two further principles. Firstly, the principle of wider Highland development: the investment by government into transport infrastructures, improving crofters' livestock and agricultural education to strengthen and diversify the regional economy. This was administered via a government agency established for the purpose, the Congested Districts Board, established in 1897.[11] Secondly, the policy of land purchase by government was extended, and was likewise overseen by the Congested Districts Board. These policies had been of debatable success; by the time Dr Grant began to write on the question regularly (from around 1904 onwards), land hunger and raiding was still prevalent across the western Highlands, and later, the 1920s saw unprecedented levels of out-migration from the region, a process which was widely regarded as a key indicator of failure of government policy towards the Highlands.[12] Certainly, Dr Grant saw the matter in these terms, and was determined to make a contribution towards its solution. As early as 1908, he identified the limitation of opportunity for young Highland people, and its root in the land:

> Many of the grown ups, especially the young men, wished to secure a holding of their own in the land of their birth. This was surely a

9 *Oban Times*, 3 Dec. 1904.

10 Cameron, *Land for the People*, 40–1.

11 Cameron, *Land for the People*, 81–4; A. S. Mather, 'The Congested Districts Board for Scotland,' in W. Ritchie, J. C. Stone and A. S. Mather (eds), *Essays for Professor R. E. H. Mellor* (Aberdeen, 1986), 197.

12 Hunter, *Crofting Community*, 205–6; I. J. M. Robertson, *The Later Highland Land Wars* (Ashgate, 2013).

laudable ambition showing good sense and healthy sentiment; and
the Crofters Holdings Act of 1886 had repeatedly demonstrated
how successful such settlers became. But then the cruel fact stared
them in the face that no land is available, and they have either to
migrate or eke out a bare subsistence at home in over-crowded,
unhealthy conditions, too often leading to disease and despair.[13]

So, first of all, what was Dr Grant's analysis of the land question? Like
many of his contemporaries, he turned to the past to foreground his
view of the contemporary problems facing crofters and cottars in the
Highlands. He called the land system in the Highlands 'diseased' (an
example of the medical terminology he often used in his writing). The
root of this disease, as he saw it, lay in the policy of landowners towards
amalgamation of land into firstly, large sheep farms, and latterly, sporting
estates, often evicting smallholders to achieve this. As Dr Grant put it,
wryly, 'for some years this system seemed to work well for the landlords'.[14]
But, he argued, it did not work well for the crofters, the 'healthy, industrious peasantry'.[15] He placed the blame for extensive emigration onto
these historical factors, as well as the other economic, social and political ills facing the Highland population and building up a picture of an
economy and society that could not support its people.[16]

Although he acknowledged that the 1886 Crofters Act had gone some
way to addressing these problems, Grant argued that it had not gone
far enough, and had not been able to stem the tide of pessimism.[17] The
Act had protected crofters from eviction, and established their right to
pass their crofts on, but the core problems of poverty, overcrowding and
the related consequences of poor health, education, sanitation: 'modern
Highland problems' as Grant called them, remained.[18]

Dr Grant was not alone in holding these views on the Highlands
in the early twentieth century; this was a period when vocal political

13 *People's Journal*, 1 Feb. 1908, report of a speech made by Dr Grant in Oban on
    23 Jan. 1908.
14 *Oban Weekly News*, 20 Feb. 1907.
15 Ibid.
16 See Grant, *A New Deal*, 6.
17 This pessimism has undergone some academic analysis in J. Burnett, *The
    Making of the Modern Scottish Highlands, 1939–1965: Withstanding the 'colossus
    of advancing materialism'* (Dublin, 2011).
18 *The Hospital*, 3 Nov. 1906.

campaigners were actively attempting to address the deep social and economic problems facing Britain as a whole.[19] The Liberal Party in particular, under various political stars such as Lloyd George, were proposing radical new legislation in the first decade of the twentieth century.[20] From state pensions, to a land campaign and a proposed super tax on the wealthiest in the land, the wider political atmosphere was conducive to reform.[21] Add to this Dr Grant's own record of activity outwith his medical duties – during the Ballachulish slate quarriers' dispute, and through his various publications and journalism, and his political activism – and we can see that his activity, though unusual on a personal level, was part of a much wider urge at the time for reform.[22]

Dr Grant believed that land, and reform of land tenures, was central to improving the overall wellbeing of the country and its population. As land was at the root of so much, only by distributing the rights to land more fairly could other aspects of society (health, housing, emigration), improve. In his own words: 'It was in the interests of all classes that the land should be developed to its utmost extent, and not allowed to be idle, or to be made use of entirely for sport.'[23] In Dr Grant's view, however, it was both futile and unhelpful to criticise or blame landlords as a class for this situation, a fairly unusual position to take at this time. Indeed, in 1909 Tom Johnston published *Our Scots Noble Families*, an assault on the Scottish landed classes, exposing the roots of their economic, political and territorial dominance in cheating, legal shenanigans and downright

19　See for example NLS, Lachlan Grant Collection, Acc. 12187/6, f. 156, J. F. Duncan, 'Sentiment about the Highlands and Some Hard Facts: The Small Holdings Delusion', *Forward*, 1 Feb. 1936; Cameron, *Land for the People*, 102–13; A. G. Newby, *Ireland, Radicalism and the Scottish Highlands, c. 1870–c. 1912* (Edinburgh, 2007), 186.

20　B. K. Murray, *The People's Budget 1909/10: Lloyd George and Liberal Politics* (Oxford, 1980), 4–5, 173–5; N. Blewett, *The Peers, the Parties and the People: The General Elections of 1910* (London, 1972), 68–70; H. V. Emy, *Liberals, Radicals and Social Politics, 1892–1914* (Cambridge, 1973), 189–201.

21　I. Packer, *Lloyd George, Liberalism and the Land: The Land Issue and Party Politics in England, 1906–1914* (Suffolk, 2001), 83–4; A. Tindley, 'The system of landlordism supreme', 24–43: David Lloyd George, the 5th Duke of Sutherland and Highland Land Sales, 1898–1919', *Britain and the World*, 3:2 (2010); E. A. Cameron, *Impaled Upon a Thistle: Scotland since 1880* (Edinburgh, 2010), 90–2.

22　MacLeod, *Talent and Tenacity*, 40, 53–6.

23　*Oban Weekly News*, 16 May, 1900.

brute force.[24] Dr Grant took a rather different line; one which was less personalised, and defined by his belief in systems of land holding. As he said in 1906: 'There was no personal animus against any landlord or group of landlords. They were as much the victims of the system as anyone, so that they could even appeal to them for co-operation in developing the country's best interests, which were always associated with mother earth.'[25] Although not a landowner, Grant was one of the professional upper middle classes, and never demanded complete social revolution. Greater fairness and stability were his aims, not equality for its own sake. This view may have been informed by Dr Grant's immediate Highland context. Although he had worked in Skye, where several notorious (at least historically) landlords were based, perhaps he did not see the same level of conflict in the Ballachulish area, dominated as it was by the slate company.[26]

Now we have examined his analysis of the Highland land problem, what were Dr Grant's proposed solutions? In a nutshell, Grant wanted to see the land in the hands of the people, so that it could be exploited effectively enough to retain the Highland population. For Grant, this would stem the flow of emigration, which he argued carried away the, 'gold of the country, and le[ft] the gilt and the dross'.[27] Instead, Dr Grant urged Highland crofters and cottars to combine, to form a trades union of sorts, to stand up for their rights and demand reform – a view clearly formed during and after his experiences with the quarry dispute.[28] So far convinced was Dr Grant that this would be the most effective way forward, that he was himself instrumental in setting up the Highland Crofters' and Cottars' Association in May 1906. As Dr Grant stated at the inaugural meeting of this association at Connel Ferry: 'Combinations of people existed for every imaginable purpose, and surely one for the betterment of the long-suffering Highlander was a laudable object on which they might ask the blessing of the nation.'[29]

24 T. Johnston, *Our Scots Noble Families* (Glasgow, 1909), 61–71; J. MacLeod, *Highland Heroes of the Land Reform Movement* (Inverness, 1917), 13–23.

25 *Oban Weekly News*, 16 May, 1906; I. Packer, 'The Land Issue and the Future of Scottish Liberalism in 1914', *Scottish Historical Review*, 75 (1996), 56.

26 Hunter, *Crofting Community*, 131–45; MacLeod, *Talent and Tenacity*, 24–36, 41–2.

27 *Oban Weekly News*, 20 Feb. 1907.

28 MacLeod, *Talent and Tenacity*, 42–3, 53–7; Grant, *New Deal*, 6, 10–11, 21–3.

29 *Oban Weekly News*, 16 May 1906.

Grant wished to see nothing less than a large-scale land nationalisation scheme in the Scottish Highlands; that is, to make the British state the main landowner, and landlord, in the region.[30] In his own words: 'They demanded justice; and nothing short of the acquisition of large tracts of the country by the nation, to be let out at reasonable rents to those who could till the soil.'[31] Again, land nationalisation as a concept had been swirling around the Highlands from the late nineteenth century, and the creation of the Congested Districts Board in 1897 had taken the first tentative steps towards state-owned land schemes, most famously at Glendale in Skye.[32] But what Grant, and other like-minded reformers, was suggesting was land purchase by government on a much larger scale.[33] Of course, large land purchases would require large sums of money, especially at market prices – something the Congested Districts Board had found out to its cost.[34] Dr Grant did not bog himself down in the detail of these proposals, however; his role was one of raising awareness by ceaseless activity and publishing, rather than developing detailed financial and legal plans. Aside from pointing out that as the richest nation in the world, Britain was in a better position than most to help her poorest, Grant left the details to 'Statesmen'.[35] True to his medical education and career, he was most interested in the diagnosis of what he called the 'social and economic disease – its cause and cure', rather than the detailed philosophising of political theorists or the practical compromises of politicians.

Dr Grant was nothing less than committed to the causes he espoused, and would continue to 'send around the fiery cross' even as the decades passed.[36] In 1935, on the back of his wide-ranging and influential publication, *A New Deal for the Highlands*, his ideas about land reform received another airing and Grant again stressed his view that only through combination could the Highlands receive the attention and

30 L. Grant, 'Modern Highland Problems', *BMJ*, 2:2345 (9 Dec. 1905), 999.
31 *Oban Weekly News*, 16 May 1906.
32 Cameron, *Land for the People*, 96–8.
33 For context on the role of the state see: Leah Leneman, *Fit for Heroes? Land Settlement in Scotland after World War One* (Aberdeen, 1989), 53–70.
34 Cameron, *Land for the People*, 112–13; A. Tindley, *The Sutherland Estate, 1850–1920: Aristocratic Decline, Estate Management and Land Reform* (Edinburgh, 2010), 133–6.
35 *Aberdeen Press and Journal*, 'Highlander Rally', 12 Sept. 1935.
36 Ibid., 'Highlander Rally'; Grant, *A New Deal*, 16.

amelioration that they deserved from the government. 'I believe that were the cottars, crofters, farmers, fishermen and agricultural workers of the Highlands and Islands thoroughly organised like some of the great unions, they would have full satisfaction from the British Legislature in a very short time.'[37] Grant's vision included all agricultural, forestry and fisheries workers, once again emphasising his inclusive view, one which placed land and land issues – ownership, use, management – at the heart of any permanent solution to the Highland Problem.

Conclusions

How important Dr Grant was in the early twentieth century land reform debate? And were his views unusual in any way for the time – and were they listened to? There is no doubt that Dr Grant was very active on behalf on his community in Ballachulish and the surrounding area, as well as for the Highland population more generally, through his activities on land reform. He was indefatigable in writing, publishing and publicising the challenges facing the region in the early twentieth century, and his central role in establishing the Highland Crofters' and Cottars' Association was a classic example of that. Another was his correspondence with the prime minister, Ramsay MacDonald, whom he knew personally – a good example of going 'straight to the top', if ever there was one.[38] However, his decided view that land nationalisation was the core solution to the land question in the Highlands was probably not entirely in step with either the common view among the crofting community, nor, indeed, the political community he was trying to influence. Initial land purchase schemes made under the Congested Districts Board had not been entirely successful and the practical realities of state land ownership – such as the day-to-day challenges of the state as landlord, enforcing the payment of rents or policing behaviour – severely undermined utopian visions of state ownership, full economic productivity and national self-sufficiency in agriculture.[39]

Overall, Dr Grant's voice was often ignored or drowned out in the crowded field of land politics and publishing; although probably quite influential in the Ballachulish area and the western Highlands more

37 'Highlander Rally'.
38 See for instance his publication of some of this correspondence in his *A New Deal*, 7–14.
39 Cameron, *Land for the People*, 126–7.

generally, he is not remembered today as one of the great thinkers or campaigners on the land issue, active though he certainly was. Perhaps we can see his greatest contribution to the question locally as being in his attempt to boost the confidence of the crofting community – to encourage them to speak out, to combine and organise themselves so that their legitimate demands would be heard and pressed upon the government's attention. Dr Grant was a man of wide views, interested in medical reform, health provision reform, land reform, the issues surrounding emigration, the preservation of the Gaelic language – all issues he saw as closely interrelated. It is perhaps not surprising then, that his views on land reform have been relegated to a more neglected position, but they formed an integral part of his overall vision for the betterment of the western Highlands.

CHAPTER 5

'A vicious and soulless propaganda'
Dr Lachlan Grant and the Inter-War Emigration Debate

MARJORY HARPER

Scotland's first official 'year of homecoming', in 2009, was a prolonged and multi-faceted celebration that, in the words of the Scottish government's website, highlighted 'Scotland's great contributions to the world' and wooed the Scottish diaspora in the hope that genealogical tourists would set cash registers ringing the length and breadth of the land.[1] At time of writing – in 2014 – it is being repeated, part of a plethora of activities in a year which sees the Commonwealth Games come to Glasgow and the Ryder Cup being played at Gleneagles. As well as being the year of the independence referendum, 2014 is, of course, the 700th anniversary of the battle of Bannockburn.

Ancestral tourism is nothing new. In the inter-war decades, when Dr Lachlan Grant was most heavily involved in debates about the economic and social future of the Highlands, newspapers frequently reported the disembarkation of 'tartan tourists' from the United States at Greenock, Scotland's main port of entry and exit for immigrants and emigrants, returners and tourists. At two-year intervals, between 1924 and 1938, the Order of Scottish Clans – founded in the USA in 1878 – chartered a succession of Anchor line vessels to transport large contingents of emigrants, or their descendants, back to the land of their birth or ancestry. Organising holidays which ranged from a fortnight to several weeks' duration was an obvious way for the Order to fulfil its objective of cultivating 'fond recollections of Scotland' among its membership, which by the 1920s stood at 24,000 men, with 21,000 women involved in partner organisations.[2]

---

1 www.scotland.gov.uk/News/Releases/2008/09/17134306. Accessed 12 May 2014.
2 *The Scotsman*, 3 Aug. 1926, 5; 10 July 1932, 10; 17 July 1934, 7a. See also M. Harper, *Scotland No More? The Scots Who Left Scotland in the Twentieth Century* (Edinburgh, 2012), 77–8. For insights into genealogical tourism in the Highlands, see P. Basu, *Highland Homecomings: Genealogy and Heritage Tourism in the Scottish Highlands* (London, 2006).

From Greenock, the homecoming holidaymakers dispersed across the country, often combining family reunions with civic welcomes in Glasgow and organised tours to Burns' country, the 'Scott-land' of the Trossachs and more distant parts of the Highlands. Their reactions were a mixture of nostalgia and relief. A *Scotsman* reporter, covering the arrival of the SS *Caledonia* in July 1932, singled out one passenger 'who must have felt thankful, as he looked at the empty shipyards and mouldy slipways, that he gave up working in a shipyard in Scotland some years ago, and went to America', where Prohibition had not prevented him making a good living as a clandestine bar tender in a club, 'dispensing alcoholic drinks with an entirely open mind on the question, if not always in an entirely open manner'.[3]

The visitors may have had fond personal recollections – or inherited images – of Scotland in their heads, but they had return tickets to America in their pockets. That so many Scots had traded sentiment for substance – or the perception of substance – overseas was a source of huge concern. Between the wars, over 545,000 Scots left the country for non-European destinations, almost 91 per cent of them in the eleven years between 1920 and 1930. During the 1920s the outflow – to all destinations – exceeded the natural growth of population, and the 1931 census revealed that Scotland's population had dropped by 0.8 per cent in the preceding ten years, the first inter-censal decline since records began.

Perspectives on Scottish emigration, 1770–1939: Brickbats and Bouquets

Debates about whether emigration enhanced or undermined the well-being of donor and host nations, as well as the participants themselves, had always been an integral part of Scotland's diasporic narrative and were to set the context for Lachlan Grant's interventions in the 1930s. In the eighteenth century, when the dominant mercantilist theories had equated national health and wealth with the retention of population, recruitment agents had been demonised by government and landlords for siphoning off money and muscle and jeopardising the modernisation of Highland estates. Following his travels in the region, Samuel Johnson added his voice to the criticism, deploring the 'epidemick disease of wandering'.[4]

3 *The Scotsman*, 19 July 1932, 9.
4 Samuel Johnson, *A Journey to the Western Islands of Scotland* (London, 1875), ed. R. W. Chapman (Oxford, 1924), 87.

Political antagonism was tempered slightly after 1783, when the West-minster government saw the case for promoting settlement on the borders of its redefined and vulnerable American empire, but Highland landlords did not modify their criticism until their estate development projects began to unravel during and after the Napoleonic wars. By the 1820s, against a backdrop of national recession, unemployment, pauperism and social unrest, emigration was more widely and emphatically defined as a lifeline, rather than a threat, not least in the Highlands, where wartime boom had given way to post-war slump and complete economic disloca-tion. The deliverance interpretation, which persisted in the Highlands for several decades, but faded in other parts of the country as conditions improved, was rekindled in national debates during the depression of the 1870s, when it was harnessed to a vociferous, but unheeded, campaign for state-aided emigration.

At no time, however, was there a single, unanimously endorsed, narrative of the objectives and consequences of emigration. The idea that emigration could relieve pressure on finite resources slowing down the growth of the population – a Malthusian safety-valve approach – was criticised in the domestic press and in Parliament as costly, ineffec-tive or unethical. Further, critics in host locations complained that their countries were being used as repositories for the redundant or disaf-fected population of the British Isles. Equally contentious were the more selective recruitment strategies implemented in the mid-nineteenth century under the auspices of Edward Gibbon Wakefield's theories of 'systematic colonisation'. Complaints – not least from Scottish commen-tators – that the best were being enticed overseas failed to eradicate negative public and political opinion in colonial host lands, while policy-makers struggled to promote empire settlement in the face of unequiv-ocal evidence that the vast majority of emigrants were heading for the United States. At the same time, newspapers, periodicals, pamphlets and guidebooks bombarded readers with voluminous and sometimes conflicting advice about different destinations, as well as about the pros and cons of emigration *per se*, while criticisms of policy and practice sat alongside celebrations of the achievements of individual emigrants.[5]

5 Attitudes to emigration in eighteenth- and nineteenth-century Scotland are discussed in M. Harper, *Adventurers and Exiles: The Great Scottish Exodus* (London, 2003), 23–31. See also T. M. Devine, *Scotland's Empire, 1600–1815* (London, 2004); M. Fry, *The Scottish Empire* (East Linton, 1947); A. Murdoch,

It was against such a complex backdrop of persistent contention and confusion that the debate resumed after the First World War. In 1907, Scottish emigration to Canada had exceeded the movement to the United States for the first time since 1846, and did so consistently from 1910. In 1922, Westminster reversed its traditional non-interventionist stance when it passed the Empire Settlement Act, by which up to £3 million a year was made available to subsidise fares, land settlement and training courses in partnership with dominion governments, or with public and private organisations in the UK or the dominions. But it was a rearguard attempt to bolster relations with the empire by implementing a strategy that had been advocated in the very different conditions of the 1820s and 1870s, and, although the exit valve opened fully in the 1920s, the earmarked state funding was not fully utilised, with only 36 per cent of British migrants leaving under the Act's auspices before the legislation came up for renewal in 1937.[6]

During the 1920s emigration was recommended not only by individuals and political parties with an imperialist agenda, but by battalions of recruitment agents from the dominions whose campaigns continued to be built around the tried-and-tested format of the public lecture and private interview. As well as taking advantage of new illustrative technologies, they were now able to enhance their encouragement with the possibility of state sponsorship. Advertisements for jobs and land settlement schemes, particularly in Australia and Canada, also appeared regularly in national and provincial newspapers, alongside glowing recommendations in published correspondence, while some emigrants – not least those who left the Hebrides for Patagonia – continued to be persuaded by word-of-mouth encouragement offered by homecoming family members, friends and acquaintances, or amateur agents such as the Reverend Donald MacCallum of Keose in Lewis.[7] Most emigrant Scots came, however, not from Hebridean crofts but – as they had done

---

Scotland and America, c. 1600–c. 1800 (Basingstoke, 2010).

6 Stephen Constantine, *Emigrants and Empire: British Settlement in the Dominions Between the Wars* (Manchester, 1990), 15–16. The Act was renewed at fifteen-year intervals until 1972, when it was finally removed from the statute book.

7 G. Mackenzie, *Return to Patagonia* (Kershader, 2010), 6–7, 15; D. E. Meek, 'Preaching the Land Gospel: The Rev. Donald MacCallum (1849–1929) in Skye, Tiree and Lochs, Lewis', in Ewen A. Cameron (ed.), *Recovering from the Clearances: Land Struggle, Resettlement, and Community Ownership in the Hebrides* (Kershader, 2013), 102.

in ever-increasing numbers since the 1860s – from the urban-indus-
trial central Lowlands. By the 1920s they were preoccupied with the
poor prognosis for a nation which appeared to be in 'terminal decline',
although many of those who left were artisans whose marketable skills
allowed them to capitalise on overseas opportunities, rather than the
unemployed and impoverished.[8]

Commendation of emigration in the inter-war years was completely
eclipsed by the sustained lament of opponents who portrayed it as an
unremitting saga of exile, loss and disappointment. Critics included not
only disillusioned emigrants, but public figures from across the entire
spectrum of political and civil society. There were some strange bedfel-
lows. On the right, they included the shipping magnate, Sir Alfred Yarrow,
who complained that every young emigrant represented a waste of £400
that had been invested in his or her education, and west Aberdeen-
shire MP, Sir Charles Barclay-Harvey, who articulated his constituents'
complaint that aggressive agency canvassing was denuding the countryside of its best farm servants.[9] On the left, Wal Hannington, a founding
member of the Communist Party of Great Britain and organiser of the
National Unemployed Workers' Movement, boarded transatlantic liners
in the Clyde in 1923 in an attempt to persuade emigrants to change their
minds and not let themselves be 'shipped off to an uncertain future'.[10]
Socialists claimed that the Empire Settlement Act was a disingenuous,
short-term expedient that was designed to impede the extension of state
welfare, while from the Liberal benches, Western Isles MP Sir William
Mitchell Cotts warned in his maiden speech in July 1923 that emigrants
who left 'with bitterness in their hearts' would 'never forget' the unful-
filled promises of land settlement that had driven them out, however
much they might subsequently prosper.[11]

Nationalist politicians and activists added a new and unequivocally
critical voice to the inter-war debates. From its inception in November
1926 the *Scots Independent*, the journal of the Scots National League,
inveighed against emigration, and pledged itself to end a situation in which

8 R. J. Finlay, 'National Identity in Crisis: Politicians, Intellectuals and the "End
   of Scotland", 1920–1939', *History*, 79 (1994), 244.
9 Marjory Harper, *Emigration from Scotland Between the Wars: Opportunity or
   Exile?* (Manchester, 1998), 202, 209–10.
10 G. M. Thomson, *Scotland That Distressed Area* (Edinburgh, 1935), 5.
11 *Hansard's Parliamentary Debates*, 25 July 1923, vol. 167, col. 570.

Scots were 'compelled to emigrate in scores of thousands every year'.[12] Five months later it accused all other parties of concerning themselves, 'actively or by passive consent, with the concocting of emigration schemes for the further depopulation of Scotland' and in December 1927 it asked, rhetorically, 'If emigration is the cure for unemployment, how comes it that Scotland is in such a plight?'[13] Meanwhile the nationalist journalist and author, George Malcolm Thomson, described Scotland as a country of 'second-hand thoughts and second-rate minds' where 'the hands of the clock have begun to move backwards'.[14] In his pessimistic and pejorative opinion, Scots were a 'dying people' who were being driven to the ends of the earth by Irish Catholic immigration, even more than by economic decline.[15]

The nationalist movement was a broad church, which was represented on the left by the National Party of Scotland and on the right by the Scottish Party. In 1936, two years after they had come together as the Scottish National Party, Sir Andrew Dewar Gibb was appointed chairman of the SNP. An academic lawyer and imperialist, who claimed that Scotland's traditional role at the heart of empire was being destroyed by the country's loss of a distinct identity, he also shared Thomson's xenophobic view that the country's 'eclipse' was attributable to heavy Irish immigration, combined with a simultaneous exodus of Scots.[16] It was a sentiment that was further articulated in the Church of Scotland's notorious call in the 1920s for the wholesale repatriation of Irish Catholic immigrants, who, it claimed, were contributing to unemployment and undermining Scotland's religious identity by taking the jobs and identities of stalwart Presbyterian Scottish emigrants.[17]

12 *Scots Independent*, Nov. 1926, 1.
13 Ibid., April 1927, 3; Dec. 1927, 20.
14 Thomson, *Scotland That Distressed Area*, 5.
15 G. M. Thomson, *Caledonia, or the Future of the Scots* (London, 1927), 10; see also G. McKechnie, *The Best-hated Man: George Malcolm Thomson, Intellectuals and the Condition of Scotland Between the Wars* (Glendaruel, 2013).
16 E. A. Cameron, 'Gibb, Andrew Dewar (1888–1974)', *Oxford Dictionary of National Biography* (Oxford, 2009), online edn, 2010, www.oxforddnb.com/templates/article.jsp?articleid=58792&back= Accessed 13 May 2014. See also A. Dewar Gibb, *Scottish Empire* (London, 1937).
17 *Report of the Committee to consider Overtures on Irish Immigration and the Education (Scotland) Act 1918 to the General Assembly of the Church of Scotland*, 29 May 1923, in *Reports of the Schemes of the Church of Scotland with the*

'Unpatriotic and Treacherous':[18] Lachlan Grant's War on Highland Emigration

It is hardly surprising that Lachlan Grant should have added his voice to this acrimonious debate. He too was in no doubt that emigration represented impoverishment rather than enrichment, and like many of his contemporaries, he deplored the unemployment and social deprivation which he believed were to blame for Scottish enterprise and skill being transplanted elsewhere rather than invested at home. By the 1930s, when he began to engage explicitly with the issues, emigration had not only ground to a halt in the face of the global depression: it had moved into reverse gear. But Grant, aware that this was likely to be a temporary cessation, hammered home his denunciations repeatedly in speeches, newspaper articles and correspondence with politicians.

Grant had connections across the political spectrum and maintained a correspondence with leading politicians. He was a personal friend of Ramsay MacDonald, but a Liberal, who was also active in the early days of the Scottish National Party, and his concerns echoed much of the nationalists' agenda. Unlike most critics, however, he trained his fire almost exclusively on emigration from the Highlands. It was a region where the debate had always been particularly polemical, focusing on the competing claims of inescapable economic reconstruction and inexcusable social dislocation.

In the 1840s and 1850s Donald MacLeod of Strathnaver had lamented the tragedy of clearance-related exile, a theme that was reiterated during the land wars by crofters' spokesmen such as Alexander MacKenzie and John Murdoch.[19] Bards, novelists and outside observers too equated

---

     Legislative Acts passed by the General Assembly, 1923 (Edinburgh, 1923), 749–63. It was a stance that was still maintained by the Free Church of Scotland in the 1970s. (See *Acts and Reports of the General Assembly of the Free Church of Scotland, Report of the Committee on Public Questions, Religion and Morals*, 9, 1972, 163–4).

18 Quoted in 'No more emigration', letter from Grant to editor of *Glasgow Weekly Herald*, 4 Jan. 1936, clipping in Lachlan Grant's scrapbooks, NLS, Acc. 12187/8, f. 112. All subsequent newspaper references are taken from Grant's scrapbooks.

19 D. MacLeod, *Gloomy Memories in the Highlands of Scotland: Versus Mrs Harriet Beecher Stowe's Sunny Memories: A Faithful Picture of the Extirpation of the Celtic Race from the Highlands of Scotland* (Toronto, 1857); A. MacKenzie, *A History of the Highland Clearances* (Inverness, 1883); J. Hunter (ed.), *For the People's Cause: From the Writings of John Murdoch* (Edinburgh, 1986).

emigration with dispossession. The exilic sentiments of the anonymous *Canadian Boat Song*, which first appeared in *Blackwood's Edinburgh Magazine* in 1829, articulated the destructive impact of economic transformation on Highland society.[20] Half a century later John MacLean of Tiree, *Bàrd Bhaile Mhàrtainn* (the Balemartine Bard), reflected not only his own personal sorrow, but also that of the community, in his poem, *Oran Mhanitoba*, composed in 1878 when a group of islanders left for that landlocked prairie province.[21] In the twentieth century the novels and short stories of Ralph Connor, Hugh MacLennan and Alistair MacLeod reinforced themes of loss, dislocation and sometimes success in the teeth of adversity, while more recently the emigrants portrayed in Runrig's *Dance Called America* and *Rocket to the Moon* were simultaneously banished from the old world and enticed to the new.[22]

Lachlan Grant therefore had a rich heritage of anti-emigration polemic on which to draw in his own campaign against the 'damnable system of coercion' that he claimed had compelled so many Highlanders to leave their homeland, enriching other lands to 'the detriment of our own'.[23] He attacked the exodus on various fronts, and his fourteen scrapbooks of cuttings, held in the National Library of Scotland, demonstrate that his statements found their way not just into Scottish and British newspapers, but into the press of the dominions as well.

His opening salvo was particularly controversial. In a letter to the prime minister, Ramsay MacDonald, in March 1934, he linked depopulation with an increase in the number of pauper lunatics in the Highlands and Islands. He returned to that theme in lectures, as well as in an article in the *Caledonian Medical Journal* in 1937.[24] It was a eugenic argument which claimed that the physically and mentally strong had been encouraged, and 'passively compelled' to emigrate, leaving behind a disproportionate

---

20 'From the Gaelic', *Blackwood's Edinburgh Magazine*, xlvi (1829), 400.

21 D. E. Meek, 'Gaelic Township Bards: An Introduction to their Songs and Functions', unpublished lecture to the Gaelic Society of Inverness, 1995, http://meekwrite.blogspot.co.uk/2013/04/gaelic-verse-and-song-gaelic-township.html, last accessed 1 April 2015.

22 Harper, *Scotland No More?*, 159, 193.

23 Lachlan Grant, 'Lunacy and Depopulation', lecture to the MacColl Society, reported in the *Weekly Herald*, 16 Jan. 1937, NLS, Acc. 12187/10, f. 115.

24 Grant to MacDonald, 3 Mar. 1934, NLS, Acc. 12187/8; Lachlan Grant, 'Highland Life, Its Past and Future', *Caledonian Medical Journal*, 15 (1935), 404–11.

and increasing number of old, infirm and degenerate. 'So long as depopulation continues,' he concluded, 'the vicious circle will remain unbroken,
the Highland stock will become progressively poorer and ultimately
become extinct.' In a lecture on 'Lunacy and Depopulation', delivered
to the MacColl Society in January 1937, he reminded his audience that
the Highlands and Islands still topped the table of pauper lunatics in
Scotland. 'Surely the reason for the unenviable position of the Highlands
and Islands is obvious to any person with even an elementary knowledge
of the history of the area,' he argued, but in case they lacked that insight,
he added, 'Emigration and the resultant depopulation is the cause.'[25]

Emigration was all the more repugnant to Lachlan Grant because
it threatened fundamentally the foundations of his 'New Deal for the
Highlands'. A major pillar of that proposal, which he published in autumn
1935 (and which led in February 1936 to the creation of the Highland
Development League under Grant and the Reverend Tom Murchison)
was the need to repopulate the region and give people 'a rooted interest
in their country', if, Grant declared, 'we are to avoid national and racial
suicide'.[26] Land reform could not be achieved, he wrote in the *Northern
Times*, without first stemming the age-old but 'abnormal' tide of migration and emigration. If that prerequisite were ignored, a distinctive
people, language and culture would become extinct.[27] Writing in the
same newspaper two months later, under the strapline 'Churches and
Emigration. A vicious and soulless propaganda', he argued not only that
the Highlands had suffered disproportionately from emigration, but that
publicity about the emigrants' experiences was weighted misleadingly
towards the 4 or 5 per cent who had made good. At least 95 per cent, he
asserted, would have been as well off, or better, at home. While acknow-
ledging that 'adventurous spirits, for whose ambitions the confines of
Scotia are too small', should be released 'with our blessings', he reiterated
his plea that 'the bulk and best of our people [should not] be attracted
abroad by subtle promises', quoting from the Book of Proverbs to drive
home his point and remind readers of the vision of his 'New Deal'.

> The future of Scotland and the Highlands particularly calls for less
> glorification of overseas countries, and more concentration on our

25 *Weekly Herald*, 16 Jan. 1937, NLS, Acc. 12187/10, f. 115.
26 *The Dunfermline Press*, 11 May 1935, NLS, Acc. 12187/8.
27 *Northern Times*, 16 May 1935, NLS, Acc. 12187/8.

own land. 'The eyes of the fool are on the ends of the earth.' The eyes of the Scot are too often bent in the same direction. We require less pioneering abroad, and more men of vision, courage and determination at home. Scotland may not be 'a land flowing with milk and honey', but under wise and courageous guidance she could, as pointed out in the New Deal for the Highlands, become a great influence for good in the world, and capable of giving to her children those homely comforts, that congenial environment through which the body is strengthened and the soul nurtured; in short, all which is worth while, and which so often eludes the wandering exile, seeking imaginary and often elusive fortunes in foreign lands.[28]

Lachlan Grant readily took up cudgels against those who held different views, especially if they played the cards of unemployment or overpopulation. 'Emigration as a cure for our national ills should not be considered, and any advocate of emigration schemes should be considered as a traitor to his country,' was his uncompromising opinion.[29] Recruitment agents were an obvious target, but at the centre of his firing line in July 1935 was the Church and Nation Committee of the Church of Scotland, which had recommended to that year's General Assembly that single women and youths in particular should be encouraged to emigrate to the dominions under the terms of the Empire Settlement Act.[30] In accusing the committee of either 'woeful ignorance, or flagrant audacity', he suggested that such a step would be unwelcome in the dominions, at least in Canada, which was already struggling with farming unemployment, and he quoted from the Saskatchewan section of the United Farmers of Canada that in current circumstances 'it would be almost criminal to allow people to be brought into the country to face almost certain disillusionment'.[31] Grant was more favourably disposed towards the Free Church, whose denunciation of depopulation he contrasted with the 'myopic policy' of the Church of Scotland.

28 *Northern Times*, 4 July 1935, NLS, Acc. 12187/8; see also *Glasgow Weekly Herald*, 4 January 1936 in NLS, Acc. 12187/8. The biblical quotation is from Proverbs 17.24.
29 NLS, Acc. 12187/8, *Glasgow Weekly Herald*, 4 Jan. 1936.
30 'Migration', in *Report of the Committee on Church and Nation*, in Church of Scotland, *Reports to the General Assembly with the Legislative Acts, 1935* (Edinburgh, 1935), 468–9.
31 *Northern Times*, 4 July 1935; *Glasgow Weekly Herald*, 4 Jan. 1936.

Within a fortnight Grant's forthright denunciation of the Church and Nation Committee had elicited trenchant support from veteran Highland Land Leaguer and NPS member, Angus Clark. In a letter to the editor of the *Northern Times*, Clark urged 'every man who has the welfare of the Scottish nation at heart' to 'do his utmost to expose and overthrow these fallacious ideas'. He added that for the national Church 'to remotely suggest further doses of emigration as a remedy for our ills, is almost enough to make the most optimistic despair of organised religion taking its stand truthfully and fearlessly for the cause of our own land and our own folk'. He rounded off his letter with a nationalist rallying call, asserting that the Highlands could only be repopulated if Scotland secured for herself the powers of self-government 'which are our birthright'.[32] A year later he took up his pen again, describing as 'flatulent humbug and pernicious nonsense' the pro-emigration policies that he claimed constituted one of the greatest scandals in Europe:

> Probably a few muddle-headed nonentities will tell us that our loss has been a gain elsewhere, to which we reply that we don't care a sprig of heather for elsewhere: our duty, our responsibility and our affections are or should be for our homeland, and it is up to us to learn well the lesson which past experience teaches.[33]

Grant, meanwhile, also had sharp words for those whose support he felt was cosmetic rather than meaningful. In a speech to the Edinburgh Argyll Association in 1938, he took to task *An Comunn Gàidhealach* and the Highland and Gaelic societies of Scottish and English towns for their failure to lobby the government over the Highland problem. Expatriate Highlanders who had done well in the towns and cities of the Lowlands and England were particularly culpable, having 'almost without exception' been 'conspicuous failures in so far as helping to save their own land and people is concerned'.[34]

Grant's persistent press interventions, as well as the publicity given to his lectures and statements, ensured that Highland emigration remained in the public arena in Scotland, England and in the diaspora. His 'New Deal' pamphlet was, reported a Queensland newspaper, distributed 'all

32 Angus Clark to the editor, *Northern Times*, 18 July 1935.
33 Angus Clark, 'Must the Scot emigrate?', *Weekly Herald*, 25 Apr. 1936.
34 *Inverness Courier*, 14 Oct. 1938, NLS, Acc. 12187/12, f. 78.

over the Empire', while in New Zealand, an editorial in the *Christchurch Star Sun*, which commended the Highland Development League to 'the sympathy and support of the people of all parts of the Empire', claimed that the Scottish Highlands was 'the saddest area in the British Isles to-day'. Meanwhile, in the Transvaal, support for the Highland Development League took tangible form when a group of expatriate Scots founded a 'Help the Homeland' Society to raise money to progress the venture that Grant and Murchison had launched.[35]

Most commentary either endorsed Grant's views, warned would-be emigrants about the disingenuous promises of recruiters, or challenged readers to more effective action in support of Grant's agenda. But he did not go entirely unchallenged. In 1939, the provost of Fort William urged young Highlanders to seek their futures elsewhere. During a recent tour in an unspecified overseas location, he had met 'thousands of Highlanders who have made good, and there is certainly no comparison between the standard of their lives and those of people living in the Highlands today'. Not only were they 'unanimous' in urging young people to emigrate, but 'I asked many of them if they would like to come back to the Highlands, and they all said, "Never again."'[36]

Outcomes: A Battle Lost?

Statistics suggest that, for much of the twentieth century, Highlanders were more inclined to act on the advice of advocates of emigration like the Fort William provost, than on the warnings of Lachlan Grant and other critics. While the issues were less pressing in the 1930s, when international depression had brought the outward movement to a virtual standstill, Grant was anxious to avoid any repetition of the exodus of the 1920s, notably the extraordinary Hebridean haemorrhage of April 1923. Then, in the course of a single week, two transatlantic vessels, the *Marloch* and the *Metagama*, had embarked – at Lochboisdale and Stornoway respectively – a total of over 600 emigrants, who were bound

---

35 *Courier Mail*, Brisbane, 30 Nov. 1935, NLS, Acc. 12187/8, f. 127; *Christchurch Star Sun*, 29 Feb. 1936, NLS, Acc. 12187/9, f. 94; letter from D. MacLeod, Milton House Boys' High School, Polchefstroom, Transvaal, *Evening Times*, 9 May 1938, NLS, Acc. 12187/12, f. 30.

36 Provost MacDonald of Fort William, *The Bulletin*, 2 Aug. 1939, NLS, Acc. 12187/13.

for destinations in Alberta and Ontario.[37] The objective of Grant's rehabilitation strategy, epitomised in the 'New Deal', was to ensure that Highlanders would never again feel the need to take such action. It was not to be. Grant's disappointment that the region was not accorded Special Development Area status in the 1930s was compounded when the outbreak of the Second World War put paid to the Highland Development League, and the cessation of hostilities was soon followed by a renewed wave of emigration from all over Scotland.

Moreover, evidence from passengers on the *Marloch* and the *Metagama*, as well as from subsequent emigrants in the 1920s, suggests that their decisions were not rooted only in need or despair. Of course, the lingering legacy of exile still hung heavily over the Hebrides, where it was reinforced by post-war depression, unemployment, alarmingly high tuberculosis rates, the spectre of famine and frustration at delays in the implementation of land settlement schemes. It was, moreover, invested with a particular pathos in Lewis following the drowning of 175 islanders in the wreck of the troop-carrying ship SS *Iolaire* on 1 January 1919. For some survivors, emigration was a means of escaping from haunting memories and encounters with the families of those who had died.[38]

Despondency and disillusionment were tempered by positive expectations. Wartime encounters with fellow servicemen from other parts of the country had broadened the horizons of Highlanders, who began to attribute their poor living standards not only to official neglect but to the sheer climatic and topographical challenges of their environment. As crofting legislation – for all its limitations – and state pensions began to offer a degree of security to elderly parents, it became easier for young emigrants to leave with a good conscience, and even the *Highland News*, a crofter-supporting newspaper, hailed the departure of the *Metagama* as 'the first glimmer of the dawn of better things'.[39] And although many were suspicious of the obligations associated with the Empire Settlement

37 The events of 1923 are analysed in Harper, *Emigration from Scotland Between the Wars*, 97–108. For a specific study of the *Metagama* emigration, see J. Wilkie, *Metagama: A Journey from Lewis to the New World* (Edinburgh, 2001, first published 1987).

38 J. MacLeod, *When I Heard the Bell: The Loss of the* Iolaire (Edinburgh, 2010); author's conversation with Donna Macleod, Bayble, Lewis, 18 Nov. 2009. Donna's uncle, Murdo, a survivor of the *Iolaire*, emigrated to Canada shortly after the tragedy because he could not cope with the memories or the questions.

39 *Highland News*, 28 Apr. 1923.

Act, it was, unlike previous subsidies, a nationwide piece of legislation, which did not single out Highlanders as particular objects of charity.

The recollections of individual participants can offer an insight into some of the ambiguities and paradoxes associated with the emigrant experience. Morag Bennett was ten years old when she left Benbecula for Alberta with her parents and six siblings. She relived the experience in an interview 82 years later, recalling that the decision to leave was taken because there was 'nothing in Benbecula for the family'. The voyage on the *Marloch* was a source of wonderment, as was her childhood experience of the prairies, although she acknowledged the challenges faced by her parents and others as they struggled to make a living in a remote, climatically hostile community that was bedevilled by inadequate preparation and poor after-care on the part of the recruitment agent, Andrew Macdonell, and the emigrants' reluctance to learn from their neighbours.[40]

In his denunciation of Highland emigration, Lachlan Grant did not take account of the positive tradition of wanderlust that was often passed from generation to generation. It is illustrated clearly in the experiences of the Murray family from Shader in Lewis. In 1907 Donald Murray left for Canada, along with several other islanders, and worked on grain elevators at Thunder Bay (then called Fort William) in northern Ontario. He came home during the war with the intention of joining up, but actually stayed in Lewis, where he married in 1917. After seven years he returned to Canada, moving west to Prince Rupert on the Pacific coast in 1926. A year later he was joined by his wife and five children, but Margaret Murray brought the family back to Lewis after her husband's death in a workplace accident in 1933. Calum, however, was to follow in his father's footsteps. Like many islanders, he initially saw the world with the merchant navy, but in 1954 he returned to Canada, where he found a job freighting grain from Thunder Bay to ports on the Great Lakes and the St Lawrence. In a pattern that was also familiar to many islanders, he then settled down to the life of the long-distance commuter, spending the next thirty years moving between his seasonal work in Canada and his marital home in Lewis.

Calum Murray, and his sister Cathie (who later emigrated to New Zealand), were part of a significant post-war resurgence of emigration,

40 Author's telephone interview with Morag Bennett, nee MacLeod, Sechelt, British Columbia, 21 Feb. 2005. See also Harper, *Scotland No More?*, 197, 206–7, 210.

and their positive sentiments offer a different perspective from the unambiguously exilic scenario painted by Lachlan Grant. But there was no single diasporic narrative, either of compulsion or choice. Perhaps the last word should go to another post-war emigrant, Ena Macdonald from North Uist. She went to the Antipodes on a £10 passage, but as a newly-wed to Australia in the 1960s rather than as a single woman to New Zealand in the 1940s, and with a sense of trepidation rather than excitement. Like Cathie, she also returned to the Hebrides, but after less than four years, with bitter memories of a heart-wrenching and incurable homesickness and a broken marriage. 'I was homesick before I even went,' she recalled in 2011. 'It was crazy, absolutely crazy. I should never have – I should never have gone.' A visit back to North Uist in 1964 did nothing to assuage her homesickness, and when the time came to return to Australia with her month-old son, she was 'dreading going back, absolutely dreading it. And I can still remember, I think everybody in the village came down to say cheerio to me, when – just going out the gate there, and I looked behind and my father was running after the car. Oh, I nearly just said "Stop, I'm not going."'[41] Had it been available 70 years earlier, Ena's testimony would surely have provided Lachlan Grant with powerful fuel for his campaign to eradicate the 'vicious and soulless propaganda' which, he argued so vehemently and persistently, was the scourge of the twentieth-century Highlands.

41 Author's interview with Ena Macdonald, Kyles, Bayhead, North Uist, 7 Sept. 2011; Harper, *Scotland No More?*, 214–16.

CHAPTER 6

'Outside the ranks of those who stand for the traditional and sentimental'?
Lachlan Grant and Economic Development

EWEN A. CAMERON

This chapter concerns Lachlan Grant's ideas about the economic development of the Highlands. The focus will be on the 1930s for the most part, the decade in which he published his *New Deal for the Highlands*, but his views had been maturing for many years, as the essays in this collection show. As is also clear from the other contributions, Grant did not see economic development as isolated from, far less in tension with, plans for the land question, the survival and promotion of Gaelic or means by which emigration could be halted and depopulation slowed down. Although Grant was regarded as an important voice in the discussion about the Highlands he was also subjected to significant criticism from those who took different approaches, notably those on the left. This was also a topic on which he disagreed with his friend J. Ramsay MacDonald, who took a rather romantic view of the Highlands. This emerged clearly over debates about the construction of a road through Glencoe. Grant's view of the Highlands was thoroughly unsentimental. One newspaper developed this theme accurately in its response to the formation of the Highland Development League in 1936:

> Dr Grant is outside the ranks of those who stand for the traditional and sentimental illusion that the wheels of industry run on bearings which must always lead to the deterioration of the cultural qualities of life. Nor does he accept readily that the theoretic ideal of the romantic beauty of the countryside depends on the ruthless exclusion of an occasional chimney stalk or the elimination of tunnels and pipelines penetrating areas where the foot of man is now that of a trespasser on preserves.[1]

1 *Ross-shire Journal,* 28 Feb. 1936.

This was an important element in Grant's outlook in the 1930s, a decade which saw the formation of the National Trust for Scotland, the Association for the Preservation of Rural Scotland and concerted opposition from landowning interests to the development of hydro-electric schemes designed to provide power for industrial projects.[2] Grant regarded such views as counter-productive and designed to block the economic development of the region. He outlined his views in an important article in 1937, one of the themes of which was to draw attention to the importance of slate-quarrying and, more widely, to the broader industrial potential of the region:

> It is nonsense to suggest that the highlander is not an industrialist. The highlander has shown that where industry is made available in his own land he is there heart and soul, but because of the lack of facilities he has perforce to go willy-nilly to become an industri-alist wherever opportunity offers in various parts of the Britain and many parts of the world.[3]

This discussion of attitudes, perceptions and assumptions about the limits within which the Highland problem could be discussed is impor-tant in considering this aspect of Grant's career. As Andrew Perchard will show in his chapter, Grant, as medical officer to the British Aluminium Company, and before that in the Ballachulish slate quarries, had a firm appreciation of the potential contribution of manufacturing and extractive industries to the Highland economy. This can be seen in three particular episodes, two important and one relatively trivial but quite telling. The first concerns the discussion over the building of a road through Glencoe in the late 1920s. Grant was firmly in favour of this project; he believed it would stimulate the tourist industry in the area. Indeed, when the road opened in March 1934 Grant was the first motorist to use it.[4] This was something about which he disagreed with Ramsay MacDonald, who described the road through Glencoe as a 'plutocratic abomination' and 'a perfect horror which completely destroys the spirit of Glencoe and turns it into a mere insignificant incident in the road

---

2 Hayden Lorimer, "'Your wee bit hill and glen": The Cultural Politics of the Scot-tish Highlands, *c.* 1918–1945', PhD thesis, University of Loughborough, 1997.
3 *Highland News*, 4 Sept. 1937.
4 This was the subject of a letter of Grant's to the *Oban Times*, 26 Nov. 1927; see also *Oban Times*, 31 Mar. 1934.

between John O'Groats and Lands End'.[5] MacDonald did have the grace to admit that he was partly responsible for the construction of the road. In 1927 Grant had written to MacDonald to press him to bring influence to bear to have the project begun, as it would help relieve unemployment and benefit 'our old Highlands and the famous Glencoe'. MacDonald did, indeed, use his influence with the Ministry of Transport to have the work expedited and pressed Labour colleagues, such as Thomas Johnston (to whom he forwarded Grant's letter) to raise the matter in the House of Commons.[6] MacDonald was, as ever, sensitive to the accusation that his opposition was in league with preservationist landowners such as Lochiel and Lord Strathcona, owner of Glencoe. He told Grant that his opposition was based on his fatigue over 'destruction of peace and undisturbed nature' and the extent to which the new road would have 'spoiled' the glen. He further remarked that he could understand why 'vandalism tempts you', faced, as Grant was on a daily basis, by the 'terrible conditions in the Highlands'.[7] MacDonald raised himself to almost absurd rhetorical heights when Grant confronted him with the idea of turning Glencoe into a national park when it was put on the market by Lord Strathcona in 1931:

I suppose a park in the highlands is one of the inevitabilities of this machine run and mass producing age. I remain a solitary, and love to take to the mountains as one of two or three at the most. For this confession you will put me down as an incurable and think of some of your beneficent and admirably run asylums. If there are chara-bancs and public parks in Heaven, I will keep out of it and take the consequences, and when you get there and undergo enlightenment which all just men do in the course of their being made perfect, I am sure you will agree with me. It is no use kicking against the pricks. The age is a park age, a waste-paper age, and a rotting-remnant-of-pork-sandwiches-on-the-grass-age, and I am a voice crying in the

5 MacDonald to Grant, 19 Aug. 1932, NLS, Lachlan Grant Collection, Acc. 12187/6, f. 149; Rose Rosenberg (MacDonald's private secretary) to Grant, 25 Oct. 1932, f. 153.

6 Grant to MacDonald, 3 March 1927, TNA, James Ramsay MacDonald Mss, PRO 30/69/1172/2 ff. 598–9,; MacDonald to Wilfred Ashley (Ministry of Transport) 7 Mar. 1927, f. 600; MacDonald to Johnston, 21 Mar. 1927, f. 609; Grant to MacDonald 29 Mar. 1927, ff. 612–13.

7 MacDonald to Grant, 28 Nov. 1927, TNA, James Ramsay MacDonald Mss, PRO 30/69/1172/2 ff. 621; MacDonald to Grant, 5 Dec. 1927, f. 622.

wilderness – a wilderness, by the by, which will soon disappear from our civilisation – so I leave you to enjoy your triumphs.[8]

As we shall see in later parts of this essay, these views were the polar opposite of Grant's vision for the Highlands. He had seen the idea of a national park as a means of providing employment, attracting tourists – with their pork sandwiches – and, ultimately, countering national 'degeneracy'. This was evident from a second episode – the controversy over the Caledonian Power Scheme in 1937 – which was a plan by the British Oxygen Company (BOC) to develop a large carbide factory at Fort William that would provide extensive local employment. The construction of the associated hydro-electric power generation facilities required legislative approval from Parliament and this stimulated a fierce debate. Alexander MacEwan was closely associated with BOC and Grant was a strong advocate of the scheme on the grounds of its potential contribution to the Highland economy. He found the opposition to the scheme from the Highlands puzzling:

> In view of the clamour for development it is difficult to understand that extreme opposition on the part of a few influential people to the Caledonian Power Scheme. Here, we have a progressive measure which, exploiting an untapped natural resource, would create a prosperous new community in the Highlands. Surely, in an area where depopulation has gone hand in hand with our decline, this is a step in the right direction, and anticipates in some measure the development and reconstruction, at which the Highland Development League aims.[9]

This point of view was opposed by those who saw industrialisation as unacceptable for the Highlands. One critic argued that he did not want to see the Gael dragged down to the 'physical and mental level of the chemical workers of Jarrow and South Wales'. The example of Lord Leverhulme's failure to convince some of the population of Lewis of

8 MacDonald to Grant, 26 Dec. 1931, NLS, Lachlan Grant Collection, Acc. 12187/6, f. 133.
9 C. M. Birnie, '"New Deal" or Raw Deal? Public Administration and Economic Development in the Highlands and Islands of Scotland, 1929–39', unpublished MSc dissertation, University of Edinburgh, 2003, 47–62; Lachlan Grant, 'Caledonian Power Scheme must go on', *Glasgow Weekly Herald*, 2 Jan. 1937.

the value of his ideas demonstrated that industry was not 'congenial' to the 'racial aptitudes' of the Gaels. Highland development, for some, but not Grant, could only proceed along the lines of extension of traditional industries such as fishing, forestry and agriculture.[10] There were also critics of Grant's stance on the Caledonian Power Scheme from a left-wing point of view. The Communist novelist James Barke was a vocal example. He argued that the scheme demonstrated the capitalist lust for profit and he expressed his opposition to the recurrence of the industrial revolution in the Highlands.[11] Grant's resistance to romantic viewpoints is a telling feature of his outlook. It helps to contextualise his loyal, uncritical, support of the activities of the BACo at Kinlochleven and Fort William, some elements of which bore out the leftist criticisms of Grant's approach. These episodes cannot, however, be considered in isolation. Grant was a contributor, albeit a prominent one, in an extensive debate about conditions in the Highlands. This debate was, in turn, a component of wider discussions about conditions of rural areas in Britain and Ireland. In the remainder of this essay these issues will be discussed.

Grant's contributions were a prominent part of a general debate about the condition of the Highlands. This was not new in the 1930s, of course, but the discussion did take a distinct turn, perhaps back towards older ideas, in that decade. A combination of factors after 1929 changed the context for thinking about Highland development. The most important was the onset of a major economic depression. This was much more serious and widespread than those of the mid-1880s or the mid-1900s. Not only did it cover most sectors of the Scottish economy, including agriculture, it was part of a global downturn. Although the depression brought to a halt the large-scale emigration of the 1920s, and may have induced modest return emigration, the legacy of the exodus was a sense that much valuable 'human resource' had been lost and that Scottish identity was under threat.[12] Nevertheless, the 1930s also saw the

10 Colonel W. Campbell Galbraith, 'Power Scheme a menace to the Highlands: reply to Dr Lachlan Grant', *Glasgow Weekly Herald*, 9 Jan. 1937.

11 James Barke, 'Scheme must not be allowed to proceed: Highlands would be despoiled', *Glasgow Weekly Herald*, 16 Jan. 1937.

12 Ewen A. Cameron, *Impaled on a Thistle: Scotland since 1880* (Edinburgh, 2010), 46–54; R. J. Finlay, 'National Identity in Crisis: Politicians, Intellectuals and the "end of Scotland", 1920–1939', *History*, 79 (1994), 242–59; Richard Anthony, *Herds and Hinds: Farm Labour in Lowland Scotland, 1900 –1939* (East Linton, 1997), 14–55.

beginnings of proactive suggestions for economic development from
interests within the Highlands; hitherto, the process had been rather
top-down and driven by central government or private economic interests. The Highland Reconstruction Association attempted to capitalise
on the immediate post-war moment to argue for government investment in the Highlands.[13] This was an organisation which was drawn
broadly from different layers of opinion in Highland society, including
some landowners such as Lord Lovat and Cameron of Lochiel, as well as
Alexander MacEwen.[14] In the 1930s the Highland Development League
drew more on the contemporary inspiration of Roosevelt's 'New Deal' in
the USA than on the historical precedent of the Highland Land League.
The moving forces in the new League were Rev. Thomas M. Murchison,
the Church of Scotland minister at Glenelg, and Dr Grant. They had
been working independently towards a similar end: a new organisation to lobby for the cause of Highland development. Murchison had
presented a petition to the Scottish Office on behalf of crofters in his
parish who were saddled with debts to the Board of Agriculture, having
taken on holdings at times of very high prices.[15]

The Highland Development League was founded in Glasgow in
1936 and proved to be an effective cross-party lobby for Highland
economic diversification.[16] In his important pamphlet, *A New Deal for
the Highlands*, Grant argued such development had to be comprehensive
and diverse, including 'farming, fishing, tweed-making, afforestation,
mineral industries and quarrying and all the probable local industries
[. . .]'.[17] This pamphlet had begun life as an element in his correspondence
with Ramsay MacDonald. In October 1934 Grant sent a memorandum
to MacDonald outlining his ideas for planning for Highland development by dividing the area into districts and undertaking a detailed
survey to ascertain the possibilities for further land settlement and other
improvements. MacDonald promised to have them examined by the

13 Hugh F. Campbell, *Highland Reconstruction* (Glasgow, 1920).
14 D. W. Cameron of Lochiel to Grant, no date (but *c.* Feb 1936), NLS, Lachlan
    Grant Collection, Acc. 12187/9, f. 21.
15 Donald E. Meek, 'Preacher, Prose-writer, Politician, Journalist and Scholar:
    The Very Rev. Dr Thomas Moffat Murchison (1907–1984)', *Scottish Church
    History Society Records*, 36 (2006), 5–27.
16 *Aberdeen Press and Journal*, 20 Jan. 1936, 7.
17 Lachlan Grant, *A New Deal for the Highlands* (Glasgow, 1935).

Scottish Office. This examination concluded that the greatest proportion of land settlement activity was in the Highlands, but that the focus was now shifting to the Lowlands for the purpose of unemployment relief. The official conclusion was that 'It does not therefore appear to be opportune at the present time to undertake a survey of the Highlands and Islands for the purpose of ascertaining what more can be or ought to be done there.'[18] This official caution would not have surprised Grant had he been privy to these comments. He informed MacDonald that the activity around the 'New Deal for the Highlands' had 'caused the biggest ripple on the placidity of Highland affairs in our generation, and it is still rippling'.[19] An important point made by both Grant and Murchison was that, although official policy initiatives were required to deal with the problems of the highlands, the people of the region also had a responsibility to be active and apply pressure on the government. Murchison argued that land settlement would inevitably be compromised without improvements in other areas, such as transport, but that 'it lies with the highlanders themselves to apply themselves to the up-building of the Highlands that ought to be'.[20] The supporters of the New Deal and the Highland Development League were presented with an ideal opportunity to encourage this activity when a by-election was called in Ross-shire on the elevation to the peerage, as Lord Strathcarron, of the sitting MP, J. Ian MacPherson. This was an unusually highly publicised election campaign, as among the candidates were Malcolm MacDonald (National Labour), son of Ramsay MacDonald, and Randolph Churchill (Independent Unionist), son of Winston Churchill. It was, however, the Labour candidate, Hector McNeil (a future Secretary of State for Scotland) who articulated the general position of the HDL most effectively.[21] The HDL's position had quite wide support in sections of the Scottish press, notably in the *Northern Times*, for which Grant frequently wrote, the *Highland News* and the *Stornoway Gazette*, as well as some

18 Observations on memorandum submitted to the prime minister by Dr Lachlan Grant, TNA, J. R.MacDonald Mss, PRO30/69/1518, Department of Agriculture for Scotland.

19 Grant to MacDonald, 25 Nov. 1934, TNA, J. R. MacDonald Mss, PRO30/69/1445, f. 546.

20 T. M. Murchison, 'Why I support the New Land League', *Glasgow Weekly Herald*, 10 Aug. 1935.

21 Ewen A. Cameron, 'Rival Foundlings: The Ross and Cromarty By-election of February 1936', *Historical Research*, 81 (2008), 507–30.

more progressive titles in the Lowlands.[22] The principal source of opposition to Grant's views on Highland development came from the left and was articulated in the columns of *Forward*, a Glasgow newspaper associated with the Independent Labour Party and once edited by Thomas Johnston. A range of writers lined up to argue that Grant and the HDL were insufficiently radical on this and other questions. Lachlan MacNeill Weir proposed an extreme solution:

> If the good doctor had proposed that the Highlanders shoot their enemies, the Highland landlords, beginning with their greatest and most treacherous enemies of all, the so-called clan chiefs, then Whitehall would sit up and take notice, and there would be some hope for the economic salvation of the Highlands. To suggest this is not to advocate assassinating a bed bug. Extirpate is the word. The Highlanders learnt how to eradicate parasites in France. A delousing drill in the Highlands would be effective for Dr Grant's purpose.[23]

Forward's report on the establishment of the HDL in January 1936 concluded that it was merely proposing a 'rejuvenation of Highland life under capitalism', a plan which they opined was 'impossible'. Joseph Duncan, who had helped Grant with the Crofters' and Cottars' Association in 1906, was equally scathing. He argued that there was nothing particularly distinctive about the problems of the Highlands. Other areas of rural Scotland, such as the north-east, had equally pressing problems. He also concluded that the basic solution was the eradication of the landlord class.[24] Duncan would have his chance to influence Highland policy when he was appointed to the Scottish Economic Committee's investigation of the problems of the Highlands.

The mid-1930s was a period in which government and a wide range of political opinion was interested in the idea of economic planning. Indeed, 'Political and Economic Planning', one of the main pressure groups in this interest, produced a publication on the Highlands. This gave a positive reference to the HDL and argued for a programme broadly similar to that advocated by Grant, Murchison and their colleagues.[25] The effect

22 *Stornoway Gazette*, 24 Jan. 1936; *Northern Times*, 25 Jan. 1936; *Daily Record and Mail*, 13 May 1936; *Highland News*, 16 May 1936.
23 *Forward*, 28 Sept. 1935.
24 *Forward*, 25 Jan. 1936; 1 Feb. 1936.
25 'The State of the Highlands', *Planning: A Broadsheet Issued by PEP*, 8 Sept. 1936.

of the economic depression had broadened the spectrum of politicians prepared to grant to the government a role in the economy. The National Government had passed the Special Areas Acts in 1934 and 1936, designed to address the problems of areas of high unemployment, rather than the issues facing the Highlands. The problems of the Highlands were viewed by officials as being rooted in the physical conditions of the region and the historical experience which it had undergone since the eighteenth century. It was argued that this could not be dealt with by the economic activities that the Special Areas Acts were designed to stimulate. This view extended to members of the business community in Scotland, some of whom expressed the view that economic policy made in London was insensitive to the Scottish economy, in which older heavy industries were over-represented. Organisations such as the Scottish National Development Council (of which the Highland Liberal and nationalist politician Sir Alexander MacEwen was a founding member) and its offshoot the Scottish Economic Committee, articulated this view to a wider public.[26] Among the series of reports which the SEC published in the late 1930s was a penetrating analysis of the condition of the Highlands. The committee which drew up this report was chaired by a Skye landowner, Edward Hilleary, included the agricultural trade unionist Joseph Duncan and was supported by Adam Collier, later killed in a mountaineering accident. Collier's posthumously published *The Crofting Problem* (1953) was a very important analysis of the economic and social issues facing the region. Although the SEC was a non-official body there had been consultation with the government at the time of its appointment, and when its investigation concluded there was a private admission that its report could not be ignored.[27]

The Hilleary Report was the most broad-ranging investigation of the condition of the Highlands since the Napier Commission in the 1880s.[28] It revealed a series of deep-seated problems which could not be dealt with by further reform to land tenure or the extension of the

---

26 Angus MacKenzie, 'Self-help and Propaganda: The Scottish National Development Council, 1931–1939', *JSHS*, 30 (2010), 123–45; R. H. Campbell, 'The Scottish Office and the Special Areas in the 1930s', *Historical Journal*, 22 (1979), 167–83.

27 Notes of a meeting of officials at the Scottish Office, 7 Dec 1938, NRS, DD 15/2.

28 Birnie, '"New Deal" or Raw Deal?', 66–8.

land settlement programme. More fundamental shifts in the economy of the region were required. The introduction of new industries based on development of the water power resources of the Highlands, promotion of the tourist industry, expansion of forestry and stimulation of traditional activities such as fishing and Harris-tweed weaving were at the centre of their recommendations. There was a recognition that both full-time and part-time employment opportunities were required and that crofting 'though modified by state action [. . .] persists in the face of economic and social forces working against its survival'.[29] The most important recommendation of the Committee, however, was for the appointment of a Highland Development Commissioner. This suggestion did not carry universal agreement. Alexander MacEwen, for one, was opposed, referring to the Commissioner as a potential 'dictator for the highlands'. He felt that a commissioner could easily become an agent of government policy rather than an advocate for Highland development. A permanent board led by someone with extensive experience of the Highlands would, in his eyes, be more effective. MacEwen, as befitted a nationalist, also argued that 'absentee government is as bad as absentee landlords' and that a 'spiritual and cultural awakening was necessary for any economic revival'. Indeed, another nationalist, Hugh Quigley, a friend of Grant, had advanced essentially the same argument in 1936. These were typical of the approach of moderate nationalists of this period who sought to reform the position of Scotland within the United Kingdom.[30]

Across the political spectrum there was strong support for the implementation of Hilleary's recommendations. One leading Unionist wrote to John Colville, the Secretary of State for Scotland, confessing his alarm 'at the decay of rural life' in the Highlands and expressing his unwillingness to 'inter it in the interests of financial orthodoxy'. A nationalist argued that a 'government who can afford to give a loan of £30 million to Czechoslovakia can surely afford a few millions to save the highlands

---

29 Scottish Economic Committee, *The Highlands and Islands of Scotland: A Review of the Economic Conditions with Recommendations for Improvement* (1938), 21.

30 Sir Alexander MacEwen, 'A Dictator for the Highlands? The Strengths and Weaknesses of the Scottish Economic Committee's Report', *Scots Magazine*, 30 (1938–9), 293–8; see also Alexander MacEwen, *Act Now for the Highlands* (Edinburgh, 1939); Hugh Quigley, *A Plan for the Highlands, Proposals for a Highland Development Board* (London, 1936).

from depopulation and relegation to the status of a sportsman's paradise or a desert'.[31] Nationalist opinion tended to argue that the evidence of government neglect of the Highlands indicated the need for a Scottish parliament.[32] Grant was firmly behind the main recommendations of Hilleary's committee and was supportive of the notion of a Highland development commissioner.[33] The first newsletter of the HDL, published in July 1939, devoted its columns to urging the government to adopt these ideas and the Edinburgh branch of the HDL wrote to the Secretary of State for Scotland to demand legislation 'to assist Highland development on the lines laid down in their report, or are the Highland people to be left entirely to their own resources'.[34]

In some senses the context of the late 1930s contained positive elements for the task of Highland development. Although a nationalist politics was emerging in partisan form with the formation of the SNP in 1934, it was marginal in electoral form. The late 1930s, however, saw a bolstering of Scottish administration with the Gilmour Report which recommended reorganisation and strengthening of the Scottish Office. This betokened an increase in the status of Scottish affairs in central government. There were also negative features and this can be seen in the government response to the Hilleary Committee's Report. The drift towards war in 1939 meant that detailed consideration of the funding of Highland development took place in a very unpromising climate. Much dissatisfaction arose from the announcement in August 1939 of limited funding, amounting to only around £65,000, for the Highlands. This had, of course, been the outcome of negotiations with the Treasury in London and the perceived miserliness of their outlook placed the Secretary of Scotland in a difficult position given the expectations generated by the report and perceived governmental generosity in

31 P. J. Blair (Scottish Unionist Party) to Colville, 3 Feb. 1939 and James Fraser (secretary, London Branch of the SNP) to Colville, 17 Dec. 1938, NRS, DD 15/4. This file also contains representations from other Unionists, the Highland Development League, the Convention of Royal Burghs and the Scottish Land and Property Federation. There are representations from local authorities and other bodies at DD15/5 and /11.
32 *Scots Independent*, Aug. 1939.
33 *Northern Times*, 23 Feb. 1939.
34 Edinburgh HDL to Secretary of State for Scotland, 17 Jun. 1939, NLS, Lachlan Grant Collection, Acc. 12187/13. f. 54; *Highland News Letter*, No. 1, July 1939, f. 62.

other areas.[35] The disappointment was compounded by the coincidence of an announcement on the same day of funding for the development of Newfoundland worth several million pounds. This led some politicians, and not only nationalists, to argue that Scotland might be better off as a dominion than as part of the United Kingdom. Bob Boothby, the independently-minded Conservative, articulated this argument. There were other views, however. The *Inverness Courier* argued that the Commission had wasted two years investigating well-known issues and that its conclusions were rather predictable.[36]

Although there were times in which this debate was conducted in a tone of Highland exceptionalism, there were parallels in other parts of the country. In Wales, where government intervention in the land question had been less pronounced than in Scotland or Ireland, the debate also turned towards the idea of development and diversification through such exigencies as hydro-electricity. Industrial unemployment was also a major theme in Wales and land settlement was seen as one possible way to deal with that problem.[37] In Ireland, however, the 'land question' reigned supreme. Although land purchase had been extensive prior to partition, both Cumann na nGaedheal and, in the 1930s, Fianna Fáil governments, especially the latter, stuck to the idea that breaking up estates and creating new smallholdings was the correct response to the injustices of rural Ireland. In the Irish case the land question was at the heart of the national movement but there was another contrast: the victims of the economic depression in the industrial region around Belfast were not the problem of the government of the new Free State. Had partition not occurred and had De Valera and Fianna Fáil been governing the thirty-two counties, as they wished, it would have been much more difficult to pursue the settlement of the land question in the way that they did in the 1930s. They too might have had to

---

35 See the correspondence between the Scottish Office and the Treasury in NRS, DD15/15, esp. John Colville to John Simon (Chancellor of the Exchequer), 20 Jul. 1939.

36 *Inverness Courier*, 8 Aug. 1939.

37 Denis Linehan and Pyrs Gruffudd, 'Unruly Topographies: Unemployment, Citizenship and Land Settlement in Inter-war Wales', *Transactions of the Institute of British Geographers*, 29 (2004), 46–63; Pyrs Gruffudd, 'Back to the Land: Historiography, Rurality and the Nation in Interwar Wales', *Transactions of the Institute of British Geographers*, 19 (1994), 61–77.

consider the same issues which were current in Scotland and Wales.[38]

The evidence provided by this debate suggests that the period immediately before the outbreak of the Second World War was a significant one. Historians who have addressed this period have, understandably, argued that the unwillingness of the government to fund the proposals of the Hilleary Commission represented a missed opportunity. Taking a slightly longer view, however, it is possible to say something different. The difficult experience of the region in the 1930s and the reorientation towards the industrial lowlands of the land settlement operation had moved the debate about the condition of the Highlands into new areas.[39] Although few of the issues raised in this debate – exploitation of water resources, how to deal with poverty, diversification of the industrial base of the Highlands, emigration – had been resolved, it was strikingly different in tone and content compared to what had gone before. The 'developmental' approach to the problems of the region was not new in the interwar period. Indeed, it might be said that the period from the 1880s to the 1920s, when the focus of government policy was largely on the land issue, was the anomalous period. The idea of developing the economy of the Highlands, not entirely neglected by bodies like the Congested Districts board (1897 to 1912) drew on ideas evident in the eighteenth century that aimed at the fundamental reorientation of the region's economy and society in the aftermath of the Jacobite rebellion.[40] In the 1930s this 'developmental' approach was recognised as the one most likely to yield results. If Grant's ideas may not have been entirely original he was a very important and articulate voice packaging these ideas and presenting them through his tireless advocacy by pen and speech.

38 Terence Dooley, 'The Land for the People': The Land Question in Independent Ireland (Dublin, 2004), 57–131, 201–27; David Seth Jones, 'Land reform legislation and security of tenure in Ireland after independence', Eire-Ireland, 32/33 (1997–8), 116–43; Nuala C. Johnson, 'Building a nation: an examination of the Irish Gaeltacht Commission Report of 1926', Journal of Historical Geography, 19 (1993), 157–68.

39 Alexander S. Mather, 'The rise and fall of government-assisted land settlement in Scotland', Land Use Policy, 2 (1985), 222–3.

40 Alison M. McCleery, 'The Role of the Highland Development Agency with Particular Reference to the Work of the Congested Districts Board, 1897–1912', unpublished PhD thesis (University of Glasgow, 1984).

CHAPTER 7

'The new paternalism in industry pays'
Dr Lachlan Grant and the British Aluminium Company

ANDREW PERCHARD

Writing in the *Caledonian Medical Journal* (*CMJ*) in January 1930, Dr Lachlan Grant ventured:

> Voltaire said that labour rids us of three great evils – irksomeness, vice, poverty. But to do this effectually the labour must be on a moralized basis, and in proportion to man's needs and capacities. Man's whole sphere of manifestation has been divided into thinking and acting [. . .] Enlightened captains of industry like the Leverhulmes, the Fords, and the Cadburys have rediscovered the fact that man is not a machine, and that his capacity for work has a psychological side. They have found from experience that sufficient leisure not only conduces to the workers' health and happiness but to loyal service, augmented output, and a higher quality of work. The new 'paternalism' in industry pays, and also makes for stability and social progress.[1]

Behind 'the Leverhulmes, the Fords, and the Cadburys', his mind was focused squarely on his own relationship with the British Aluminium Company Ltd (BACo). As Grant observed in the *CMJ* five years later:

> The enterprise of the British Aluminium Company, and the very great benefit to the Highland communities of Kinlochleven, Foyers, and Inverlochy, resulting from their operations, might well be repeated in other parts of the Highlands. To a far seeing Gael – Mr. W. Murray Morrison of the Aluminium Company – is mainly

1 The author wishes to express his gratitude to the staff at Glasgow University Archives Services, Highland Council library (Fort William), the National Library of Scotland, and the library of the Royal College of Physicians and Surgeons Glasgow (RCPSG). Lachlan Grant, 'Work and Leisure', *Caledonian Medical Journal* (*CMJ*), 14:5 (January 1930), 160, Library of the RCPSG.

due the credit for the development of this hitherto neglected, great national asset – water power.[2]

This chapter explores Lachlan Grant's relationship with British Aluminium, a role that was tempered by his social activism, as a 'Doctor of Society'.[3] It locates his public advocacy of the Company within the context of the politics of Highland development. Finally, it examines British Aluminium's cultivation of its relationship with Dr Grant as part of a broader corporate political strategy to garner support for its activities in the region, supported by nurturing networks and personal relationships amongst local power brokers in the Highlands. The policy vacuum in the Highlands and Islands – given the indifference of government to the region for much of the first half of the twentieth century – enabled BACo to pursue a 'quiet politics', developing networks and personal relationships which would pay dividends in promoting legislation and opening doors; providing insights into the means of, as well as the motivations behind, corporate political activity.[4] This management of 'political risk' at local, as well as national and international, levels became increasingly important in the twentieth century. As Geoffrey Jones and Christina Lubinski have observed of the shifting global political economic environment from the First World War: 'In the broadest sense, the management of distance was replaced by the management of governments as a central challenge.'[5] At a national level, British Aluminium pursued a close relationship with government. Key to BACo's 'quiet politics' was the personal relationship established by the Company's *pater familias* (himself a Highlander), William Murray Morrison, and prominent political figures and landed elites in the region.[6]

2 NLS, Dr Lachlan Grant Collection (LGC), Acc. 12187/8, Lachlan Grant, 'Highland Life, Its Past and its Future', *CMJ*, 15 (July–October 1935), 125–8.

3 S. Taylor, *A Natural History of Everyday Life: A Biographical Guide for the Would-be Doctors of Society* (London, 1988), cited in R. Cooter, 'The Rise and Decline of the Medical Member: Doctors and Parliament in Edwardian and Interwar Britain', *Bulletin of the History of Medicine*, 78 (2004), 64.

4 P. D. Culpepper, *Quiet Politics and Business Power: Corporate Control in Europe and Japan* (Cambridge, 2010).

5 G. Jones and C. Lubinski, 'Managing Political Risk in Global Business: Beiersdorff 1914–1990', *Enterprise & Society*, 13 (2012), 86–7.

6 For more about BACo's corporate political activities, as well as their operations, see: A. Perchard, *Aluminiumville: Government, Global Business and the Scottish*

'Saviours to the Highlands'? British Aluminium in the Highlands

Formed in 1894, British Aluminium established their first aluminium smelter in the west Highlands of Scotland at Foyers on the banks of Loch Ness in 1896. Plants at Kinlochleven in Argyllshire and at Fort William, the Lochaber smelter, followed in 1907 and 1929 respectively. These smelters formed the backbone of the Company's global operations, which stretched eventually from the Highlands to Australia, British Guiana (present day Guyana), Canada, France, India, the Gold Coast (Ghana) and Norway. In view of the energy intensiveness of electrolytic aluminium production, British Aluminium were attracted to the Highlands and Islands by the potential of cheap electricity promised by harnessing the region's water catchment areas and fall. In what was considered a 'problem area', in which many communities remained heavily reliant on subsistence (and seasonal) activities – like crofting and fishing – for survival, the benefit of attracting jobs and capital investment of this nature was significant. It should also be noted, contrary to persistent stereotypes, that the region had a long history of industrial development including chemical manufacture, coal mining, iron smelting and slate quarrying.[7] Of added benefit was the fact that British Aluminium offered 'crofting and fishing leave' to allow smelter workers to return to crofts and the fishing in season. BACo also built Company housing and settlements at Foyers, Kinlochleven and Inverlochy (the last close to the Lochaber smelter), and invested heavily in amenities and infrastructure, and their contribution in terms of rates benefited not only the immediate localities but the landward areas and islands as a whole. Some indication of this can be seen from the fact that by 1920 the Company employed between 250 and 300 in the west Highland area, paying out £170,000 in wages (£5.985 million in 2013 prices). By 1937 British Aluminium were the largest single employer in Argyllshire and one of the largest across the

---

Highlands (Lancaster, 2012); A. Perchard, '"The salvation of this district and far beyond": Aluminium Production and the Politics of Highland Development', *Northern Scotland*, 4 (2013), 43–65; A. Perchard, '"Of the highest imperial importance": British Strategic Priorities and the Politics of Colonial Bauxite, *c.* 1915–*c.* 1958', in R. Gendron, M. Ingulstad and E. Storli (eds), *Aluminum Ore: The Political Economy of the Global Bauxite Industry* (Vancouver, 2013), 53–78.

7　A. Perchard and N. G. MacKenzie, '"Too much on the Highlands?" Recasting the Economic History of the Highlands and Islands', *Northern Scotland*, 4 (2013), 4–22.

whole of the Highlands. In addition, the Company contributed one-fifth and one-twentieth of the rates to Inverness-shire and Argyll respectively. They also became one of the biggest landholders in Scotland. In 1949 the Company owned a total of 150,000 acres of land in the Highlands, and managed four sheep farms and a dairy farm. By 1977, despite the sale of around 22 per cent of their landholdings in the intervening years, they were the largest landowner in Inverness-shire (with estates of 6,300 acres in Argyll), and the eighth largest in Scotland.[8]

These undertakings were accompanied by a sense of moral obligation and 'political risk' too.[9] Constructing large hydro-electric schemes and installing modern industrial plants predictably drew their share of criticism, admittedly less than subsequent ventures, especially from Victorian conservationists. In such a capital-intensive industry, and initially staid market expansion and then subsequently exponential growth, meant that potential delays arising from obstructions of the passage of the relevant legislation or planning agreements to these large-scale developments could be extremely costly. Equally, discontent manifested in industrial action could be disastrous in a process where a prolonged stoppage would cause metal to freeze in furnaces causing thousands of pounds- worth of damage, not to mention lost output, and meant that eliminating the potential for disruption was very important. For all of these reasons, establishing networks and good working relationships with Highland political elites and other notable figures in the region was imperative. Increasingly, the relationship developed with local smelting communities took on the vestiges of the old clan system of *dùthchas* – heritable trusteeship – built around a 'moral economy' of sorts.[10]

The failure to nurture these relationships and the implied social contract associated with them was brought starkly into focus for British Aluminium on a number of occasions, such as their defeat during the Lochaber strike of 1936, when the wider occupational committee of Inverlochy and the town of Fort William mobilised behind the demands

8 The equivalent in 2013 prices has been calculated through a history opportunity cost using www.measuringworth.com; Perchard, *Aluminiumville*, 245–6.

9 Jones and Lubinski, 'Managing Political Risk in Global Business', 85–119.

10 Perchard, *Aluminiumville*, 245–71; Perchard, 'The salvation of this district'; E. P. Thompson, 'The Moral Economy of the English Crowd in the Eighteenth Century', *Past and Present*, 50 (1971), 76–136; Andrew Sayer, 'Moral Economy and Political Economy', *Studies in Political Economy*, 61 (2000), 79–103.

of BACo's striking workforce. It was also revealed when the Company failed to prepare adequately for the passage of legislation to enable the extension of their Kinlochleven smelter in 1918, resulting in the shelving of the Bill at great cost to BACo. Their success over the long durée in cultivating and maintaining these relationships paid dividends. The groundwork laid with Inverness County Council in 1895, for example, served them well in overcoming the 281 objections, and considerable adverse press coverage, including from prominent and powerful figures, raised over the Foyers scheme.[11] The lesson was learnt for the Lochaber scheme where relationships were fostered with many of the local elites – amongst them Grant, as well as Cameron of Lochiel and Mackintosh of Mackintosh. The Bill passed into law.

'Boosterism' in the Highlands: Lachlan Grant and Industrial Development

Dr Lachlan Grant, as a physician and Highland development campaigner, offered British Aluminium a number of attractions. This was immediately apparent from the outset. Grant, who become the medical officer for BACo, first at Foyers and then for Kinlochleven, observed to the 1907 Royal Commission on Canals and Waterways: 'it is a matter of great gratification to me that I happen to be connected with companies who have done something towards that part of the country'.[12] Grant was no less effusive in his praise of British Aluminium's role in the Highlands in his 1919 book *Ballachulish and its Quarries*:

> A great statesman said that 'individuals may form communities, but it is institutions alone that can create a nation'. Herein is the key to progress and repopulation of the Highlands and Islands. The British Aluminium Company has led the way in the harnessing of water power in the Highlands, and the possibilities of its development are great. Whatever form its extension may take, this enterprising company deserves our warmest commendation as progressive in its methods, and enlightened in its attitude to the workers.[13]

11 'Inverness County Council and the Falls of Foyers', *Scotsman*, 18 Oct. 1895.
12 *Royal Commission on Canals and Waterways, Minutes of Evidence and Appendices*, vol. 3, PP, Cd 3718, 1907, Q. 30,154.
13 NLS, Acc 12187/5, Lachlan Grant, *Ballachulish and its quarries* (Glasgow, 1919), 15–16.

Grant's boundless enthusiasm for British Aluminium's developments was as evident in his florid description of Kinlochleven in March 1923 for the *Oban Times*:

> Perhaps the most remarkable and romantic example of Highland, or even of Scottish, industrial development is that of the British Aluminium Company at Kinlochleven. Here, in a remote and once almost inaccessible spot, has sprung up, as if by magic, in less than twenty years a large and up-to-date factory with the necessary accommodation for the workers and their families. The haunt of the sheep, the deer, and the lonely shieling have given place to a hive of industry and a modern town of about 2000 inhabitants [. . .] This Highland town was planned and built on modern lines, and has benefited from the lively practical interest in it continually shown by the Chairman and Directors of the Aluminium Company. The houses are modern, electrically lighted, and comfortable, and the streets are well laid out and lit all night. There is an excellent water supply, and drainage and scavenging are thorough [. .] Kinlochleven by night bears an impressive scenic aspect, which makes it worth the visitor's while to tarry until the shades of evening fall. Hosts of brilliant electric lights, every home illuminated, and the twinkling aluminium furnaces in a sombre setting of frowning bens and darkened sea, raise up fancies of fairyland and the magical power of Pluto. The resounding hum of the great power house, dominating a chorus of minor undertones, might pass for music of the Titans, and as we leave the romantic panorama behind, we involuntarily repeat Rossetti's line:- The sighing sounds, the lights around the shore.[14]

This directly mimicked British Aluminium's own presentation of the Company's activities as complementary to the landscape and local culture. Not all observers were so complimentary.[15] The value of Grant's advocacy in the public was amply illustrated by his testimony to the Lochaber Water Power Bill, the statutory tool for establishing the Fort William smelter, in 1921. Using the example of the Company's housing at Kinlochleven, he declared:

14 Lachlan Grant, 'The city among the hills: present day industrial activities – Kinlochleven', *The Oban Times*, 24 Mar. 1923.
15 Perchard, *Aluminiumville*, 273–84.

The houses are well finished and well ventilated. All have W.Cs.,
sculleries, coal cellars, large kitchens, 2 or 3 bedrooms, water supply
and electric light introduced [. . .] In the men's temporary hostels
the accommodation is similar [. . .] From the public health point
of view these buildings are constructed on modern lines [. . .] The
planning of the village is good, the space at disposal being well laid
out. There are no slums or anything approaching such a description.
The Health of the community all along has been very satisfactory
[. . .][16]

A decade later, in 1931, Grant extolled the healthy environments both
of Kinlochleven village and the smelter in a letter to the *Lancet*, judging
the health of local residents to be 'exceptionally good'.[17] His views were
not shared by others, with one local noting acerbically of Grant's recent
letter, the renowned Highland physician would not know as he rarely
spent much time in the village, choosing instead to leave the rounds
to his assistants.[18] Just how out of touch Morrison was with conditions in the village of Kinlochleven is evident from the conclusions of
BACo's own factor for Highland estates (and William Murray Morrison's brother, Edward Shaw Morrison) after BACo's own audit of their
properties in 1936; in his judgment, 48 of the flats, built less than 30
years previously, should be 'pulled down', the hostel for single workmen
should 'cease to be used', 97 per cent of the houses had no baths or space
for them to be installed, and 18 per cent of houses were overcrowded.[19]
This scarcely reflects Grant's picture of the village, and suggests that his
Lancet detractor's observations were well founded. Indeed, it is quite
possible, given the intimate knowledge and the publication outlet, that
it was one of his assistants. Grant's observations were motivated by his by
now unswerving belief that the Company were saviours of the region. In
this he was not alone amongst members of the medical profession in the

16 Minutes of evidence to the select committee on private bills: Lochaber Water
Power Bill, Dr Lachlan Grant, 6 May 1921.
17 'Aluminium and Health', *The Lancet*, 14 Sept. 1931, 622, NLS, Acc. 12187/6,
18 His two assistants were Drs Murdie and Falconer: *The Lancet*, 14 Sept. 1931; *The
Lancet*, 23 Apr. 1932, NLS, Acc. 12187/6.
19 British Aluminium Company, minutes of managers' annual meetings, 30 Nov.
1936 – report of E. S. Morrison, Glasgow University Archives, British Alcan
collection, UGD 347 21/2/2

area, either at the time or in the decades that followed, as debates over occupational health and safety illustrate.

Lachlan Grant as Company Physician

Lachlan Grant's services were employed as a Company physician from an early stage. By the 1920s, Grant's roles included consulting medical officer for the Company at Kinlochleven, as well as being the district medical officer for the village and for Ballachulish.[20] As well as his prominence as a Highland development campaigner, Grant, as a physician, had other attractions for the Company; ones which would become apparent increasingly as questions over risks for consumers associated with aluminium, and occupational and environmental health in BACo's smelters started to be raised. By the 1930s, mounting concerns and speculation about the apparent risk posed to consumers by aluminium were being expressed in both medical journals and other publications. Suggestions Grant swiftly rebutted in *The Lancet* in 1931 and the *British Medical Journal* the following year declaring there to be 'no grounds whatsoever for the campaign against aluminium'.[21] He also reiterated the importance of the industry to the area and region. Grant had become such a passionate advocate of the metal and its applications that he penned a pamphlet on *Aluminium Throat Swabs* in 1922, and sent aluminium grape spoons to his old friend, Prime Minister Ramsay MacDonald.[22] The value to British Aluminium of such an endorsement was clear from the statement of company secretary R. W. Cooper to BACo shareholders in March 1931:

> The evidence of scientists is overwhelmingly in favour of the absolute non-toxicity of aluminium, and it will interest you to know the verdict which has been pronounced upon this question

---

20 *Report of the Committee on the Highlands and Islands Medical Service*, PP, Cd 6920, 1913, Evidence: Dr Ronald Cadell Macdonald, 19 Aug. 1912 (Qs. 1,808–908, and 1,942); Dr Lachlan Grant, 28 Oct. 1912 (Q. 19,719); Rev. Malcolm McCallum, 30 Oct. 1912 (Q. 21,180); *The Medical Press and Circular*, 18 June 1924, NLS, Acc. 12187/6.

21 *The Lancet*, 14 Sept. 1931; *British Medical Journal*, 9 Apr. 1932, LGC, NLS, Acc. 12187/6,

22 Lachlan Grant, *Aluminium Throat Swabs* (London, 1922); Ramsay MacDonald to Lachlan Grant, 26 Dec. 1933, NLS, Acc. 12187/7.

by two medical journals whose names are household words, namely, *The Lancet* and *The British Medical Journal*, which have satisfied themselves by practical experiment and by studying the scientific evidence on the point.[23]

If the charges of aluminium's toxicity for consumers lacked credence, then Grant and British Aluminium were being decidedly more disingenuous about workplace health issues. In his 1931 defence in *The Lancet*, Grant declared that during his period of service with BACo:

> I have had no evidence whatever of any industrial disease (such as is to be found in some other metal industries) resulting from the ingredients which are used in the manufacture of aluminium ingots. The pure bauxite clay and cryolite used in the manufacture of the metal are of the highest purity. The former is carefully calcinated and much of the fine alumina dust and hot furnace fumes must be inhaled or swallowed by the workers in the factories. Yet I have never observed the slightest signs of ill-health, temporary or chronic, which could be attributed to the inhalation of alumina. Numerous workers who have spent the greater part of their working lives, some for thirty years, are in excellent health, and show no sign of nervous depression.[24]

In December 1936, William Murray Morrison wrote to Grant expressing his gratitude for the latter's public defence of the health of BACo workers:

> I am obliged to you for your letter of the 10th instant and for having sent me the paper containing a report on your recent speech in London, which as a matter of fact I had seen in another paper. I was very pleased to observe the clean bill of health which you give to our employees as a result of your long experience of the health of our community at Kinlochleven.[25]

23 British Aluminium Company Ltd, Proceedings of the 22nd Ordinary General Meeting, 31 March 1932, GUA, UGD 347 21/19/2.
24 *The Lancet*, 14 Sept. 1931.
25 William Murray Morrison to Lachlan Grant, 18 Dec. 1936, NLS, Acc. 12187/10.

And the following year at a Masonic meeting in London, Grant once again testified to the 'excellent health' of BACo workers, and the idyllic and model 'hydro-electric industrial community of Kinlochleven'.[26]

The previous year, the Medical Research Council's (MRC) Industrial Pulmonary Diseases Committee had conducted a survey (on behalf of Black Country pottery owners) of the West Highland smelters to examine for chest complaints arising from alumina dust. Whilst their terms of reference for the study precluded any wider deliberation of occupational health, their observations of conditions within the Company's furnace rooms and carbon factory were less than favourable. Factory inspector J. K. Goodall provided a telling observation of effects of the fumes that came off the uncovered furnaces:

> Digressing for a moment, in connection with the discussion of the materials present, as dust and gases in the furnace room, it may be stated, that none of the workers to whom I spoke, complained at all of the dust, but they objected to the fumes which they had to stand on the furnace crust during the process of removing and fixing the anodes, in the process of 'blocking'.[27]

Goodall further noted that the concentration of dust present in the furnace rooms would not have been tolerated had it been in the Black Country potteries. The fumes that Goodall noticed would have included polyaromatic hydrocarbons and sulphur dioxide, both highly toxic and later discovered to be very carcinogenic. Whilst medical science had not arrived at these conclusions in the 1930s, Goodall's observations are still damning. Radiological screening of furnace workers had found 14 with abnormalities, with seven of these showing abnormal levels of fibrosis and emphysema. Equally telling was the remark by Professor E. L. Cummins that the team's methodological approach should have included pathological tests, implying that the IPDC had suspicions that there was cause for concern. The following year, Norwegian factory inspectors raised concerns with BACo's Vgieland works about the pronounced rates of occupational asthma amongst furnace workers. The problems of emissions and effects on local farmers' crops had been raised by the

26 'Factory Chimneys in Highland Glen', *Sunday Mail*, 10 Jan. 1937, NLS, Acc. 12187/10.

27 Quoted in Perchard, *Aluminiumville*, 213.

manager of another of their Norwegian plants at Stangfjorden in 1932 and 1933. However, the manager's appeal for capital to invest in fume extraction systems had been turned down by the head office in London on the grounds that: 'Capital expenditure and purchases have to be kept to the absolute minimum, and in the circumstances it is considered preferable to incur the risk of possibly having to pay some compensation rather than the capital expenditure on the proposed scheme.'[28] Similar concerns about pollution had been raised by the Lochaber manager, John Bullen, in 1936, and in 1941, Edward Morrison had condemned pollution from the plants and the parlous state of housing in Kinlochleven as a result of this. Reports by the Association of Scientific Workers in 1943, alongside a book by sociologists from the University of Edinburgh, painted a dismal picture of the atmospheric pollution in Kinlochleven. Subsequent reports by the MRC in the late 1940s confirmed widespread fluorosis chronically affecting flora and fauna in the area. Visiting French aluminium engineers reiterated these damning conclusions about workplace conditions within, and environmental pollution from, BACo plants in the west Highlands in 1951.[29]

At the same time that BACo and Lachlan Grant were extolling the health of BACo workers and the communities, and presenting a picture of idyllic planned bliss, they were aware that they were being disingenuous about this. In BACo's case, this was driven by a deliberate tactic of avoiding the cost of further capital expenditure. For Grant, BACo was a highly important employer and investor in the area, and a case to promote further industries coming into the region. Grant was not alone amongst physicians in the area extolling the virtues of British Aluminium; in language that shared much in comment with Grant's own praise of BACo's developments, Dr Cameron Miller, medical superintendent for the Belford Hospital, declared of their Lochaber scheme:

---

28 Ibid., 213, 219–20.

29 Ibid., 222–9; the two reports were, respectively, Association of Scientific Workers, Scottish Area Committee, *Highland Power. A Report of the Utilisation of Hydro-Electric Power envisaged in the Hydro-Electric Development (Scotland) Act – 1943* (Glasgow, 1943); M. F. Gregor and R. M. Crichton, *From Croft to Factory: The Evolution of an Industrial Community in the Highlands* (Edinburgh, 1946).

It is a matter of common knowledge that the fountain and origin of the present scheme has been the determination in the general public interest to utilise the waste water-power of the Highlands so as to provide profitable employment, both in the immediate and in the permanent sense, for the indigenous people, and to enrich the   producing capacity of the nation as a whole. That enormous Electrical Energy lay latent in the lakes and rivers of the Highlands was known as a truism, but the difficulty of tackling the problem on a massive scale with the above double object in view seems to have baffled the minds and the means of enterprising men; until, finally, the British Aluminium Company under the direction of a master Highland brain resolved to make essay.[30]

Miller made little of the heavy human cost in constructing the scheme; between 1925 and 1926 alone, there were 78 admissions to the Belford Hospital in Fort William from the site – 60 per cent of these as a result of direct traumas (explosions, rock falls and machinery) – with 28 fatalities. At his retirement many years later, another local medic, Dr Shay Connachie, attributed 48 fatalities to tunnel development alone on the scheme. Confronted by this evidence, Miller chose to downplay the fatalities, instead praising the engineering ingenuity. For Miller, the deaths were unfortunate but inevitable as part of the development of the scheme: 'unhappily, but perhaps inevitably in a work of such magnitude, several fatal accidents occurred, including misadventures not due to the work'.[31] Crucially, Miller's response also absolved the Company of any responsibility. In view of the constraints on both the Factory Inspectorate and the Mines and Quarries Inspectorate, because of numbers and also the remoteness of the site, the importance of the endorsement of a safety record by such prominent local physicians was significant. Whatever the motivations, the effect was to place workers and communities at risk, and to damage the environment, as well as the livelihoods of local farmers. Not all local physicians were so complacent. Dr Isaac Maciver, originally from Lewis, became a vocal critic of the health and

30 A. C. Miller, 'Medical Work on the Lochaber Water-power Scheme', *CMJ*, 13:2 (April 1926), 63.

31 A. C. Miller, 'Medical Work on the Lochaber Water-power Scheme', *CMJ*, 13:3 (July 1926), 108; See also, *CMJ*, 13:2 (April 1926) and 5 (Jan. 1927), 63–70, and 183–8, and 'editorial', *CMJ*, 14:8 (Oct. 1930), 257–9.

safety record on the construction of the schemes, lobbying the Scottish Trades Union Congress on the subject. Maciver would go on to chair skilfully the strike committee of BACo Lochaber smelter workers in 1936 in their successful campaign against the Company's assault on working conditions and attempts to raise rents.[32]

Conclusion

Lachlan Grant was indubitably a valuable ally for British Aluminium in the Highlands, both in terms of promoting them as an employer and investor in this 'problem area', and in providing them with a clean bill of health. This involved him, and BACo, in being disingenuous both about environmental conditions in Kinlochleven and within the Company plants. British Aluminium's deployment of medical professionals and scientific knowledge to counteract emerging evidence of occupational and environmental health issues was prevalent in a number of industries, as the battles over coal-dust pneumoconiosis, asbestosis, mesothelioma and silicosis illustrate.[33] However, he was undoubtedly well intentioned – if flawed – and motivated by a lifelong commitment to seeing the Highlands developed and removing the scourge of unemployment and rural poverty.[34] His passion for what he saw as the Company's paternalistic vision also included Grant giving lectures for improvement on reading to Kinlochleven audiences.[35]

BACo's cultivation of relationships with figures like Grant in the Highlands was clearly part of a sophisticated corporate political strategy to counteract opposition and promote their business. However, to attribute William Murray Morrison's relationship with Grant exclusively to the cynical pursuit of corporate interests would be to diminish the former's idealistic sense of being able to contribute to Highland development. In correspondence with Grant, which struck a familiar note, in

32 Perchard, *Aluminiumville*, 147–9.
33 See, for example, A. J. McIvor and R. Johnston, *Miners' Lung: A History of Dust Disease in British Coal Mining* (Aldershot, 2007); G. Tweedale, *From Magic Mineral to Killer Dust: Turner & Newall and the Asbestos Hazard* (Oxford, 2000); G. Markowitz and D. Rosner, *Deceit and Denial: The Deadly Politics of Industrial Pollution* (Berkeley, 2002).
34 For example, Lachlan Grant, *Modern Highland Problems* (Glasgow, 1906), NLS, Acc. 12187/3; 'Unemployment and degeneracy', *Glasgow Evening Times*, 22 Nov. 1922.
35 *Oban Times*, 2 Jan. 1909.

January 1935, Morrison declared: 'It is a most pleasing recollection in my career that I have also been able to do some practical and lasting good to my beloved Highlands.'[36] A former student and subsequent colleague of Lord Kelvin, Morrison's sentiments should rather be viewed as combining both a pragmatism and an idealism; the latter, like his mentor and erstwhile tutor, in an post-enlightenment view that science and natural resources harnessed for mankind could advance social progress.

36 William Murray Morrison to Lachlan Grant, 1 Jan. 1935, NLS, Acc. 12187/7.

Two men splitting slates in Ballachulish, Argyll, c. 1950. National Museums Scotland: SCRAN

Staged photograph of the Dewar Committee, with secretarial staff, 1912. Editor's private collection

Images of the Dewar Committee on visits, with their signatures, October 1912.
Editor's private collection

Images of the Dewar Committee on location taking evidence, October 1912.
Editor's private collection

HIGHLANDS AND ISLANDS MEDICAL SERVICE BOARD.

County of ARGYLL.   Districts of COWAL and KINTYRE.

1. The HIGHLANDS AND ISLANDS MEDICAL SERVICE BOARD hereby give notice to all whom it may concern that they have entered into Agreements with the Practitioners named in the annexed Schedule whereby medical attendance is made available to certain classes of the community in the districts and on the terms and conditions set forth below :

2. PERSONS ELIGIBLE TO RECEIVE MEDICAL ATTENDANCE AT MODIFIED FEES :

The families and dependants of insured persons, uninsured persons of the cottar and crofter classes and their families and dependants, and others in like circumstances to whom the payment of the Practitioner's ordinary fee for medical attendance would be an undue burden.

3. FEES CHARGEABLE TO THE PERSONS REFERRED TO IN SECTION 2 HEREOF :

A fee *not exceeding* 5/- for the first visit and 2/6 for each subsequent visit in the same illness. Midwifery fees (including fees for any subsequent visits that may be necessary), £1.

THE FEES WILL BE THE SAME WHATEVER BE THE DISTANCE OF THE PATIENT FROM THE DOCTOR'S PLACE OF RESIDENCE.

An additional and moderate charge will be made for medicines supplied by Practitioners. Where medicines are not dispensed by the Practitioners, patients must themselves pay the chemists' charges.

4. The treatment to be given by Practitioners in respect of the fees specified in Section 3 hereof is treatment of a kind which can be properly undertaken by a general Practitioner.

5. In the event of any dispute as to whether any patient comes within the scope of the arrangements between the Board and the Practitioners, the matter shall be decided by the Board. The decision of the Board in such cases will be based on the circumstances of the patient in each case, and such evidence as the Board may require in regard thereto must be forthcoming in all cases where an appeal is made to the Board.

6. Persons desiring to participate in the benefits of the Board's scheme must be prepared to comply with all such reasonable requirements of the Practitioner as will enable him to make the best arrangements for his patients.

Messages requesting the attendance of the Practitioner should, if possible, reach him before the hour on which he ordinarily begins to visit patients, and, if sent later in the day, they should invariably state whether his attendance is urgently needed that day or whether a visit on the following day is regarded as sufficient.

In cases where the Practitioner is accustomed to make fixed visits on certain specified days to particular localities, all calls for his services, except in urgent cases, should be reserved for these days.

Where duly qualified district nurses are available, special calls for the services of the doctor, outside ordinary visiting hours, to patients living at a distance should be made through the nurse wherever practicable.

7. In cases where two or more Practitioners practise in the same area, the patient may select the Practitioner whose services he desires to have, but urgent calls for medical assistance should, as a rule, be sent to the nearest available Practitioner.

8. It should be clearly understood that Practitioners called to cases outside the area in which they have undertaken to give attendance under arrangements with the Board, as shown in the annexed Schedule, may charge their ordinary visiting fees.

9. The Agreements between the Board and Practitioners do not interfere in any way with any private arrangements which may be in existence between Practitioners and their patients, whereby the latter receive attendance under a system of annual payments per individual or per family.

10. If it is proved to the satisfaction of the Board that the privilege of a medical service at modified fees is misused in any district or by any individual, the Board res_ve the right to withdraw the service from any such district or individual. In such cases the Practitioner's ordinary fee will be payable.

L. McQUIBBAN, *Secretary*,
HIGHLANDS AND ISLANDS MEDICAL SERVICE BOARD,
4A ST. ANDREW SQUARE, EDINBURGH, 1st Ja ary 1916.

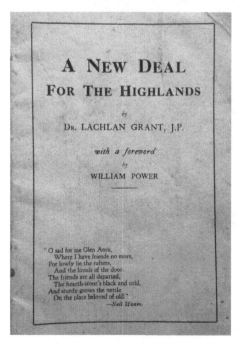

Above. An example of a public notice of the work of the Highlands and Islands Medical Service, Argyll, 1916. Editor's private collection

Left. The front cover of Lachlan Grant's *A New Deal for the Highlands*, 1936. Editor's private collection

A postcard showing Kinlochleven village, c. 1920. A. Perchard, contributor, private collection

Lochaber Furnace room. A. Perchard, contributor, private collection

PART II

*A Selection of the Writing and Speeches
of Dr Lachlan Grant*

Introduction

An edited selection of the writing and speeches of Dr Lachlan Grant have been transcribed and collected here, to allow the reader to track Dr Grant's thinking on the key themes covered by this volume in his own words.

The transcriptions have been organised to reflect the themes of the foregoing essays, and as such are not in full chronological order, although they have been arranged chronologically within each theme. Grant was a prolific contributor to the general and medical press, and a range of his research articles and notes are transcribed here from Highland newspapers as well as *The Lancet* and the *British Medical Journal,* to give a flavour of this aspect of his professional activities. Related to this is his thinking and writing on healthcare provision for the Highlands and Islands, and his important evidence to the Dewar Committee (1912) has been transcribed in full here.

One of the areas in which Grant is most keenly remembered and discussed is in his contribution to the debate and passionate support for Highland development in the 1930s. Of course, Grant had long regarded this as a key policy area, but it is in that decade where the bulk of his publications lie. As well as his important pamphlet, *A New Deal for the Highlands,* transcribed here is a selection of his correspondence with James Ramsay MacDonald, when the latter was prime minister, in which he urges direct political action, and in which he sends all relevant publications and memorandums. How MacDonald and his colleagues dealt with and regarded these efforts is illustrated here. It is in this section that his concerns over emigration are most frequently articulated, and so this theme has also been included. It is significantly the largest section, a reflection of Grant's efforts in this field.

This is not meant to constitute by any means a full and complete collection of Grant's work; that would be beyond the scope of this volume. Instead, it tries to display as fully as possible the huge range of Grant's interests, to indicate to the reader how broad these were, but also the ways in which, for Grant, they all connected up into a holistic vision for the Highlands and Islands.

SECTION 1

Medicine and Medical Research

'Bile as an Antidote in Variola', letter to the editor, *British Medical Journal*, 2 (17 Sept. 1898), 842

Sir – I read with great interest in the BRITISH MEDICAL JOURNAL of September 3rd Professor T. R. Fraser's eminently practical Further Note on Bile as an Antidote to Venoms and Disease Toxins.

In this note he states that it is indicated that 'a special antidotal constituent additional to the ordinary constituents, is present in the bile of an animal whose body contains a poison of the nature of the venoms or toxins.'

As experiments with the serum of vaccinated calves or heifers have not proved very successful in antagonising the virus of small-pox or its toxins, is it not more probable after what Professor Fraser has shown in connection with the bile of other animals, that the bile of calves after an attack of cowpox may possess an antidotal constituent as well as the ordinary constituents?

It would be important to test (if it has not yet been experimentally demonstrated) whether such bile contains antidotal properties, and if it would have any curative action in cases of small-pox. Should the bile of these calves be found to have such an antidotal action, it would also help to prove that variola and vaccine are identical diseases. – I am etc,

Lachlan Grant, M.D. Edin., Edinbane, Skye, N.B., Sept. 6th

'Strychnine as a Factor in Causing a Cerebral Haemorrhage', *Lancet*, 155: 4000 (28 Apr. 1900), 1204–5.
By Lachlan Grant, M.D., C.M. Edin., Medical Officer, Gesto Hospital, Isle of Skye

A man whose arterial walls are healthy stands very little chance of being attacked with spontaneous cerebral haemorrhage; but if his blood-vessels want their normal elasticity through being affected with degenerative changes such as arterio-sclerosis or miliary aneurysms, he is liable to apoplectic seizure from one of the weakened vessels giving way when it is subjected to any extra strain. This extra strain results from an increase of the blood pressure, as when the individual is engaged in occupations involving more than usual muscular exertion – for example, in lifting heavy weights, or in defecating, or from some mental excitement causing acceleration of the heart's action. Knowing this we quietly caution patients in whom we may suspect apoplexy against such exciting causes and against such stimulating agents as alcohol which increase the blood pressure. The following case occurred whilst the patient was, of his own accord, taking a mixture containing strychnine, a drug which is known to have a powerful action in raising the pressure in the circulatory system.

The patient, a man aged 64 years, of apoplectic build, with atheromatous arteries, had been exposed to a great deal of hard wear and tear. Latterly he had been in the habit of dosing himself, whenever he felt below par, with the syrupus ferri phosphates cum quinine et strychnine (syn. Easton's syrup), generally taking it along with some bicarbonate of sodium, which gave him what he termed a 'fizzing' drink. One morning he fortified himself with a larger dose than usual of the syrup and about an hour afterwards he began to feel uneasy with giddiness and numbness in his extremities. He became quiet and drowsy and when I saw him two hours later symptoms of right-sided cerebral haemorrhage were well marked. There was hemiplegia on the left side of the body, for when the left arm or leg was raised and allowed to drop it fell as if it belonged to a lifeless person. The limbs on the opposite side of the body had jerky movements which continued for half an hour; the hypoglossal nerve was involved as the tongue could not be put out straight, but deviated towards the paralysed side. The patient's face was of an ashen-grey colour, the pupils were equal and moderately dilated, the pulse was 70 and was full and regular, the temperature was normal, the sphincters were relaxed, and the evacuations were passed involuntarily. The urine contained neither sugar nor albumin. Complete unconsciousness gradually developed, the respirations became stertorous, and on the second day the face became injected [sic] and the temperature reached 101 F, the pulse being 110. The fundi oculi were examined and appeared to be normal. There was little or no change until the fifth day, when the breathing assumed the Cheyne-Stokes rhythm, the coma deepened, the temperature reached 103, and he succumbed without having regained consciousness. I was informed that a week previously to this fatal seizure he had premonitory symptoms, being attacked with headache, vertigo and syncope.

When the action of strychnine is considered it is not unreasonable to suppose that in this case it was the actual exciting cause of the rupture. Strychnine increases the blood pressure in several ways. It is a cardiac tonic, making stronger the contractions of the cardiac muscle. It is also a vaso-motor stimulant. Experiments have shown that strychnine is a great stimulant to the respiratory centre. Then it has a general tonic action, greatly increasing reflex sensibility and strengthening people generally so that the patient may be tempted to undue exertion and thus overstrain himself. It is also a gastric tonic, and, being one of the bitters, is hunger-producing, so that the patient may eat more and the overloaded viscera will also tend to raise the arterial tension. There is, however, another action of the drug which is dangerous – namely, that when strychnine has been taken for some time, there may appear the so-called cumulative action, when the full physiological effect of the drug may suddenly develop. It is, then, conceivable that in this patient there was a cerebral vessel on the point of rupturing; the strychnine might have so raised the pressure within the artery as to cause the weakened wall to give way.

From the above it is apparent that older patients should be warned against drugging themselves promiscuously with tonic syrups and tabloids containing preparations of the seeds of *strychnos nux vomica*, remedies which are largely sold by druggists nowadays. By comparison with other prescriptions it has been found that strychnine in the form of nux vomica is more used than any other drug whatever in this country. It is evident, however, that great care should be taken in administering this stimulating drug to patients who have arrived at the degenerative age, and especially in all cases of cirrhotic Bright's disease, chronic gout, and syphilis, or where a patient has thickened and tortuous blood-vessels, or even where there has been an hereditary tendency to apoplexy. In many of these cases it should only be given when absolutely necessary, as in cardiac failure, to endeavour to tide the patient over his threatened dissolution.

'On Haemophilia and its Treatment', *Lancet*, 164: 4236 (5 Nov. 1904), 1279–80.

By Lachlan Grant, M.D., C.M. Edin., Medical Officer, Ballachulish

It is still uncertain whether abnormal conditions of the vascular system or morbid conditions of the blood itself are the cause of the dangerous haemorrhage occurring in those affected with haemophilia; in fact the etiology and pathology of this distressing disease are practically unknown. However, this much is known, through observations extending over several centuries the hereditary transmission of haemophilia has been conclusively demonstrated. One important circumstance concerning the 'bleeder's disease' is that it nearly always affects members of the male sex and although women can transmit to their sons the tendency to bleed it is a striking fact that they themselves very seldom suffer from the disease. So rarely does it affect females that Legg, who has written one of the most important papers on the subject, goes the length of saying: 'I have never seen a true case of haemophilia in a woman and I am inclined to think that the diagnosis of cases of haemophilia in women is founded on mistaken observations.'

That females mostly escape is a very important element in the problem and it led me to think that it might possibly have some bearing on the treatment of this disease which is still largely empirical. The condition is in all probability present in the females of haemophiliac families, although it would appear to be in abeyance throughout life in an as yet unknown way. That there must be some restraining influence in the blood or tissues of the female is evident when we take into consideration the opportunities for haemorrhage during the separation of the placenta. Were this not so the contraction of the uterus would not of itself be sufficient to control the haemorrhage. But it seems that parturition has no special danger for haemophiliacs, the daughters of bleeders who marry 'often show an average fecundity nearly double that of the ordinary population.'

It naturally suggests itself whether this female immunity is not due to some constitutional influence emanating from the female reproductive centre – this probably through an internal secretion of some kind, possibly ovarian – and further, whether the internal administration of extract of ovaries, mammary gland, or other tissues peculiar to the female would have any effect in lessening the tendency of dangerous haemorrhage in cases of haemophilia. It is well known that the ovaries have a profound influence in the female. Thus, as a result of a double ovariotomy, the climacteric with its train of symptoms is induced, and the symptoms are in turn said to be ameliorated by the administration of ovarian extract.

During the past ten years I have had under my care four individuals, all males, for conditions aggravated by the haemorrhagic diathesis. They were all offshoots of a certain family. One was a boy, aged eight years. The others were his uncle and his uncle's two cousins. Through this article I will refer chiefly to the boy's case, I may in passing mention that, of the others, one bled to death as a result of an abscess of the thigh, another had round his right ankle suffered extravasations which took months to absorb, and the third suffered from epistaxis of three days' duration, which ultimately ceased after the local application of adrenalin and the internal administration of chloride of calcium.

The boy, whose case came under my care last, had dangerous haemorrhage from a deep cut one inch in length on the plantar surface of his right foot, between the fourth and fifth metatarsal bones. The cut was the result of his having stepped on a piece of glass the previous evening. The wound, which bled considerably, was first washed and dressed by his mother. It continued to bleed all night and next morning the mother, becoming alarmed, had the child carried to my house. There was then steady capillary haemorrhage, the blood showing no tendency to natural thrombus formation. The wound was cleansed with hot carbolic lotion 1 in 40 and cautiously examined to see if it contained glass or any other foreign body. Knowing that he was of haemophiliac stock I did not stitch the wound for fear of setting up further bleeding. Instead I applied a pad of sterile gauze, boric dusting powder, and firm compression by means of a bandage, and at the same time elevated the wound. The dressing, however, became saturated in a quarter of an hour; gauze soaked in 1 in 1000 adrenalin solution was then applied and the leg was kept elevated for three hours. This considerably lessened the flow and the boy was removed home. In a few hours the oozing was again serious and a fresh adrenalin gauze was applied. This had to be repeated during the night. On the second morning after the accident the boy complained of much pain and the oozing of sanguineous fluid was considerable. On the third day his temperature rose to 102 F and the wound had evidently become septic. The foot was much swollen round the wound, the tissues in proximity looked unhealthy, while the oozing still went on. Iodoform gauze soaked in adrenalin was packed into the wound but this just seemed to dam back the blood, causing it to penetrate into the surrounding tissues. When this plug of gauze was removed the pressure of the surrounding tissues caused the collection of blood to spurt out. A small drainage tube was then inserted into the centre of the gauze but the pressure necessary to prevent external oozing caused such pain that it had to be withdrawn.

By this time the boy was getting very anaemic and the prognosis was undoubtedly grave. Having procured some extract of ovarian substance prepared from sheep, by Messers Burroughs, Wellcome and Co., I commenced to give him two and a half grain doses thrice daily. At the same time the local treatment of the wound was continued, corrosive sublimate solution 1 in 2000 being used for cleansing. During the next two days, the fourth and fifth, the condition was much the same but on the sixth day the oozing of blood gradually lessened, the temperature came down to 99 F and the pain ceased. On the eighth day the wound became healthy looking. After this granulations formed and the wound gave no further trouble. At the end of the sixth week it was completely healed. From the third day following the injury the ovarian extract was continued as well as the four-grain doses of the citrate of iron and ammonia. My colleague Dr A. Dingwall Kennedy, who assisted me in this case, also noted that, shortly after the commencement of the ovarian opotherapy, not only was there a marked improvement in the boy's general condition, but that the tissues in the vicinity of the wound rapidly assumed a healthy appearance. At the same time the oozing of blood ceased.

When it is considered how critical the patient's condition was there is some hope that the ovarian extract had some effect in bringing about his recovery. At the same time, it is difficult to assert dogmatically that the boy's own system did not of itself naturally overcome the morbid condition. And one has to be cautious in a disease like haemophilia in attributing a favourable result to any special remedy, the more so as we know that occasionally in this disease the bleeding will cease spontaneously. Only further tests in this direction can prove conclusively whether this was a case of *propter hoc* rather than *post hoc*.

We are living in an age when organic extracts are extensively used and when we recognise the immense benefit already derived from thyroid and suprarenal extracts it seems not unreasonable to go further afield and to try any method of treatment which might reasonably be expected to influence the course of obscure diseases in which up to now all remedies have been uncertain. Happily cases of haemophilia are not of frequent occurrence and it might be some time before I had experience of another case. I therefore deemed the foregoing worthy of record, so that others who might have the opportunity could try the effect of ovarian opotherapy in such cases. If a sufficiently large experience of this treatment proved of benefit its continuous use in haemophilia would be indicated. But if this suggestion should not be supported by further investigations we must, of course, put it aside and endeavour to discover some other remedy.

Ballachulish.

'Vaccines in General Practice', *Lancet*, 172:4439 (26 Sept. 1908), 931–3.
By Lachlan Grant, M.D., C.M. Edin.; T. H. Campbell, M.B., CH.B. Glasg.; and W. D. Anderson, M.A., M.B. Cantab., M.R.C.S. ENG

The following cases, having resisted the older forms of treatment it was decided to try the effect of vaccine therapy, and in these notes we will give a brief history of the cases, the *modus operandi* employed and the results obtained.

CASE I. – A man, aged 35 years, with a tuberculous history, consulted us in September 1907, regarding a large swelling of two months' duration, on the left side of the neck, which extended from the angle of the jaw almost to the manubrium sterni. The case was one of advanced tuberculosis of the cervical glands which were evidently in a state of caseation and liquefaction. A few days later an incision was made into the dependent part of the swelling and the fluid content was evacuated. The swelling subsided considerably and during the following three weeks the disease seemed to be held in abeyance. The improvement, however, was only temporary and the swelling advancing downwards another incision became necessary. In the course of another month, owing to the disease having spread over the manubrium, it was found expedient to make a third incision. The wounds were throughout treated antiseptically and all precautions were taken against the possible occurrence of mixed infection. Absolute rest in bed was enjoined, the patient's diet was regulated, and the best hygienic measures possible were adopted. This proved of little avail. The wounds remained open, sinuses discharging tuberculous debris. Indeed, an extension along the deep fascia into the mediastinum was feared. The affected part, after remaining unchanged for about three months, was subjected to the x-rays. Irradiation was given on three separate occasions at intervals of one week, the dose on each occasion being 15 minutes of a soft tube with 0.35 milliamperes passing and the anticathode 12 inches from the diseased tissue. After each irradiation a thin friable cicatrix formed over the wounds, but it invariably broke down again after a few days. The patient had been in our care for seven months and we now decided on a vaccine treatment.

On May 11th, 1908, an estimation of the patient's opsonic index for tubercle bacillus was made and the index was found to be 0.7. On the same day 1–5000 cubic centimetre of T.R. was injected into the infrascapular region. This was followed on the 12th by a slight mnammatory reaction in the neck, and the temperature, which had previously been normal, rose a degree, otherwise there was no constitutional disturbance. On the 13th the inflammatory signs passed off and the temperature fell to normal. On the 15th the wounds were covered by a thin delicate skin. On the 17th this skin was shed and the wounds were once more open. On the 20th another injection of 1–5000 cubic centimetre of T.R. was given, the opsonic index being again at 0.7. This injection caused, 12 hours late, inflammation in the wounds with distinct pain, which lasted for 24 hours. In four days the inflammation had subsided.

On June 1st, a bluish-white line of epithelium began to appear round the wounds. On the 3rd 1–5000 cubic centimetre of T.R. was again injected and the same clinical phenomena followed as on the previous occasions. On the 10th the condition was as follows: the upper wound was closed by thin, young, healthy cicatrix; the second wound was partly closed and showing healthy margins; and the third of lowermost wound was still open but was surrounded by healthy edge and floored with pink healthy granulation tissue. On the 15th 1–2500 centimetre of T.R. was injected, the opsonic index being at this date 0.89 (practically normal). On the 17th the two lower wounds were almost closed and three days later all were completely covered and the patient was now allowed to go out in warm weather. On the 25th 1–2500 cubic centimetre of T.R. was injected, the patient remaining in bed on the two following days. This procedure was followed after each injection till the termination of the treatment.

On July 2nd 1–2500 cubic centimetre of T.R. was injected, the opsonic index being now 0.98. The patient was feeling in splendid health.

The wounds had remained quite closed and the cicatrices were beginning to contract. On the 13th 1–5000 cubic centimetre of T.R. was injected. The scars were white and anaemic in some places. On the 24th 1–5000 cubic centimetre of T.R. was injected. The scars looked strong, tough and white. An area about one-eighth of an inch in diameter in the centre of the lowermost scar had broken down. On the 29th this breach was diminished to half its previous size.

On August 19th 1–25000 cubic centimetre of T.R. was injected. On this date only an area the size of a pin's head remained bare. On the 25th the wounds were entirely closed and the cicatrices appeared fine, white and strong. There was wonderfully little marking. The patient has remained well ever since and started work on Sept. 3rd [. . .]

CASE 3. – A boy, aged ten years, was brought to us in the beginning of June, 1907, complaining of pain, stiffness and swelling over the metatarsal bone and proximal phalanx of the great toe of four months' duration. The case was one of tuberculous disease of the metatarsophalangeal joint. Calmette's ophthalmic reaction was positive. The boy was put to bed, the foot was immobilised in a splint, and cod liver oil and nutritious diet were prescribed. The general condition was asthenic. In the course of a month the swelling had increased and showed signs of liquefaction. The question of an excision was considered, but it was decided to incise and evacuate. This was done at the beginning of August. Shortly after this the skin broke at two other places, and there were now three sinuses discharging. Treatment by Bier's method was initiated, the congestion being kept up for two hours twice daily. This had a distinctly salutary effect. The swelling began gradually to subside and the discharge lessened. One sinus closed completely, but the other two still remained open, discharging a little serum every day. During February, 1908, a second sinus closed, but opened again in a few days. This was repeated on two of three occasions during the next three months; the third wound never closed. The boy's general health had improved.

On June 13th, 1908, 1–10000 cubic centimetre of T.R. was injected and the patient was kept in bed the following day. There were a well-marked local reaction with congestion and increased discharge from the sinuses. On the 15th the reaction had subsided and during the following seven days there were a continued diminution of the swelling and a lessening of the discharge. On July 2nd another 1–10000 cubic centimetre of T.R. was injected. After the reaction had passed off further improvement had occurred. One of the sinuses closed, while the other remained open, discharging a little serum every second or third day. At the beginning of August the remaining sinus closed, but opened up again about the middle of the month. On the 19th 1–10000 cubic centimetre of T.R. was injected. After the reaction had passed off the remaining sinus closed and remained so. On Sept. 1st the scars were white, soft, pliable and depressed. Comparatively little thickening was present at the site of the lesion. The joint remained stiff. On this day an injection of 1–10000 cubic centimetre of T.R. was followed by a very slight reaction. The last closed sinus opened on the 2nd and omitted a drop or two of blood-stained serum. On the 3rd the dressing was absolutely dry, no discharge being present nor has there been any reappearance of the discharge since that date [. . .]

Conclusions. – The results in the foregoing cases have so far been most satisfactory, and we venture to attribute this to the action of the vaccines. In those cases treated with tuberculin the following points are of note:–

1. The scars resulting were soft, pliable and the disfigurement slight.
2. Recovery under the treatment seemed rapid, and this implied saving of suffering and expense to the patient and anxiety to the medical attendants.
3. The absence of severe surgical measures minimised the risk of a general tuberculous infection and obviated that slight risk which always attends of general anaesthesia.
4. Although opsonic estimations were only made occasionally during the treatment, they suggested that the index was being steadily raised, and from this it is probable that for some time at least the patient will be less susceptible to attacks by the same bacterium. Surgical measures alone may achieve this indirectly, inasmuch as they rid the body of the focus of the disease, but it is questionable if they are capable of raising the standard of defence to the same high level as that induced by vaccine therapy.

It may perhaps be right to conclude by saying that much expense and valuable time were saved to the patients and to ourselves by the fact that the microscopical work, the electrical treatment, the preparation of vaccines, and the opsonic estimations were all conducted in our own laboratories.

Ballachulish, Argyllshire.

British Medical Journal, 2 (18 Dec. 1909), 1763

In a paper on books and reading, read before the Kinlochleven Literary Society, and now reprinted from the *Caledonian Medical Journal*, Dr Lachlan Grant, of Ballachulish, discourses on the value of the reading habit, which he says can be acquired by all, especially in these days of public libraries. But Dr Grant urges that the private collection should not be neglected, and we are sure all writers of books (which was the description given of himself by Thomas Carlyle) will highly approve his recommendation that all those who can afford the luxury should buy as many of their favourites as they can. He utters a needed note of warning against too much reading of newspapers, which, as he truly says, becomes a form of mental dissipation. He himself is catholic in his literary tastes. He does not frown at novels, which, it may be remembered, were an unfailing relaxation to Darwin. One of the greatest physicians of the present day used to read novels on his daily rounds, tearing out and flinging out of the window the pages as perused; a better use of them would have been to give them to hospitals, the inmates of which are often even now but ill supplied with light reading. Napoleon, who carried about with him on his campaigns a library of three thousand volumes, also read in his travelling carriage. In the matter of novels he was somewhat difficult to please, and he threw away those which did not hold his interest from the first. Thus, as Andrew Lang says, he marked his steps of conquest through Europe with bad novels. The only rule as to reading is to read what interests one and gives pleasure. At the present day the snippet magazine and the novelette have almost killed the taste for anything deserving the name of literature; while the lady novelist, with her eternal sex problem, has to a large extent taken the place of Scott, Dickens and Thackeray, who are treated as 'back numbers'. Has not the half-baked intellectual condition which we call 'education' much to answer for? We would add that if the mind is to be instructed, books must be digested, not merely skimmed through; the spirit of the old maxim *non multa sed multum*, which is reversed by our present system of education, still holds true.

'Growing Up', *British Medical Journal*, 1 (4 May 1912), 1031

Dr Lachlan Grant recently delivered an address on growing up to senior scholars of the Ballachulish public school, which Mr Charles Stewart, of Achara, Duror of Appin, Argyllshire, has had printed and circulated. It is an address full of good sense, and preaches the gospel that the human body, so far from being treated as the Brother Ass of the *Poverello* of Assisi, is a sacred gift and should be dealt with accordingly. Dr Grant says: 'Treat your bodies with respect; keep them sweet, clean and beautiful; study yourself and find out what is best for you: what to eat and drink, how much sport and recreation.' He insists on the need for fresh air by night as well as by day and regularity in meals. He contrasts this country to its disadvantage with France in respect of cooking, but thinks that a time is coming when every girl will be expected to serve a short time in a good cookery school. From this it would seem that the voice of the 'feminist' has not yet made itself heard in the Arcadia of Ballachulish. To serve in a cookery school indeed! To serve in a prison for breaking windows appears to be more the ambition of militant women of the future. Dr Grant gives much sound advice that should help make the body strong and healthy; but as he says, strength and beauty in man without wealth and wisdom will not avail him much at the present day. By 'wealth' he is careful to explain that he does not mean money, but a calm, well-balanced mind, stored with useful knowledge and the highest development of one's powers, gifts and faculties. Wealth, he insists, is not what a man has, but what he is. He points out that many fail in business or professional life through slovenly habits of mind. 'If asked about something, such people will beat about the bush and enter into a long conversation instead of going straight to the question. Or, if asked to repeat what they have heard, they will add here and there, and what they forget will be filled up by the imagination.' Unluckily this is a universal human failing which no amount of 'growing up' seems to be capable of eradicating. A famous judge who was asked whether in his experience lying witnesses were common, replied that most of those he had had before him tried hard to tell the truth, but could not succeed in doing so. It is this that makes human testimony so untrustworthy and observation of such doubtful value. Carlyle somewhere says that the best test of clearness of mental vision is the capacity to give a concise account of any event shorn of all needless detail. Dr Grant rightly says that inaccuracy is often due to defective early training and a bad memory, both of which defects can be remedied by proper attention and mental exercises. One golden piece of advice given by Dr Grant is: 'If you don't know a thing just say so straight out.' Lord Rosebery tells us that when Napoleon took the reins of government in his hands he did not know the barest elements of administration, but he was never ashamed to ask for an explanation of the simplest things – and he never asked twice. Here we may take occasion to point out that inaccuracy and ignorance which may remain with a man throughout life are often the fault of the teacher. A pupil may be too shy to ask a question on some point as to which he is not clear, and his mind may thus permanently harbour a fundamental misconception which a word or two spoken in season would have removed. We have known distinguished teachers who apparently thought it beneath them to help a beginner over the stones of stumbling in his path [sic].'

'How is the Early Diagnosis of Pulmonary Tuberculosis to be Made?' *British Medical Journal*, 2 (8 Dec. 1917), 776–7

Sir – In your issue of November 24th Dr A. Garvie rightly expresses the views of the profession on the difficulties of an early diagnosis of cases of pulmonary tuberculosis. He asks for the practical experiences of fellow general practitioners in connexion with the earliest diagnosis of incipient cases. In an article published in 1914 by Dr Wm. Murdie and myself we pointed out that one of the chief difficulties was to ensure that patients consult a medical practitioner at an early stage of the disease. The onset of this trouble is so insidious that, unless there is an attack of haemoptysis or pleuritic pain, it may never occur to a patient that there is anything much wrong. Coughs and colds are so prevalent in this country, especially in the winter, that, as a rule, nothing very much is thought of catarrhal attacks, and it is only when a patient begins to feel weak, loses weight and suffers from anorexia, or one of the complications of the disease appears, that a medical man is consulted. An effective plan to meet this difficulty might be to distribute at intervals a short circular to every household explaining in a judicious manner the mild onset of symptoms and the harmfulness of delay in having an infection of this kind attended to. This is already done by some municipal councils in connexion with cancer. With one-fourth of our population insured, and so entitled to free medical advice, any patients in this section could be assured as to whether or not they were suffering from consumption.

The earlier the stage the easier it is to miss a definitive diagnosis. The most careful percussion and auscultation may reveal little or nothing. Diagnosis by means of the *x* rays, tuberculin tests, or serum reactions, cannot be generally applied. The simplest and one of the most valuable tests at our disposal is the careful use of an accurate clinical thermometer.

It is advisable to leave the thermometer in longer than usual to ensure a correct reading. When from the history and symptoms a suspicion of incipient tuberculosis arises, if an elevation of temperature occurs at some time of the day of even a half to three-quarters of a degree above the normal for some days, we hold that such a case should have the most careful observation so as to endeavour to prevent it going on to be an 'open' case of pulmonary tuberculosis.

Unfortunately, many patients at the present time do not present themselves for diagnosis or treatment until they are already producing sputum. In such instances it is strongly advisable to have the most thorough and repeated examinations of the secretions for the tubercle bacillus. We should not be content with one or two negative results; but in all clinically suspicious cases should persevere with the search, examining the sputa at different intervals, even six, eight or nine times, until we are fairly certain of the presence or absence of the bacillus of tubercle. Again, a complete bacteriological and cytological examination of the sputum is of great value in distinguishing between a pneumonic or influenzal infection, simple bronchial catarrh, and a tuberculosis infection of the respiratory tract. This should be made at the earliest opportunity at the nearest laboratory – I am, etc.

Lachlan Grant, Ballachulish, Nov. 26th.

'A Note on Septic Carriers', *Lancet*, 216:5585 (13 Sept. 1930), 579–80.

By Lachlan Grant M.D., C.M., D.P.H. Edin., F.R.F.P.S. Glasg., bacteriologist, district committee Argyll County Council consulting medical officer, British Aluminium Company, Kinlochleven

A common group of diseases with which medical practitioners have to deal is that of boils and local inflammatory and pustular skin infections, which occur more particularly on the fingers, hands, wrists, forearms, back of the neck, and other skin areas, and at the nasal orifices. In other papers[1] I have fully discussed the probability that some of these troublesome and painful local infections result from the daily use of the present type of toilet and wash-hand lavatory basins. Most people wash their hands and faces several times daily in stationary water contained in the common unsterilised basins. They deposit in this water and on the walls

---

1 *Medical World*, 31 (1929), 38; *Caledonian Medical Journal*, 45 (1929), 47.

of the basin the dust and dirt particles from the skin surfaces, which carry minute harmless or harmful 'bacterial passengers'. By the usual bacteriological methods these latter can be shown to be present in the polluted basins. It is thus plain that by washing in such a concentrated, contaminated fluid-medium, any micro-organisms present are applied and re-applied, again and again to the surfaces of the parts usually supposed to be correctly and properly cleansed. The result is that they are, to a large extent, deposited on the towels during the wiping and drying process. All this is surely quite unhygienic and insanitary. After such washings it is little wonder, whenever we get a wound of the skin, an abrasion, or an epilated hair leaving an open follicle, that staphylococcal, streptococcal or other pathogenic organisms frequently enter the open and exposed injured surface. These may then set up the complete infective and inflammatory process. At any rate, one must admit there is every possibility of this happening.

RECURRING BOILS

Recently instances have been noted where several members of the same family suffered at intervals from recurring boils, or a too-ready inflammation of even simple wounds sustained in the course of the day's work, and it naturally occurred to me to go more fully into the medical history. In several instances an obvious origin for these inflammatory repetitions was soon apparent.

In the case of two patients from the same household, both of whom suffered within the past three years from numerous boils, and several wrist infections – one of a severe type with abscess formation necessitating incision, following a traverse wound of the wrist – I found that the mother had a long-standing, chronic and open varicose ulcer of the lower leg, about 2 in. by 3 in. in size. In another male case with persistent periodic boils, it was discovered that the mother had a large, chronic, septic leg sore. These two poor and middle-aged women informed me they were quite distressed at their sons' frequent loss of work and wages through boils and abscesses which developed, in spite of repeated morning saline laxatives, a common method of prevention in many families. They did not realise that their own unhealthy integumentary systems were the likely carriers and distributors of the virulent organisms which caused these periodical infections; cultures from the chronic ulcers gave the usual staphylococcal growths.

In the treatment of these cases prophylactic aseptic daily cleansing by every member of the family was advised, and special mention was made of the downward flushings from an elevated water tap. With one patient, in whose house no gravitation water-supply was laid on, the difficulty was overcome by washing at a nearby water spout – a natural running tap. Clean towels and garments were also recommended and, subject to local and general attention, with the occasional exhibition of a polyvalent staphylococcal vaccine, the boils and inflammations were cured, and for the past year there have been no recurrences. Meanwhile, with the aid of prolonged rest for the mothers, the open ulcers have responded to suitable treatment. It ought to be of interest to state that the men affected were outdoor manual workers, liable to abrasions and other surface injuries.

HAND-BASIN CONTAMINATION

This note is published with the suggestion that when these suppurative inflammatory infections persistently recur, and where there is no systemic condition such as glycosuria or a chronic furuncular state and where, in spite of pure water cleansing success is not achieved, it might be helpful to make fuller and tactful enquiries in order to discover if there is not some carrier or harbourer of septic conditions in the home. Similar casual inflammatory attacks in families may also result in the presence of septic teeth, chronic sinusitis, tonsillar infections, otitic abscesses, leucorrhoel discharges and furuncular conditions generally. It is obvious that pus from patients suffering from such diseases must daily enter the wash-hand basins, contaminating them and rendering them bacteriologically unclean. Against infection from such sources the only effective precaution is to avoid washing in the stationary fluid, and to use pure running water for all the daily ablutions. This can easily be carried out by using a combined elevated hot and cold water tap with a spray or single medium-sized jet inlet. Such modern and improved water faucets have already been described by the author in previous articles. Towels can always be boiled, but the sterilisation of every wash-hand basin after each usage is an absolute impossibility.

Hence the necessity for the raised flow as a simple preventative remedy for these and other largely avoidable organismal infections. By the downward flush the dust and dirt particles, harbouring the pathogenic bacteria, are carried off direct to the waste and soil pipe. In this way there is no reapplication of any infected microscopic suspended matter. This method is so obviously correct that it seems almost incredible that such faucets are not installed forthwith in every home and institution where gravitation is laid on. Instead, the old-fashioned, primitive and dangerous toilet and lavatory basins, with their close-up taps, are being used and fitted for washing in the stationary water. This, as already pointed out, favours the direct application of any aggressive bacteria present, not only to the half-cleansed skin areas but to the nasal-oral orifices as well. These microbiotic organisms, being 'considerately' rubbed in during the cleansing processes, tend to inoculate the system, and any wounds or abrasions of its cutaneous surface, with the possible risk of subsequently setting up one of the acute or chronic, local or general infectious diseases.

'Cerebro-spinal Fever', letter to the editor, *Lancet*, 217:5609 (28 Feb. 1931), 497–8

Sir – Your leading article emphasises the necessity for open air, the avoiding of crowded assemblies and excessive fatigue, the importance of increased cubic space, and the taking of precautions whilst coughing and sneezing in order to avoid the scattering of infectious droplets. One other very necessary precaution is that of washing the hands and face by means of pure running water from a single elevated nozzle, in the form of either spray, wave, or straight jet. The present wash and lavatory basins are unsanitary, being bacteriologically unclean as no regular and correct sterilisation of the basin wall is attainable. The basins are just minia- ture baths and, when used with stationary water for the various daily ablution purposes, favour direct naso-oral inoculation and a spread of infectious disease. I believe the abolition of the waste plug and the use of the elevated tap in wash-basins would lower the incidence of infectious diseases all over the country.

I am, Sir, yours faithfully, LACHLAN GRANT, Bacteriological Laboratory, Ballachulish, Argyllshire, Feb. 23rd, 1931.

'Prevention of Puerperal Sepsis', *British Medical Journal*, 1 (23 Jan. 1932), 148

At a meeting of the Edinburgh Obstetrical Society, on December 9th, 1931, with the president, Dr James Young, in the chair, Dr Lachlan Grant read a paper entitled 'Puerperal Temperatures and their Prevention'.

Dr Grant said that it was realised that, to improve the quality of the race, we must begin with the child. To that end a happy, healthy, enlightened and safe motherhood was the first consideration. No longer should there be so many shameful conditions that made maternity a martyrdom and childhood a tragedy. The mothers must have the best that science could offer, in addition to any material adjuncts to a safe and efficient discharge of the greatest of all human duties. Every practitioner undertaking obstetric work should be familiar with the various etiological factors which might cause febrile attacks in the puerperium. Further, it was advisable to consider from time to time whether or not it was necessary to alter or revise any part of the practitioner's supervising work or any details of his operative technique. Dr Grant compared the average surgical operation with the obstetrical one, stating that, in both, blood vessels were opened up and direct channels suddenly exposed to external or internal infection. The conditions and nature of the maternity operation, however, differed greatly from those present in ordinary surgery. Ante-natal care was necessary, but it should be agreed to by the patient and carried out by the patient's own medical attendant, supplemented by specialist obstetrical assistance in any difficult or doubtful diagnosis. Things could then be prearranged for the labour, and for dealing with likely emergencies.

'Medical Contributions to Lay Journals', *British Medical Journal*, 1 (10 Mar. 1934), 459

Sir – An article with the dramatic title 'Motherhood is safe – if you are poor', was published in the *Scottish Daily Express* of February 21st. It calls for some comment. Dealing with maternal mortality, 'A Famous Gynaecologist' states: 'The first most important cause is puerperal sepsis or infection. By that is meant the introducing of bacteria into the mother during or shortly after the birth of her child, and the giving rise to localised or general disease. The tragedy is that the medical attendant may carry the germ on his hands or clothes; or that, as has been shown comparatively recently, the germ may be present in the attendant's throat without causing any personal inconvenience. Without any symptoms to reveal its presence, a doctor may be his patient's most deadly menace. All women, at such a time, are vulnerable to infection, but Nature renders assistance in the fight.'

Such a statement appearing in the lay press serves no useful purpose to the public, and might only bring a highly conscientious colleague, the victim of circumstance, into professional disrepute. The 'Famous Gynaecologist' – I am certain he or she is not an obstetrician – by telling only half of the truth, and indeed the lesser half, indicates that sensational effect has been his main object: or, to be more charitable, he may be a young writer of limited experience, with little penchant for reflection and *savoir-faire*. The contributor has been content to pillory the medical attendant. He has failed to mention the well-recognised possibilities of intrinsic and auto-infection.

From the lay reader's point of view, also, the article in question is undesirable and harmful. Where is the encouragement for the expectant and potential mother in a contribution the reading of which would inculcate only a dread and fear of pregnancy and parturition into the mind of any woman? Consider the effect of mental anguish and worry during pregnancy on the subsequent labour and puerperium, and their total effect on maternal mortality figures. Five years ago I wrote in a medical newspaper: 'Expectant mothers should, if at all nervous, be told that the vast majority of confinements are easy, natural and safe. They should not be frightened by articles on maternal mortality in the public press, as such are apt to prove a harmful policy.' This should, I think, indicate to the 'Famous Gynaecologist' the type of message of hope, comfort and encouragement which does so much to fortify the expectant mother and render her pregnancy and parturition less morbid.

In conclusion, I would express my extreme disappointment at the increasing number of tactless professional contributions to the lay press by colleagues, and would suggest that 'the code' be readjusted to obviate the menace – for so it is. I would appreciate the opinions of other colleagues. – I am etc.,

Lachlan Grant, Ballachulish, Feb. 27th.

SECTION 2

Healthcare Provision

Highlands and Islands Medical Service Committee. Minutes of Evidence taken before the Committee appointed by Treasury to Enquire into the Provision of Medical Attendance in the Highlands and Islands of Scotland, vol. 2, PP, Cd 6920, 1913, Q. 19,647–775, pp. 329–97

28 October 1912, Oban
Dr Lachlan Grant, called and examined.

19,647 (*Chairman*). You practise at Ballachulish, Argyllshire, and at Kinlochleven? – Yes.

19,648. You are a graduate of Edinburgh University? – Yes. I am M.B.C.M. and M.D. of Edinburgh University. I also hold the Diploma of Public Health of the R.C.P.S. (Edin.) and the R.F.P.S. (Glas.), and the certificate of the Medico-Psychological Association.

19,649. How long have you been in Ballachulish? – For ten or eleven years.

19,650. The Kinlochleven practice is a new practice? – Yes. I am the doctor for the parish which includes Kinlochleven.

19,651. But the population has come there recently? – Yes, within the last four and a half years.

19,652. What is the population of Kinlochleven? – Between 1100 and 1200.

19,653. And that is all in addition to your previous practice? – Yes, but they have a resident man besides me.

19,654. How long has that doctor been there? – Four years.

19,655. The population over which you practise amounts to 3500? – Yes.

19,656. You give in your statement a list of the towns and villages along with their approximate population? – Yes, – Ballachulish and Glencoe, 1400, Kinlochleven, 1100, Kintallen and Duror, 450, North Ballachulish and Onich, 500, and Ardgour, 200.

19,657. What is the farthest that you have to go to see a patient? – Twenty-two miles.

19,658. Is that one family or a township? – It is down Glen Etive where there are a series of families, including two shooting lodges.

19,659. What proportion of your practice is within three miles of your house? You say there are about 600 within two miles. Will it be about the same within three miles? – Yes.

19,660. Then you have about 300 at ten miles and about forty at twenty miles? – Yes.

19,661. How do you get about the country? – By motor car, bicycle, walking, motor boat, rowing boat, steamers and trains.

19,662. Have you much travelling to do in steamers and boats? – Yes, a good deal.

19,663. Are there some places you cannot get to except by boat? – Yes, there is one place.

19,664. What does your motor cost you a year to run? – About £60.

19,665. How much is that per mile? – I cannot say.

19,666. That £60 does not include a chauffeur? – No.

19,667. Do you keep horses too? – No.

19,668. Did you keep horses before you got your motor? – Yes, one.

19,669. You do some bacteriological work? – Yes.

19,670. Do you find that it is useful? – Extremely useful.

19,671. Do you do it for other doctors too? – Yes.

19,672. What about security of tenure? Have you had any trouble with your Parish Council? – No, none at all.

19,673. But you would approve of it? – Yes, I would.

19,674. Do you think the parish medical officer should have the same security of tenure as the county medical officer has? – Yes.

19,675. The county medical officer has to interfere very likely with the property of certain County Councillors, while the medical officer for the parish has not to do so? – Of course I am local medical officer of health.

19,676. And as that have you fixity of tenure? – No.

19,677. Do you find an increase in the number of conscientious objectors against vaccination? – Yes, at Kinlochleven more than at Ballachulish and Glencoe.

19,678. Is it really conscientious objection, or is it merely to avoid the trouble? – It is really to avoid the trouble of vaccinating.

19,679. We have had evidence to the effect that since it was possible to get relief, the doctors have practically no vaccination now? – In my district the vaccination is much the same as usual, except at Kinlochleven.

19,680. (*Dr Mackenzie*). Is that because of the difference of the imported population? – Yes.

19,681. They are a different race really? – Yes, they largely come from the south.

19,681a. Your own people fall in with it quite peaceably? – Yes.

19,682. (*Chairman*). How does your club at Ballachulish work? – It works only fairly well: it is not a great success. The workmen pay me 3 and a half pence per week.

19,683. Does that cover attention to themselves and their families? – Yes. The single men pay the same thing.

19,684. That is about 14s. a year? – 15s. 2d.

19,685. That is paid by all the men, whether married or single, and it includes medical attendance on the women and children? – Yes.

19,686. Does it include maternity? – No.

19,687. What do you get for the maternity cases? – A guinea as a rule.

19,688. Does it include operations and that sort of thing? – Yes, but supposing we use a local or general anaesthetic we charge extra.

19,689. You have forty men at Kintallen? – Yes.

19,690. How many have you at Ballachulish? – About 200.

19,691. How do you collect the subscriptions? – They have a secretary and a treasurer who collects the money each pay. It is not deducted from their wages at the slate quarries, but it is deducted at the granite quarries.

19,692. But the money is always got? – Not always.

19,693. (*Lady Tullibardine*). Taking both clubs you have 240 men in them? – Yes.

19,694. (*Chairman*). Suppose this was a private practice and there was no club, do you think you would get more or less out of your practice there? Does it amount to a fair remuneration for you? – No. If it was not for my outside practice I really could not make it up.

19,695. Do you give to these 240 men more attention than you are really paid for? – Yes.

19,696. (*Dr Mackenzie*). Supposing you were attending them as if they were not a club, but as private patients, do you think you would get more from them in the form of fees, than you are getting now? – I don't think I would. I am afraid I would have to sue them, and that would be *infra dig.*

19,697. (*Chairman*). Suppose there was no club here, and you attended them, would you be able to get £180 out of them, taking the risk of bad debts and all the rest of it? – I think I would, but they have been used with the club practice for a matter of fifty years.

19,698. What I want to get at is whether you think your income would be better or worse if they paid by fees instead of club practice? – That is a difficult point.

19,699. Do you think you are oftener called than you would be if they had to pay a fee each time? – No, I don't think so.

19,700. Are you called frivolously? – Occasionally, but not very often.

19,701. Do you think they would do that whether they paid a fee or not? – They would not be so ready to do it. Of course one goes in for a little personal admonition.

19,702. When the doctor gets to know the people it does not happen to any great extent? – That is so.

19,703. That is your experience? – Yes.

19,704. You suggest that with the payment by fees you have often to modify your charge and very often don't get it at all? – That is so.

19,705. Are those club people all insured persons? – Yes.

19,706. Do you think it is likely you will get £80 out of the wives and families? – I should think so.

19,707. How many of these 240 are married? Roughly speaking a half? – Yes.

19,708. Why do you consider payment per visit preferable? – Simply because of the check on the useless calls.

19,709. But you say that that does not amount to anything very serious with you? – That is so.

19,710. There is this to be said, that this population is just at your door? – No, there is Duror for example.

19,711. Are they all in the club there? – No.

19,712. I was referring to the club? – Kintallen is four miles from me.

19,713. You are afraid if it was a club entirely you would be called unnecessarily. As a matter of fact you have not found that to be the case? – Not so far.

19,714. Taking it from the public health point of view, would it not be an advantage if a poor person knew he could get the doctor without running up a bill? Would he not send sooner and oftener? – Yes.

19,715. And it would entail a great deal of extra work for the doctor? – Yes.

19,716. You would have more to do, but at the same time, the patients would get a better service and from the point of view of the public health it would be better? – Yes.

19,717. A good deal of your practice is unremunerated? – Yes.

19,718. That is to say, when you have a long way to go you don't get a fee adequate to pay you for your trouble and expense? – That is so. With regard to public works, some contract is in force as in my own practice. The Workmen's Medical Society in my own district of Ballachulish and Glencoe arrange for all single and married men to pay 15s 2d per annum. To become entitled to medical benefits all workmen earning their own living must pay into the fund. Confinements and vaccinations are extra. This scale of remuneration enables the doctor to give attention to the work, though there is, by no means, anything in the shape of a fortune in it, and were it not for the outside practice one could not 'make' a living. The outside private practice from the parish centres is of a varied character. The amount of professional work varies from year to year. It is done by trap, bicycle, motor car, tram, steamer, motor boat, ferry boat, when not by walking. Here, the patients, as a rule, only send for the doctor when they think the case is a serious one, or when an accident takes place. Hesitation in calling the doctor often leads to irreparable injury and death. For instance, in two families, there were cases of diphtheria that turned out fatal. Had I been called in the earliest stage of the disease the chances are that both lives would have been saved. I have never lost a case of diphtheria yet when I got in the first day and administered the antitoxine.

19,719. How far were those patients away? – One was five miles and the other was ten.

Competition. – The parish medical officer, and the local independent medical practitioners in the more populous centres like Oban, Fort William, Kinlochleven etc., are all more or less in competition. There is consequently a large amount of overlapping in rural practice. For instance, I have considerable work at Onich and North Ballachulish, though both those places are in my colleague Dr Miller's practice. This is due to my being the nearest doctor. Parish medical officers are frequently called in by patients in adjoining parishes, so that, as things are, artificial boundaries cannot be adhered to. Yet, the result is much wasted energy, and work at very inadequate remuneration. Locomotion in the Highlands and Islands is expensive and often difficult, entailing great hardships in rough weather. Take the case of Duror and Ardgour, ten and seven miles from my centre, the cost of hires – if no steamers or trains are available – is from 9s to 15s per visit. On trying to make a living I find myself in competition with colleagues in town and country, including other parish medical officers: I certainly don't enjoy any fun there may be in the scramble; but I have no option but to follow the present economic necessity.

Adequate equipment. – Bearing on this is the lack of equipment. Parish doctors make a bare living, having no free dwelling houses, and financially unable to equip themselves with the most modern medical and surgical appliances, patients cannot get the best treatment. I quite admit there is a continual improvement in this respect, but there is still a great deal of inefficiency from this cause.

Medicine. – Patients' friends have to come for medicines and dressings to the surgery – or they are sent by post.

Outline of my work. – Before giving an outline of the work I do in my practice, I may mention that I have had the following experience. House Surgeon, Royal Infirmary, Edinburgh, Assistantship in General Practice, four and a half years Surgeon to Gesto Hospital, Isle of Skye, situated in centre of island, two days weekly free dispensaries. I did ordinary and consulting practice over island. General medical practitioner here and at Kinlochleven. Have an assistant at times, but this is expensive and now they are somewhat difficult to get. At present I have the following appointments:

(1) Parish Medical Officer.
(2) Local Medical Officer of Health.
(3) Medical Officer of Fever Hospital which includes shelter for isolation and treatment of advanced phthisical cases.
(4 Medical Officer to Workmen's Society.
(5) Consulting Medical Officer to British Aluminium Coy., Kinlochleven Works.
(6) Certifying Factory Surgeon.
(7) Bacteriologist to Lorn, Ardnamurchan, and Mull districts of County Council.

In the course of daily practice I endeavour to diagnose and treat patients by the latest modern methods; and I would consider much of my efforts wasted unless I did so. I am convinced that for many diseases *laboratory methods* are nowadays absolutely necessary as an adjunct to clinical work. Much inefficient diagnosis and treatment are due to lack of the aid this modern development in medicines can give. So I should like to emphasise that bacteriological diagnosis is an important requirement in many illnesses, and is not half taken advantage of. The District Committees of some County Councils get the diagnosis of diphtheria, consumption and enteric fever done for the medical practitioners free. I do such for some of the Committees, and get paid at the usual rates; but the remuneration is so small it does not really pay me, and were it not that I am deeply interested in such work I should let such be sent away to Glasgow, Edinburgh, or London. For some years now I have been issuing vaccines mostly prepared in my own laboratory with very good results.

Ophthalmic Work. – On my district, eyework I find is an important branch of practice. I went over my lists recently and found I had fitted over a thousand people with lenses during the last eight years. If I did not do this work some of these patients would require to travel to one of the ophthalmic institutions in the cities.

Recommendations. – First and foremost comes adequate remuneration; then relief from uncertainty and useless competition, and a reasonable amount of leisure. I have given the problem considerable thought, and confess I see no adequate solution along the old lines of general practice. We require a new departure in the form of a full State medical service for our Highlands and Islands. I would tabulate the essentials of such an organised medical service as follows:-

(1) A sufficient salary increasing according to length of service and work done – also a pension system.
(2) Free house with surgery – and dispensary – if no chemist near.
(3) Periodical visits to hospitals and post-graduate classes.
(4) Provision for motor cars, motor boats, and bicycles.
(5) Consultation and assistance in serious and obscure cases.
(6) Provision for cases requiring special hospital treatment.
(7) Provision for bacteriological diagnosis.
(8) Provision for x-ray diagnosis and treatment.

(9) Provision for vaccine and other special treatments.

(10) Supply of medicine, surgical dressings and surgical appliances by the administrative authority.

(11) A committee of medical men consisting of specialists and practitioners should act as an advisory body to the Central State Department.

(12) Some leisure and an annual holiday for the medical practitioner.

(13) Regulations of an elastic nature bearing on general, medical and surgical duties and equipment should be formed and issued to the medical practitioners; or occasional visits should be paid by all-round experienced medical commissioners to each district – something on the pattern of the Lunacy Board.

With reference to point No. (3), the district medical officer should visit some general hospital at least every two years, and a fever hospital perhaps every third or fourth year, his expenses being paid, and efficient trained substitutes provided. *E.g.* in a few of the larger centres a regular staff of well-paid assistant medical officers should be available as locums or assistants for special and emergency work, or extra service in case of epidemics. Special medical men should also be retained for consultative or special operative work. In my opinion, it is highly desirable to have one or even two *bacteriological* and chemical laboratories in the Highlands. Such a modern, well-equipped laboratory, situated in the centre of the Highlands, providing for diagnosis and treatment, would prove of the greatest possible benefit, and the cost would not be very great. It would also stimulate fresh interest in medical matters not only amongst the members of the medical profession, but also amongst the whole of the general public in a way which cannot be arrived at by the delegation of such special work to distant laboratories in the larger centres of the south, where of necessity the bacteriologist is out of contact with the general medical practitioner whose work it is his function to assist. It may seem rather advanced to propose to give medicine, vaccines, and appliances free, as well as medical advice, but I believe it is bound to come to that in the end. And, after all, it is only a further division of the burden of taxation among the whole people according to the ability to pay. It will always pay the country as a whole to keep each or any section of it in the highest grade of health. A medical organisation like this is really a system of police against disease, and to make it effective a similar method to the police and post office is essential. As an illustration, last year I examined some forty specimens of sputum in my district, and eight of them were found to be tubercular. Some of them were only found positive after repeated examinations and special tests. Without examination, some of the cases would have been missed and allowed to develop into more 'open' cases of tuberculosis, with consequent danger to those around. I hold, therefore, that if a patient with incipient tubercular disease has been allowed to get the length of having sputum – that all doctors should send the suspicious sputas repeatedly to the nearest medical laboratory – I say repeatedly, as we know it is often only after repeated examinations that we find the presence of the tubercole bacillis. Supplementary to local organisations, there could be centres of easy access for various departments of specialism, say for eyes, ear and throat, teeth, women's and children's diseases. At present, special centres are available for mental and infectious diseases in our asylums and fever hospitals.

A Possible Compromise. – Some system of compromise may possibly be devised so that all may pay something for attendance, with extra fees for night visits, confinements, fractures, vaccines, treatments, and operations. But, whatever plan may be adopted, I don't think the capitation system will suit the country and the outlying district of the Highlands and Islands. The time and expense incurred in travelling to patients precludes that. And there are other considerations, such as the poverty of many of the patients. If the district medical offices were under the State, the salary hitherto paid by the Parish Councils could be utilised as a portion of the standardised remuneration under a new scheme. The minds of the officers being free from the details and anxieties of fee-collecting would be better able to concentrate on the duties of disease prevention and health betterment of the individual and the community. The question would naturally arise who was to be medically attended to and who not by the district medical officer. It would probably be found that the system should be of universal application, and any who wished extra-official attention could have it by individual payment to private practitioners. But as district officers would be confined entirely to official work, the salaries and conditions would have to be adequate and reasonable in order to attract the best talent to this branch of the medical profession.

Supplement. – Some details of my Isle of Skye experiences may be of service. I have seen:

(1) Cases of women having large families who never had the skill or service of a medical man or skilled nurse.

(2) Cases where the distance from the nearest doctor was many miles – frequently I drove ten and twenty miles, and sometimes having to stay over a night.

(3) Cases where, after a long fatiguing journey and a difficult case, no fees were ever paid.

(4) Cases of people very poor, with little or no comforts and hygienic conditions very bad.

(5) Cases where the services of a trained nurse were essential to recovery.

My experiences would indicate that, in addition to district medical officers, some organised system of 'medical patrol' at stated and regular intervals would best suit the outlying sections of our Highlands and Islands. There should also be telephonic communication direct between medical outposts and also to the base of supplies, and to the nurses' homes – so that nursing or extra-skilled assistance, and special remedies, can be had freshly prepared without any undue delay.

Nursing Service. – An efficient medical service for the Highlands and Islands necessarily carries with it an auxiliary in the form of a staff of well-trained nurses available for service anywhere. These nurses would require a special equipment of items for the sick, and perhaps little comforts for the destitute. It should be part of their duty wherever they went to teach elementary general health conditions, and even sick-room cookery. Amongst the corps of nurses should be some specially trained in midwifery (mental cases) etc., to send to cases in isolated parts (glen or island) where doctor is not easily available.

Intelligence Department. – A series of tracts or handbills should be officially prepared by the medical headquarters in plain language dealing with the essentials of healthy living and avoidance of illness. Also, perhaps, warnings of various dangers, etc., for broadcast distribution. Each county might issue timely bulletins dealing with anything special, as well as a monthly circular, for public perusal (churches have their Records etc.). A system of popular medical lectures might be given every year for old and young on how to try and keep well. Such should be a standing order of the new territorial medical corps. Juvenile health culture and physiology classes should be encouraged, and each district should have its first-aid or ambulance classes. In, say, two centres there ought to be a Motherhood

College (instruction largely by women graduates), where girls could obtain instruction in matters pertaining specially to their health, and in subjects necessary for mothers to know.

The Medical Man as Casual Labourer. – Some of us are frequently in the position of a casual labourer waiting for a job. It will happen there is only one job for several waiting aspirants, while not far off there will be a number of jobs and only one man available. Again, some of us are so poor, we cannot afford to let any opportunity pass for making a fee. One eye has to be kept on the patient and the other on our bread and butter. The exigencies of a lean pasture make us regretfully sparing of our science and sentiment. There is a tendency created to think meanly of, and perhaps to act meanly to, our fellow medicals, but competition, even in doing good, always does that. The casual labourer is a danger to the industrial community, and the casual competitive doctor of medicine is also a danger to the public health. In a profession demanding a large strain of altruism, a paltry commercialism is fatal to its best manifestations.

Conclusions in favour of a Complete State Service:-

(1) That the case of the Highlands and Islands requires special treatment and consideration.
(2) That medical practice as carried on in the Highlands does not give the people the benefit of those advances in medical science that they are entitled to.
(3) That medical practice as carried on in many Highland districts is unremunerative, and this because of the time taken in travelling to and from cases, heavy outlays for transit, cost of medicines, and no free houses (such as are provided for the clergy and head teachers).
(4) That the present moment is ripe for the inauguration of a complete State medical service.
(5) That the starting of such a service in the Highlands could be done with less opposition and much less friction than in the more densely populated parts of the country.
(6) That if the remuneration were adequate to attract skilful members of the profession, that both the doctors and the public would favour such a form of medical service.
(7) That such a service should include a fully equipped bacteriological laboratory at one or more convenient centres.

(8) That, in addition to the money received from the insured people and from parish and county councils, financial assistance should be obtained from the Treasury in order to make up the allowance necessary for satisfactory medical attention for each district.

(9) That only on these lines will every individual in the Highlands receive proper medical and surgical attention; no patient would be neglected and no serious cases jeopardised through dilatoriness in sending for the doctor because of the expense, the distance and the inconvenience.

(10) That such a State preventive system as I have briefly outlined is a 'coming event' all over the country in the near future.

The motive and object of all the reforms outlined is to enable the people to be well attended when they are sick, to live naturally, and to avoid to a large extent the necessity for drugs and doctors. A sure sign of progress will be when doctors have little to do but attend to accidents and the unavoidable visitations of Nature.

19,720. In regard to your proposals, who do you propose should get the benefit of this State medical system? – I should say all the people.

19,721. Without regard to their position or ability to pay? – Yes. If you remunerate the local district medical officer sufficiently, he will be pleased to attend all and sundry.

19,722. The Duke of Sutherland and Mr Andrew Carnegie and all those people should get the benefit of this service? – I suppose that would have to be.

19,723. Do you think it a feasible proposal? – I really do think so.

19,724. (*Dr Mackenzie.*) Your point is that you would put general medical attendance on the same footing as attendance for public health purposes? – Yes.

19,725. (*Chairman.*) How are these people who at present pay fees for this doctor? You will let off all those people who at present pay fees. Are you not to get anything from them? – There will be the ordinary taxation, and if you get a grant from the Treasury they will be contributing to it indirectly.

19,726. Is the whole cost to come from the Treasury? – No, there will be money from the insured people and contributions from the Parish Councils and County Councils.

19,727. Why should you take it from the Parish Council? – I get a salary from the Parish Council already.

19,728. But if you are to let off the ordinary patient from paying his doctor's fees, why should you not let off the Parish Council? – The Parish Council taxes the people for the parish medical work.

19,729. Yes, but they don't tax them in the same proportion. We have got some parishes in the county that pay 1s in the £ for their medical officer's fee, and others that pay less than 1d. Are you to continue that present rate, or are you to take the universal rate all over the country? – I should say that probably it should be a universal rate for the Highlands.

19,730. Who is to control the doctor? – That is another problem. I should say that there ought to be some system of local control as well as central control – I should say perhaps the Insurance Committee – and the appointment should be sanctioned by the Local Government Board or the central advisory body.

19,731. There should be some control? – Yes, I think I would favour that. Of course the Parish Council and the County Council have it just now.

19,732. (*Dr Mackenzie.*) You would unite all the bodies and any voluntary bodies as well? – Yes, I think that is a feasible proposal.

19,733. There is nothing contradictory in that? – No.

19,734. (*Chairman.*) You would give this body the absolute control of the kind of doctor that was to be set down to work a certain parish? – You mean local bodies?

19,735. Yes? – Of course the regulations would be framed and the work really set agoing by the central body.

19,736. And no matter how objectionable and unsatisfactory a doctor might be or might become for a parish, you would not give any right to the locality to get rid of him? – I should think they should have the right to petition the central body.

19,737. (*Lady Tullibardine.*) Do you not think there would be some fear of the average doctor not being as interested in his patients if there was a State service as he is at present? – I am inclined to think not. I should think nowadays there is such care taken in getting the best men into the profession, examinations are so difficult, and then their testimonials would be carefully investigated by the local body, and the appointment would be made by the central body. If an undue number of complaints were made, then there would be room for investigation. Then the work would be supervised by a Commissioner visiting occasionally, and reports on the doctor's work could be sent on.

19,738. Do you think that would be agreeable to the profession? – I am inclined to think it would, in the Highlands. I think most of the doctors would rather have a salary of say £500 per annum than try and work up to £200 and £300 more – they would rather be certain of the £500.

19,739. Your great objection to the present system is its uncertainty? – Yes.

19,740. Do you not think that if there was a certain sum guaranteed that would remove a good many of your objections to the current system? – It would help. It would depend upon the amount of work that had to be done and the sum allotted.

19,741. Would you not see a danger of friction between your State doctors and the ordinary doctor? – I don't think so – not any more than would have between the present public schools and the private schools.

19,742. Private schools are usually found to be in centres. I gathered that your private practitioners would be distributed about the country and would be employed by the people who did not care to employ a State doctor? – Yes, but ultimately they would have to fall into line.

19,743. What exactly do you mean? – The State doctor would ultimately take over the whole of the duties.

19,744. So you would have none but State doctors? – Ultimately.

19,745. That involves forfeiting the choice of doctors by patients? – Not entirely.

19,746. Would you not have to give your State doctor each his own area? – Yes, but there would be some choice of doctor to start with anyway. That would have to be so, because, as I have pointed out, some of us visit adjoining parishes.

19,747. You mean that other doctors visit the same parish? – Yes, and other parishes.

19,748. Do you not find that the people like to have a free choice of doctor? – Yes, I am sure they do, but they really don't have it much at the present time.

19,749. Owing to the scattered nature of the population? – Yes. Each doctor is practically in his own district at present, and the people have no choice in the selection really. I believe you would get a better set of men under this arrangement.

19,750. You do not find that in this part of the country that some of the poorer people rather like to change their doctor, perhaps not always for a very good reason? – Yes, that sometimes happens.

19,751. That would be rather difficult under your system? – If they did wish to change there might be some arrangement. As I said, the arrangements should be of an elastic nature, providing a certain amount of freedom of choice.

19,752. Do you think that as a rule the average doctor is as interested in his club practice as he is in his ordinary practice? – Perhaps there is a tendency to rush over the club patients – it is sort of human nature – but I don't think there is really much in that.

19,753. That is what I had in my mind. You don't think there would be a danger in that? – I don't think so, if the work was carefully looked after and suitable records kept. I am sure it would really be a good thing, and there is a chance just now of getting such a thing going. It is practically a State service now, with the Parish Councils – I am practically a State servant.

19,754. Surely your salary is provided from the rates? – There is a medical relief grant from the Treasury.

19,755. (*Chairman.*) Do you make a distinction between centres like Oban and centres like the Gesto Hospital? – Yes, there is a distinction.

19,756. There is a difficulty, where there are several doctors, in how the practice is to be distributed. One doctor would be apt to be overworked, and another would not have enough to do? – One would only have to do what he could.

19,757. I don't see much difficulty where there is the one doctor in the one parish? – No. You have not so very many populous centres in the Highlands to deal with.

19,758. (*Lady Tullibardine.*) But you have a good many doctors going out from the centres to adjoining rural areas? – Yes. There is a good deal of that, but still, if you had really able local practitioners and arrangements for consultations, there would not be the same necessity for that.

19,759. You would keep the town men in the town? – Yes, I think I would. They could be available for special operative work.

19,760. Do you not think the better men would tend to flock to the towns, leaving the less able men for the country areas? – I don't think so, if the remuneration was sufficient. There are often just as good men in the country as there are in the towns.

19,761. (*Chairman.*) It does not occur to you that we might continue to get contributions from the people for the purposes of the doctor? – I say that some form of compromise might be arranged in that way, but I believe it would be easier to get contributions from the people if such were advised by the arrangements you are to recommend to be made just now.

19,762. I am anxious that there should be a modified payment for the service they get, just as in the Insurance Act? – And that would include the wives and children?

19,763. Yes, it would need to be that in the Highlands, I think? – It would be very advisable. Of course that is practically creating a State service.

19,764. (*Dr Mackenzie.*) You say your contribution per family is really a State medical service – that is to say, it is a form of taxation, such as parochial or other rates, and it comes to the same thing as if it were rates and imperial contributions. That is what is in your mind? – Yes.

19,765. So therefore, as far as you are concerned, it is a matter of convenience whether you would realise your service through such direct contributions from families, or whether you would just realise it as it is at present through rates and imperial contributions? – Yes, quite.

19,766. You have read the Chancellor of the Exchequer's speech last week as given in the *British Medical Journal* and elsewhere? – Yes.

19,767. Your scheme in reality is pretty much on the same lines as he has indicated? – Yes.

19,768. You would consider that that fairly covers the ground? – Yes.

19,769. (*Dr Miller.*) There is one little difficulty under the complete scheme, and it is this, that insured persons who are now obliged to pay contributions towards medical benefit ought to be relieved of the payment of such contributions? – Yes, I think so.

19,770. So to that extent, supposing a scheme like yours was to be adopted, the Insurance Act would have to be repealed to that extent? – To that extent, unless the local Insurance Committee had powers.

19,771. You think that something like £500 a year would be a fair basis upon which parochial medical officers should be remunerated under this scheme? – Yes, provided they had houses and medicines given them. With regard to the laboratory, the cost would not be very great. Probably the site would be a factor, and then there would be all the buildings. These would not be very expensive. All that would be required would be two or three rooms well lighted, ventilated and heated and then the equipment. I would say the whole cost would be about £2000 or £3000.

19,772. (*The Chairman.*) What is the advantage of having it in centres like that when you have it in Glasgow or Edinburgh? – You want a vaccine prepared at once, and the bacteriologist and medical practitioners would be in closer touch.

19,773. (*Dr Mackenzie.*) You might explain what a vaccine is? – Many infectious diseases, e.g., common colds, are caused by micro-organisms. You get a growth of the organisms in a culture tube, and you examine this and find out what the organisms are. You rub the growth into a sterilised salt solution and sterilise this for an hour to kill them. Then you start and count them, then you inoculate so many of these organisms into the individual, and the individual's system says, 'We must manufacture an antidote.' The organisms are dead but at the same time they stimulate the system, and the defensive material goes to the most affected part. It is almost necessary to have vaccine treatment nowadays, and you must get the organism that is causing the disease. If you had this laboratory situated centrally, it would stimulate interest among the 200 doctors in the Highlands. The cost would not be very great.

19,774. What would be the cost of running it? – You would have a caretaker to inoculate the materials when they came in, when the doctor was not there. Probably about £700 a year – and about £100 per annum for materials.

19,775. About £1000 a year would run it? – Yes. I think myself that this is one of the most important of the medical schemes in connection with the Highlands.

'Health in the Highlands', *British Medical Journal*, 1 (15 March 1919), 324

Dr Lachlan Grant, whose long connection with Ballachulish as medical officer enables him to speak with special knowledge, gives an interesting account of the conditions of life and health in the Highlands in a paper reprinted from the *Caledonian Medical Journal* for January. Although the land of brown heath and shaggy wood does not offer riches to the cultivator there are commercial possibilities in farming by scientific method, the utilisation of electric power, fishing and afforestation, which have hitherto been to a considerable extent neglected. Dr Grant expresses the belief that most of the areas now allowed to run to waste and many of the deer forests will soon be things of the past, but it is to be feared that the best of Scotland's manhood will still continue to be attracted by the opportunities of a richer life overseas. Dr Grant deals with the housing question in a somewhat optimistic spirit. All will agree that in the interest of the public health and the amenities of life an 'elastic and comprehensive scheme' is imperatively required; the difficulty is to frame such a scheme and then to get it carried through the legislature. Although the Highlander is still, as the war has abundantly shown, hardy beyond most classes, men, women and children suffer from bad housing, wrong diet, and neglect of hygiene, and thus conditions are produced which make for the degeneration of the race. The root of the evil is poverty, and this can only be remedied by the intelligent use of natural resources and industrial development. The chief obstacle to this is the difficulty of transport, which may to a considerable extent be overcome by the application of modern methods, especially the motor boat. The scope of the aeroplane seems likely to be limited by the want of landing grounds. Dr Grant considers that, though the Highlands and Islands Medical Act is good, it should be replaced by a more generous scheme. He urges the provision of better housing and surgery accommodation, arrangements for the relief of doctors when overworked or struck down by illness in remote parts, improvement of the economic conditions of the service, and the grant of pensions to men who have spent themselves in the work. He also insists on the need of school clinics, more local hospitals with maternity wards and some system for the removal of serious cases to city hospitals, periodical visits by skilled dentists, and more maternity nurses in outlying districts. The powers of the medical officers of health should be enlarged, and there should be a special Highlands department in the proposed Health Ministry. We commend Dr Grant's suggestions to the attention of all those interested in the prosperity of the Highlands, which are a national asset of the highest value as a breeding ground of men who deserve well of the State, a field for manly sport which is a training for war, a source of new vigour to the wearied intellectual toiler, and a joy forever to lovers of things of natural beauty.

SECTION 3

The Ballachulish Slate Quarry Dispute

'A Scottish Bethesda', *Labour Leader*, 24 July 1902

The West Highland township of Ballachulish, famous as the home of a slate-quarrying industry, rivalling that of Penrhyn in Wales, is at present the scene of a dispute, which, though not originating in the same way as the Welsh trouble, seems likely to have serious developments, of which it will be worth the while of all Labour men to take note. In the present instance it is not a question of wages or hours of labour. The dispute centres around the personality of one man, Dr Lachlan Grant, the medical officer of the slate quarries company. Dr Grant has, without any reasons given or explanations of any kind, received a month's notice of dismissal from the company's service. The company in taking this action, have not consulted the desires of the quarrymen, and the latter, who have deductions made from their wages for medical services, are naturally indignant at the high-handed dismissal of a gentleman against whom they have no cause of complaint, and who by reason, not only of his medical skill, but of his social and human qualities, seems to have won the regard and affection of the entire community. Indeed, not only the quarrymen, but people of all classes for miles around, including clergymen of every denomination in the district, have protested against the company's action. In a matter of this kind, however, protests are not of much avail, and the men have determined to exercise their right to appoint their own medical officer, and have given notice that they will not allow any deductions to be made from their wages on behalf of any doctor who is not appointed by themselves. There the matter stands at present, and it remains to be seen whether the company will persist in enforcing deductions which would be illegal, or whether they will appoint another medical officer in opposition to the wishes of the people most concerned. It is to be hoped in the interests of common justice that

Dr Grant and the quarrymen will be enabled to fight the matter through, and if in doing so they are able to throw some light on the industrial conditions which prevail in the West Highlands, the probability is that the only persons who have cause to regret the dispute will be the management of the Ballachulish Quarries Company. Concerning this company, its shareholders, its dividends, its wages bill and its general management, we may have something to say in the LEADER before long.

'A State of War at Ballachulish', *Labour Leader*, 17 Jan. 1903

The men locked out

The Ballachulish quarrymen, in their remote corner among the Highland hills, having during the last six months come through much trouble and turmoil. It would now seem that the year that has just begun is to be more fraught with strife for these peace-loving people.

As a New Year's message from their employers they have received intimation of a lock-out. The ostensible reason for this act of war is to be found in a resolution passed by the men on the 23rd December.

The resolution was as follows: 'That on the resumption of work, on the expiry of the New Year holidays (1903) quarry contracts be taken for the period of four weeks, instead of six weeks as formerly; and they further demand that their wages be paid in full to all the workmen at the end of each four weeks.'

That is to say, the men have asked for a system of monthly pays and contracts, a perfectly moderate and reasonable request, which no employer of labour with any sense of fair play would ever dream of making the basis of a dispute. Those responsible for the management of the Ballachulish Slate Quarries Company, do not, however, seem to be endowed with any sense of fair play. Flushed apparently with their temporary victory in the law courts over Dr Grant, they have adopted a policy of no compromise, and have declared war against their workmen.

They have not even condescended to negotiate or to argue the matter.

With an autocratic disregard for right or reason, and in terms brimful of unconscious humour, these great men have issued their ultimatum. 'At a meeting of the directors of the Ballachulish Slate Quarries Co. Ltd., held on the 7th inst.' – so runs the official document – 'it was resolved to make no alteration in the terms and conditions of employment in the company's quarries, and work will be resumed and carried on under the same terms and conditions of employment as were in force immediately before the holiday; and the directors have now to intimate that those who were in the company's employment at last pay day will have an opportunity of resuming work after signing on at the company's office, Ballachulish, *on the company's former terms and conditions of employment*, and so soon as a majority of the quarrymen, labourers and tradesmen, etc., have so signed work will resume and contracts will be let as formerly. A copy of the form to be signed is sent herewith.

> By order of the directors,
> E. Brice Low, Secretary
> A. MacColl, Manager.'

Here is a copy of the previous document which the workmen are asked to sign before they will be allowed to start work: 'We, the undersigned quarrymen, labourers, tradesmen etc., hereby agree to accept employment in the company's service at Ballachulish upon the same terms and conditions of employment *as have existed in the works since the company entered as lessees of the quarries.*'

It will be seen that these terms and conditions are comprehensively retrospective. They go back to the beginnings of things, so far as the present company is concerned. Were the men to sign this document they would, by a stroke of the pen, annul all of the concessions they have won during the last six months, including the right to the appointment of their medical officer. This probably is the crux of the whole matter. So long as the men retain that right, the company, even with legal decisions behind them, are powerless to drive Dr Grant out of the district, and if the men were to forego that right they might find the directors amenable to reason, even on the question of monthly pays and contracts. Needless to say the men will not sign this document. If the directors adhere to their decision the works will remain closed and the shareholders will have to go without their dividends. It is a lock-out. The Christian directors of the Ballachulish Company have been driven back on the methods of barbarism. At one blow they hope to regain their power over the men, to destroy the newly-formed trade union, and to defeat Dr Grant.

By throwing the men out of work they seek to stop the supplies both of the men and of Dr Grant, who depends for the payment of his salary upon the ability of the men to find steady employment.

It is thus a cold-blooded policy of starvation that has been adopted.

For the purpose in view it is a fatal policy. It may be productive of much misery. It may mean the breaking up of homes and the scattering of friends; it may even mean the destruction of the slate industry at Ballachulish – these probabilities have doubtless all been considered by the management – yet when all this has been done nobody will have gained anything. Everybody all round will have been losers. The management, the shareholders, the workmen, the medical officer, and the entire community, will have suffered. For what? For whose benefit? This question has been asked over and over again ever since the beginning of this dispute, and it remains still unanswered. The arguments in the Court of Session did not touch it. This latest ultimatum does not answer it. It remains a mystery insolvable except on the hypothesis of sheer unreasoning vindictiveness.

There is no other explanation, and it is the explanation accepted by the quarrymen and by all those on the spot. Rightly or wrongly they trace all the trouble to the malign influence of the manager, and they maintain that at bottom it is as much a question of miserable personal spite and social jealousy as of industrial conditions. There are certain small natures that can brook no rival in social influence, and it is Dr Grant's misfortune that his popularity in the district is disturbant of Mr Maccoll's sense of self-importance.

These seem petty and trivial motives to breed so much mischief, but human nature is a strange thing. Whatever the causes the result in the valley of Glencoe is a state of war, in which there is ranged on the one side the company's management, and on the other the entire community from Oban to Fort William. The radical 'Highland News' and the Conservative 'Oban Telegraph' have both declared themselves against the company, and there is no doubt that they voice the sentiments and feelings of the people of the West Highlands, and indeed all the North of Scotland. The Ballachulish question has become a Celtic question.

If the lock-out is maintained it will not be the quarrymen who will go under. They are a resourceful people these Highlanders, and the clan spirit is not dead. They will find the means to help each other. They are fighting for their rights as citizens, and for the principle of combination, and beyond and above that they are animated by that chivalric spirit which has at all times been an inspiring element in the Highland character. They have made Dr Grant's case their cause, and they will stand by him till the last. So far as this lock-out is concerned the company may as well realise to begin with that apart from the quarrymen their quarries are absolutely valueless. There will be no blacklegs in this dispute. Other industries are springing up in the Highlands. The men will manage to live without the company. The company cannot exist without the men. If the shareholders are content to see all their interests sacrificed in a quarrel which is largely the outcome of personal animosities, that is their look out. If, on the other hand, they still desire to get some return for their Ballachulish investments they will make haste to get their directors to revile from the intolerant and absurd position which they have taken up.

Of one thing they may be sure. The men will not sign that agreement. Self-respecting human beings do not voluntarily walk back into a condition of slavery from which they have fought hard to escape.

As to the legal aspect of this case between Dr Grant and the company, now in course of appeal, I make no comment. Morally, the company stands condemned at the bar of public opinion.

They are seeking to perpetuate an act, which, if successful, will make the names of Malcolm of Poltalloch, Bruce Low, Arch. Maccoll, and Thomas Shaw bywords of reproach in every town and village and glen in the Scottish Highlands.

LAVROCHE.

'The Ballachulish Quarriers and their Medical Officer', *British Medical Journal*, 2 (4 July 1903), 45

Many of our readers doubtless remember the case of Dr Lachlan Grant, who for a long time past has been fighting the Ballachulish State Quarries Company on an important question of principle. In August 1900, Dr Grant was engaged as a medical officer to the company at a salary of £270. The company terminated the engagement in July, 1902, but at a meeting of the quarries it was unanimously decided that Dr Grant should be requested to remain in the district. The men undertook to pay his salary and in fact engaged him as their medical officer. The company, however, attempted to prevent his practising in the district on the ground that under the terms of his engagement he was debarred from exercising his profession there. The parties went to law and Lord Kyllachy gave judgement against Dr Grant, who appealed on the ground that the company's authority to arrange for medical attendance had been withdrawn and that the restraining clause was against public policy. The case has now again been decided in the company's favour. The Lord Justice Clerk in delivering the judgement said that the volume of practice in the district in question was necessarily limited, and if the company desired to have a medical officer of their own selection to attend on their workers it might be of the greatest importance that there should not be competition in the district by one who had been in their service, but had ceased to be employed by them, and thereby the value of the appointment would be so much diminished that their choice of candidates might be limited to less eligible practitioners. He could see no ground in public policy for the doctor being allowed to break his contract. The restriction imposed upon them related only to a very limited area, and he might practise elsewhere without interference. Lord Young, who dissented, after reviewing the facts of the case, pointed out that they sufficiently showed that the clause of the contract on which the application was founded, as the company construed it and sought to enforce it, was in restraint of trade and professional employment. The 600 men working at the Ballachulish quarries desired the services of Dr Grant as their medical attendant for themselves and their families, and he desired to attend them. At a meeting held by these workmen, and, as Dr Lachlan Grant averred, attended by the entire population, including landed proprietors, clergymen and other influential residenters, the doctor was unanimously requested to remain in the district. They had been informed that the district was not populous or important. It was, however, in his opinion, important that the 600 workmen who were most immediately concerned, and the other inhabitants of the district, though not numerous, should be free to employ Dr Grant as their medical attendant so long as they pleased, and that the Court should not impose to restrain them from doing so, unless the circumstances in which they were asked to interfere showed that the legitimate and reasonable interest of the applicants would be sacrificed or suffer seriously if the Court refused to interfere. The rule of law was that an undertaking in restraint of trade or freedom of professional employment would not be recognised and enforced by a court of law unless – and this was the only exception to the rule – it was a reasonable, proper, and useful term of the contract, the judicial enforcement of which was necessary to satisfy the interest of the party in whose favour it was given. His lordship was of opinion that this case did not come under any exception of the rule, and he would even be prepared to hold that, having regard to the terms and purposes of the contract, the clause in question was unreasonable, and quite unnecessary for the protection and satisfaction of any legitimate interest of the pursuers. He was therefore of opinion that Lord Kyllachy's decision should be reversed. The two other judges, however – Lord Trayner and Lord Moncrieff – agreed with the Lord Justice Clerk, and the appeal was therefore dismissed. We understand that Dr Lachlan Grant is taking the case to the House of Lords, and we heartily wish him success in his brave fight against what we venture to call legalised injustice.

'BLIADHNA MHATH UR DHUIT', *Labour Leader*, 16 Jan. 1904

'Bliadhna mhath ur dhuit!' 'Good New Year to you!' Such was the message that came to me on New Year's morning from Ballachulish. Of all the season's greetings which reached me this was the most welcome. I have only once been in Ballachulish, and then only for two days; yet it seems to me as if all the inhabitants of the village at the far end of Loch Leven are intimate, personal friends of mine.

Ever since that autumn evening, now nearly eighteen months ago, when I stood in front of the quaint Town Hall, and made one of the audience of the villagers who listened to the eloquence of mingled English and Gaelic with which the village orators voiced the wrongs of the quarrymen, I have felt as if I were one of themselves. Today, in the moment of victory, the memory of that meeting comes back to me, and I seem to hear the clear, calm, almost lawyer-like statement of Mr McLaren, the chairman of the meeting, followed by Dr Farquarson's advice to the men to stand together, no matter what might happen; then Mr McMurchy, the Free Kirk minister, logical, learned, yet vernacular and familiar, now phrasing his argument in the language of St Paul, now giving it voice in the tongue of Ossian; and, lastly, the rushing, burning Gaelic of Donald Maccoll. I understood not a word of it, but the quarrymen did, and their answering shout seemed like the reborn slogans of the Macdonalds' awaking again the echoes of Glencoe.

There was no talk then of strike or lock-out; on the contrary, the desire was all for 'peace with honour.' But I felt then, and said so, that if these men were forced to fight, they would prove themselves unconquerable.

And so it has come to pass. The quarrymen have won, and the New Year greeting that came to me brought with it the assurance that for the men, women and children of Ballachulish it was in very truth a good New Year. Let no one unacquainted with the history of this dispute suppose that I am in any way overstating its importance. It has been one of the most important conflicts ever fought by Labour, and to the workers in the North of Scotland it will always have a historical significance. Only some four hundred workmen were concerned in it, but the principles and the material issues involved were of the highest. Eighteen months ago the Ballachulish quarrymen were not free men, even in the limited sense in which freedom is as yet understood in this country; today whatever rights belong to the most highly-organised British workmen are also the possession of the Ballachulish quarrymen.

Remember what the grievances were, and look at the terms of settlement. Take the wages question first. 'For quarrymen, in failure of contract, 28s per week, with powder allowed all the year round.' An advance of 3s per week. 'For labourers, those formerly in receipt of 18s in summer to receive 20s all the year round, and those formerly in receipt of 20s in summer to receive 21s all the year round.' An advance of 2s and 1s respectively, with immunity from fluctuations. Similarly joiners, smiths and tippers receive proportional advances, while in the case of joiners and smiths time-and-a-half is to be paid for overtime.

So much for wages. Now look at this and compare it with the high and mighty attitude taken by the management at the beginning of the dispute. 'There shall be a Conciliation Board, to prevent strikes, which will consist of three quarrymen appointed by the workmen, and two directors of the company and the chairman of the board of directors, with the Sheriff of Perthshire as arbiter, whose decision shall be final, to which Conciliation Board it shall be competent for the company or the employees to appeal. Any individual workman having any grievance will first submit same to the manager and, failing redress, to the three local members of the Conciliation Board, who shall again confer with the manager before summoning the rest of the Conciliation Board.' Evidently the directors have had enough of war. They mean, in future, to try the methods of peace. Pity they had not done so at the beginning rather than at the end of eighteen months. I have given the whole of the conciliation clause. It is the sort of document worthy of preservation in the files of the LEADER – in case of further eventualities.

Now as to the medical question, which has bulked so largely throughout this dispute, which has been indeed the main cause of the battle, the other matters having been held as, for the time being, subsidiary both by the company and by the men. On this point the terms of settlement are brief, comprehensive and conclusive. 'Interdict against Dr Grant to be suspended; law actions against company withdrawn. Men to have unrestricted choice of doctor.' The victory is complete. 'Bliadhna mhath ur dhuit!' A good New Year – ay, and many of them – to Dr Lachlan Grant and the Ballachulish quarrymen!

They have stood together 'through good report and evil' and now they share with each other in the reward.

There has never been anything finer than the behaviour of the Ballachulish quarrymen in this matter of their medical officer. It is quite well known that they could have secured the most of the concessions very early in the dispute; that they might even have secured the right to appoint their medical officer, provided they had dropped Dr Grant.

But they are not that kind of folk in the valley of Glencoe. Chivalry may be a dying sentiment in modern life; it lives still among the Highland hills. Were it for nothing else than this revelation of fidelity and comradeship, this fight has been worthwhile. To have been associated, even remotely, in such a fight, and with such men, is an inspiring memory to be cherished while life lasts.

Such are the chief gains, but there are others, not the least of which is the pledge given that cottages will be built for the workmen. In one of my earliest articles, I described the housing conditions in Ballachulish and their insanitary accompaniments. These evils are to be remedied; in fact, the workmen have gained more in eighteen months than in some other parts of the country have won in as many years.

But the greatest gain of all has been the knowledge of their own strength and of the power of union. They went into the struggle without organisation; they have come out of it with a strong trade union, well equipped to maintain the rights they have won, and to secure others which time and circumstances may render necessary. That this trade union power will not be used intolerantly, vindictively, or unwisely may be taken for granted; but that they will uphold it, is, I think, equally certain.

The trade unions of the country came to their help in the time of trial. They are not the men to forget that. They will realise, have already realised, that the cause of labour is not a thing of one locality merely; that whenever men live by the sweat of their brow, there Labour has to fight for its own; and in that fact lies the common interest which binds all labouring men together, whether they be Highlanders or Lowlanders, Celts or Saxons.

Under a baptism of fire the men of the North have come into the Labour movement. Henceforth we may be sure, they will play their part in that movement in union with their fellows elsewhere, and with a consciousness that therein lies the true fulfilment of human brotherhood and fellowship. For the present, I say goodbye and good luck to the men of Ballachulish!

LAVROCHE.

SECTION 4

Highland Land Reform

Oban Times, 3 Dec. 1904
Report of a lecture by Dr Grant at the High School Ceilidh in Oban, titled 'The clan system in modern life'

It is not my purpose this evening to enter into any elaborate historical review or speculation but rather to consider only so much of the past as will explain some aspects of the present, and perhaps throw some light onto the future of society [. . .]

The inevitable break up of the clans by economic, political and social changes loosened the bonds that bound the chieftains to their clansmen and in time there arose, in place of the patriarchal relationship, an unsympathetic landlord class on the one hand and a landless, unfranchised [sic] people on the other. This sad change culminated in the wicked and unpatriotic clearances, which I dare say you know all about; and, at the present day, the havoc played by an irrational land system may be easily seen all over the Highlands. In many parts of the western Highlands the crofters are longing for land, and from what I know of them, I believe they would make the best possible use of further additions to their holdings, should they be able to obtain the same on suitable terms. The Congested Districts Board is doing much to mitigate the lot of the poorer crofters and the purchase of a large track of land in the Isle of Skye marks the beginning of a new and better policy from which much might be expected.

Oban Weekly News, 16 May 1906
Highland Crofters and Cottars Association
Inaugural Meeting at Connel
Stirring addresses by Rev. Malcolm MacCallum, Dr Grant and
Mr McLaren

'Unity is Strength.' This is an axiom the truth of which is evidenced by the existence of such bodies as Trades Unions and Associations by which the workers may assert their wants with employers, and also with respect to legislation in Parliament. Up to within recent weeks, however, the crofters and cottars of the Highlands and Islands have had no such fortress at their command. Recently, however, it was realised that if anything tangible was to be done it would have to be done by united effort and accordingly it was agreed to form an Association. The first meeting of the new body was held in the Reading Room, Connel, on Saturday afternoon when Dr Grant presided. Representatives were present from the following districts:- Taynuilt, Kilmore, Onich, Glencoe, Benderloch, and Ballachulish; and those present included:- Rev. Malcolm MacCallum, Muckairn; Archd. McCallum, Alex McLaren, John McTaggart, Peter McKenzie, John McGillivray, Dugald Campbell (Onich); Norman MacLeod (Tullich); Donald McNiven; Archd. McCallum, Colin Campbell, and John Rankin.

The Chairman [Grant], in his opening remarks said he need hardly say it gave him intense pleasure to take part in that day's proceedings. The birth of that Association, having for its object

The Furtherance of the Crofter Interest

was something unique in the history of their country. They must all regret that such a defensive organisation had not taken place many years ago, and perhaps prevented the constant stream of emigration from the Highlands, which they all so much deplored. (Applause.) He felt certain that had the crofters of the last century had the moral support of such a body as they were now forming, what were notoriously known as the 'Highland Clearances' could never have taken place. Their action that day did not require one word of apology. Combinations of people existed for every imaginable purpose and surely one for the betterment of the long-suffering Highlander was a laudable object on which they might ask the blessing of the nation. There had been leagues of all kinds, Liberal, Conservative, Tariff Reform, Primrose, Highland Land Reform, and Irish National, and with all due respect to those forms of political activity he submitted that none of them had the same social and economic importance as the Association they were forming that day – (applause) – which was to deal with the root problems of the national existence. (Applause). They therefore confidently appealed not only to

the crofter and cottar class, who were mostly poor in the world's posses-
sions, but to all classes of the community. If a country possessed a good
land system, and if agriculture was a prosperous industry, the first essential of a successful and happy nation had been attained. It was in the
interests of all classes that the land should be developed to its utmost
extent, and not allowed to be idle or to be made use of entirely for sport.
(Applause). They saw from the daily press that emigration from all parts
of the country to Canada and elsewhere was very active, and that the best
of their young men by the score were leaving

The Land of Their Fathers

probably forever. Everyone, irrespective of shade of politics, must admit
this to be a national calamity. As Ruskin said and others had often said,
the true wealth of a country consisted of healthy men and women, and no
true patriot could view with equanimity the continuous export of such
national wealth, but on the contrary, must have grave misgivings as to
the future. At the rate they had been going during the last 50 years, there
would soon be nobody left besides the town and city dwellers except a few
factors, hotel-keepers, ghillies, gamekeepers and millionaire's flunkeys.
(Laughter and applause.) But while thousands of people saw the evil, and
admitted the urgency of the problem, they saw no immediate solution,
and it would be the object of the Association to educate the public on the
nature of the social and economic disease – its cause and cure – and to
propound a remedy to be submitted to, and pressed on the Government
of the country. What that solution might finally be he did not know,
but his personal opinion was that no fancy, petty-fogging, philanthropic
scheme would solve the problem. They demanded justice; and nothing
short of the acquisition of large tracts of the country, by the nation, to be
let out at reasonable rents to those who could till the soil, would satisfy
those who best understood the whole question. That, of course, was his
private opinion, but as a practical man, he was quite willing to accept
instalments of reform from whatever corner they might come. No doubt
they had some very good friends in the present Parliament who were
sympathetic and anxious to do something for the Highlands, but the
fact remained that with so many interests in the House of Commons,
competing for the time and attention of the legislature, there was small
chance of their affairs receiving adequate consideration unless they had
men sent there for the express purpose of

Advocating Highland Land

and other reforms. They, however, expected the present Government to carry out their promises made in the King's Speech, and if they fell short of that, it would be the duty of the Association to press the claims of the crofters, and to keep asking for more. They were fortunate in having the promise of the services of Mr Alexander McLaren as secretary. He was a man of good common sense, and who could speak his mind clearly in both Gaelic and English, and who had a thorough understanding of every land and other problem associated with the existence of the Highland community, and he (the Chairman) was sure by the time Mr McLaren had gone his first journey among the Highlands and Islands, he would be able to report that their infant association had attained the status of a robust youth with every indication of virile manhood. (Applause.) Here then was the simple problem. Tens of thousands of people were willing to remain on the land to till the soil, and much suitable land was lying more or less idle. How then were they to bring the two factors together, land and labour, for the good of the workers as well as the country at large. They had still the land; they had still a stock of healthy and hardy clansmen; and they could reasonably appeal to the strongest Government of the richest country the world had seen, to keep its own people at home on their native and beloved straths and mountains. (Applause.) Let it be clearly understood they had no designs on other people's property, and if it was necessary to buy out some of the present landlords in compulsory fashion, value in £.s.d. would be duly paid, and such might have the satisfaction of knowing that the

Prosperity of the Country

would be thereby increased, and in which prosperity they would be partakers. There was no personal animus against any landlord or group of landlords. They were as much the victims of the system as anyone, so that they could even appeal to them for co-operation in developing the country's best interests which were always associated with mother earth. All those who advocated the preservation of the language of their forefathers and who were first to cry 'Suas leis a Ghaidhlig' must be on their side. For surely the best way to preserve Gaelic from decay was to have people in the straths and hills to speak it; and the best way to bring about repopulation of the Highlands or any other part of the country was to establish a healthy democratic land system, giving security of tenure, minimum rent charges, and the help of the public authority in developing the resources of nature. (Applause.) The Celtic revival was very interesting and the efforts to give Gaelic its due were very commendable, but if their young men and women were to continue emigrating to Canada, what was the use of it all? If the new Celtic sentiment did not get beyond the scholar's study, the schoolmaster's desk, or the collections of the museums, it was not worth their while troubling about it. How could people living a precarious hand to mouth existence, uncertain of tomorrow, and knowing their children would be forced to become exiles be expected to get up any enthusiasm for

A Mere Academic Sentiment?

(Applause.) They therefore called on all interested in the preservation of the old tongue to support them in preventing any further exodus from the Highlands and Islands. It would be the work of the Highland Crofters' Association to band together the whole crofter and cottar community in the work of securing attention to grievances; and in furthering schemes to develop agriculture, forestry and industries, to enable the largest possible number of people to live happy and healthy lives on the land. In doing this they were true Protectionists inasmuch as their object was to conserve, the best they could offer the Empire, what Oliver Goldsmith had termed a 'bold peasantry' who would in the last resort form the mainstay of the nation whether in peace or war. (Loud applause.)

The Chairman invited opinions as to the new association, and also as to whether it was the mind of the meeting that such an association should be formed.

Mr Dugald Campbell, Onich, moved, seconded by Mr Norman McLeod, 'That the crofters present form themselves into a Highland Crofters Association.' The motion was passed unanimously.

Oban Times, 18 Aug. 1906

Highland Crofters' and Cottars' Association: demonstration at Fort William

The recently formed Highland Crofters' and Cottars' Association was duly launched at Fort William on the evening of Friday last [. . .] Its objects are to establish an organisation by which the Highland crofters and cottars may have their rights asserted, their interests promoted and their grievances brought more prominently before Parliament and the country; to promote any schemes calculated not only to arrest the depopulation of rural districts but to re-people all parts of the country at present devoted to sport and grazing, but suitable for agriculture and afforestation; to investigate, and, where advisable, to defend members in cases of hardship and injustice arising from the operation of the present land laws; to raise funds to organise the voting power of the crofter counties to ensure an adequate representation of the crofting interest in the House of Commons; to assist the movement for the industrial development of the Highlands; and, if found necessary, to publish a monthly journal in the interests of the crofters and cottars.

Oban Weekly News, 20 Feb. 1907

Highland Crofters' and Cottars' Association.
Lecture by Dr Lachlan Grant

Under the auspices of the above Association an enthusiastic meeting was held in the Masonic Hall, Oban, on Monday evening last. The meeting was convened for the purpose of hearing an address on the Land Question by Dr Lachlan Grant, Ballachulish, who is a well known authority on this question. Ex-Provost MacCowan presided, and he was supported by Bailie Campbell, Messers Alex MacLaren, Dr Morrison and Norman MacLeod. The Chairman introduced the lecturer of the evening in a pithy and interesting speech. Dr Grant, who was received with applause said:-

Mr Chairman and gentlemen – It affords me great pleasure to meet the members and friends of the Oban branch of the Highland Crofters' and Cottars' Association, and to see that this branch is doing its utmost to further the aims of the Association inaugurated last May. It is only by the united effort not only of the various branches, but of the individual members of these branches, that the goal can be attained for which we are all striving – a goal which will see the repopulation of our Highlands an accomplished fact, silent glens and desolate straths but a memory. By this time you are no doubt familiar with the objects of the Association. The importance of the issues at stake justifies my reiterating them. Boldly put, these objects are:- the banding together of the crofter, cottar and small landholder for the purpose of securing to each the right to live on the land – for the purpose too, of assisting and of strengthening their cause, the organisation, also, through its various branch committees ascertain the wants of its members, and places these before the public and the Government of the country. It is in effect, to 'combine', in keeping with the trend of the present day methods, but with more of a combine's virtues and none of its vices. That reforms are urgently needed is obvious to anyone who takes the trouble to look into the diseased condition of our present land system and considering the vast importance of the land question to the country as a whole. I would like to deal shortly with that aspect of it which specially affects the Highlands. The efficiency of a nation depends on the prosperity and well-being of its various communities and, conversely, if the individuals comprising its integral parts be allowed to degenerate, the whole country must suffer. The Highlands of Scotland in the past was the nursery ground for a healthy, industrious peasantry, and would be still, were reasonable inducements offered its inhabitants to remain on the land. For the continuous depletion of the Highlands, of its strongest and best stock, we must seek a cause, and that, in my opinion, is not to be found in the desire for emigration, but in the absence of any alternative. Up till now, the people of the Highlands have shown a submissive apathy to their lot, mistaken by some for contentment; but for this we must not blame them. There is in almost every Highlander, to a greater or lesser extent, an element of inherited fatalism fostered by his environment, which impels him to regard with a like indifference the hardships of his present lot, and any measures brought forward for his betterment – the former, he regards as the unalterable decree of a Divine Will, the latter, as Utopian. This fatalistic tendency may appear of minor importance, but as a factor in the production of this apparent mental lethargy, is one not to be disregarded. Before attempting to discuss the very necessary changes which are urgently required, it might be well to retrospect a little. During the last fifty years the population of many rural districts has decreased by about half. This is almost entirely due to the fact that many smallholders and crofters were deprived of their lands, in order that these might be absorbed into single large farms, or reserved for sport; the idea of the larger farms being, that such would entail fewer tenants, and thus less trouble for the landlords. The plea that the smaller holdings were not self-supporting certainly did not hold with these; practically all their tenants being able to live comfortably on the product of their holdings. For the conversion of these small holdings into large farms, larger steadings, drains, dykes and fences were required, and such improvements gave temporary employment to some who were allowed to remain. Driven in many cases to remote corners of the various estates and left only sufficient land for the grazing of one cow, they were enabled along with the wages received for labouring to eke out a living. Even this source of income ceased when the improvements were completed. Although the old people might remain in the district, their families had to emigrate to the towns or foreign lands. When the old folks died the houses became tenantless and were allowed to decay. For some years this system seemed to work well for the landlords. Gradually, however, owing to the depreciation in the value of stock and land, the rentals from the large farms decreased, until now, some farms, the rent of which was £800 per annum, can be had at from £150 to £400. The fall in the rent is out of all proportion to the actual depreciation, and many of the landlords themselves admit that, from their point of view, the system of small holdings would be better. I am sure all of you must have observed within recent years that on the expiry of the lease many farms were instead of being re-let as such were cleared of sheep stock, and this valuable grazing ground went to swell the acres of the deer stalker and partridge breeder. Thus is the country impoverished. There is the inestimable loss to the people of farm produce, such as fresh beef and mutton, eggs, milk and butter, necessitating the importation of these commodities in ever-increasing quantities, frozen, tinned and borated, obscuring any flavour they might have possessed, and not infrequently adding flavour peculiarly their own. To what extent has the question been solved by the Crofters Holdings Act of 1886? Among many other advantages it gave security of tenure, thereby allowing the families of one generation to remain on the land, and making allowance for the succession of one member of the family, and even this was hedged in by the condition that only the nearest blood relative on the father's side could succeed. But it was incomplete in that it did not take into account the natural increase of the population, and most members of the rising generation found themselves beyond the pale of its benefits. This definite limit to the amount of land available did not make for progress, and the majority of the landowners adopted a 'policy of negation' towards all who desired land, which the Crofters Act had no powers to combat. The Congested Districts Board, entering as it did upon its duties with limited powers, has only succeeded in touching the fringe of the Highland Land question. While we admit that the little done was in the right direction, we cannot but recognise that, had its resources been greater, more would have been accomplished. Having now revived the principal fallacies of our present land system and their chief cause, let us see wherein lies the remedy. If the lot of the Highland people is to be one of peace and happiness, if one of the main sources of our Empire's strength is to be left intact, something must be done, and that without delay to check the stream flowing to other countries, carrying with it the gold of the country and leaving in its place mainly the gilt and the dross. Did Scotland's boundaries include the rolling prairies of Canada, or the illimitable plains of Australia, there were some excuse for large tracts given up to sport; but the area within our shores is too small to permit the sacrifice of its fertile portions on the altar of Nimrod. In the first place then we must give the people land worth cultivating. It is hardly fair to experiment with an unproductive and wind swept piece of land, and then condemn the system of small holdings, because, forsooth, an obviously barren soil has not brought forth an hundredfold. Further, we must have compulsory powers for acquiring the necessary land. The best agricultural lands being in the hands of the large landholders – lairds and large farmers – it is necessary to bring forward a measure by means of which suitable portions of land could be acquired for the purpose of small holdings, each of which would be of sufficient size to support a family. These allotments need not be of the same size, but could be graded within limits according to the means of the applicants and the number of individuals the allotment was intended to support – that is, each holding to have so many acres of arable land with outruns, and moorland or hill pasturage. This compulsory measure would entail little or no hardship on the landlord, and even were it found to be necessary to purchase land outright, the landlord would be assured of a proper valuation. The larger farmers should be similarly compensated for any loss. Such powers could be obtained by a special Land Purchase Act, similar to that in force in Ireland, or by an extension of the Crofters Holdings Act, such as was embodied in the Small Landholders Bill introduced last session by the Secretary for Scotland. The practical application of a special Land Purchase Act on a large scale would involve a loss of time we can ill afford; but in conjunction with an extension of the Crofters Holdings Act, the whole scheme would immediately be put on a workable basis. The regrettable postponement of the Small Landholders Bill came as a bitter disappointment to thousands in the rural districts of Scotland to whom its provisions would have applied. Despite the earnest attempt of the Secretary for Scotland to get this Bill made law, nothing has so far resulted. Had the Bill passed a great step would have been taken towards lessening many of the evils for which the present land system is responsible. Prominent among its benefits were – Fixity of tenure to those whose rent did not exceed £50 per annum; powers for the formation of new holdings, very necessary for the cottars, as well as for members of the rising generation who would otherwise be forced to emigrate; powers also for the extension of existing holdings where these were of insufficient size for the needs of their tenants; financial assistance for the purpose of establishing small landholders upon the soil on a sound economic basis; a Land Commission independent of County Council or other local influence, whose work it would be to see that the landowners received adequate compensation, and at the same time safeguard the interests of the majority; and compensation for improvements carried out on the holding, the fixity of tenure ensuring the 'working owner' all the benefit from these improvements. The Crofters Holdings Act of 1886, apart from its limitations, has been of immense benefit to the Highlands. And already we see many instances of families who have benefited under this Act, taking a new interest in their homeland and finding pleasure and profit in their work as evidenced by the improvements which they themselves have carried out. There is no reason why an extension of this Act should not have equally good results when applied to small farmers up to a £50 limit, not only in the Highlands but all over rural Scotland. Objections have been raised to the £50 limit, or any limit, but, as a line must be drawn somewhere, and the Bill of last session was intended to benefit the poorer class of farmers, it was decided by the Government that this purpose could be best achieved by limiting the application of the Acts to a £50 rental. In my opinion it could be advantageously be extended to £100 rentals. Among the arguments used against the system of small holdings, perhaps the most misleading is the one which states that a system of small holdings is not desired by the people. To my certain knowledge, the cottars who have no land are eagerly desirous of obtaining some. The majority of the crofters would be only too glad to have their small crofts enlarged, and they are, in my opinion, able and willing to make the best possible use of the same; nor is the need for land legislation felt by the Highland crofters alone, but is as surely required by the tenants of small farms throughout the whole country. It has been argued that small holders cannot live on the products of their holdings alone, and that existence from them is only possible when their incomes can be supplemented from extraneous sources, as, for example, in the vicinity of industrial and fishing centres. At the present time instances of this are to be found, due to the unproductive nature of the land and small size of the holdings, and to the fact that the younger and more active members of the family were forced to seek their daily bread elsewhere, leaving their parents, frequently old and infirm, to struggle on as best they could. This state of affairs it should be the object of the coming legislation to remedy, and I need hardly say with what keen anticipation we look forward to the new Land Holdings Bill promised us in the King's Speech. Of the advantages of instituting small holdings in the neighbourhood of industrial centres are so great, this still favours the widest application of the Small Landholders Bill. I have heard it said that under this new regime landowners would cease to take an interest in the upkeep of the holdings – well I don't think there is much to be feared from this, as under the Crofters Act the small holders have shown themselves quite competent to undertake unaided any necessary repairs. One apparent drawback to a system of small holdings is the difficulty their tenants would have in competing against the modern equipment which the large farms can afford. This difficulty could be overcome if adjoining small holders co-operated, and had for instance the larger and more expensive agricultural implements in common. The financial aspect of such an all important scheme must not daunt those who see in the repopulation of rural districts the strengthening of the nation's back-bone. And we can reasonably appeal to the strongest Government of the richest country the world has seen to do its utmost to keep its own people – its living wealth – on their own native straths and mountains. From the point of view of public health and of the physical well-being of the nation no better investment could be made. For this purpose then, help should be readily forthcoming from the National exchequer. Were the cry of 'Back to the Soil' to be answered from the street corners and slums of our great cities, I fear the resulting chaos would counterbalance any of the good results we anticipate. Let our efforts be directed towards stemming the stream that is draining from the land those best adapted by nature and environment to the requirements of rural life. It is not to be understood that we object to emigration entirely. It is the case that in every community there is to be found a certain proportion active and energetic, who will naturally seek a wider sphere for their surplus energy. Let these go, but, by all means, let us endeavour to retain on the land all those desirous of remaining. The task before our Statesmen is one not to be lightly regarded. Besides the question of Land Legislation, other important reforms should be considered. There are parts of the country more suitable for sylviculture than agriculture, and in many of the country districts there is room for the encouragement of rural industries. Briefly put, what is wanted is a healthy national land system, giving security of tenure, minimum rent charges, and the help of the public authority in developing the resources of nature. The accomplishment of this object would earn for those statesmen, who might support it, the well-deserved gratitude of the people directly benefited, and in addition the thanks of an enriched and strengthened nation. While dealing with the practical aspects and objects of the Crofters' and Cottars' Association we must not neglect its own immediate wants – that is to say – while your representative officials are pressing for reforms, urging your claims, and defending your interests, they in turn require your strongest support – in short, the machinery of your Association must be oiled, and for the lubrication of your machine I would suggest 'palm oil.' The stronger an association is financially the more successful will be its efforts. This serious attempt to arrest the gradual depopulation of the Highlands and Islands is one which merits support moral and financial, of all true patriots at home and abroad. And let me appeal not only to crofters and small landholders, but to all who have the real interests of the Highlands at heart, to give their practical support to this movement. In times of war the Highlands is called upon to fight for the motherland and home. To him the terms in many cases are a mere sentiment, and it is for the purpose of giving them a more real significance that your Association has been formed. You have in my friend, Mr Alexander MacLaren, an organising secretary exceptionally well fitted for the post he occupies – a man to whose untiring energy is due the already wide spread interest in your Association throughout the Highlands – one well worthy of the confidence you have placed in him. Gentlemen, your Association is at work on behalf of a great cause. The process is not revolutionary but evolutionary, and surely, if slowly, the time is coming when your Institution will be a recognised force in the land. Of it I would say – May its light never become dim; may its shadow never grow less; may its bow be ever full of strength, and its quiver full of arrows.

SECTION 5

British Aluminium and Health

'Aluminium Throat Swabs', *British Medical Journal*, 1 (18 March 1922), 434

A few years ago Dr William Murdie and the writer drew attention to an improved throat swab made from aluminium wire. Since then inquiries regarding it have come into this laboratory from time to time, and its further extensive use by us and others have confirmed the claims made for it.

The ordinary types of swabs now in use have several serious drawbacks and disadvantages, and a more efficient kind of instrument seems to be called for. Those made of copper, iron, steel or thin nickel wire are somewhat easily tarnished, and if left lying in a climate the least damp are very liable to become discoloured and unsuitable for use. Copper and nickel are apt to develop verdigris or a green colour from the soluble copper and nickel salts, and brown discolouration is also likely to happen with those made of iron, which develop 'rust' or ferric oxide. Such swabs, after being in use or laid aside for some time, acquire an unattractive and unhygienic appearance, and are not the sort of thing to ask a patient to admit to his throat. The pleget of sterile wool is also likely to be stained, and as the soluble copper and nickel salts are germicidal, they may more or less invalidate the bacteriological diagnosis.

By the use of aluminium wire these and other undesirable accompaniments are obviated. It is easily moulded to shape and yet is sufficiently rigid for swabbing purposes, and it keeps bright and clean. No matter how often used, or even if kept for a considerable time, the aluminium swab never has the soiled or discoloured appearance of those made from other metals. It stands boiling well and is easy to clean and redress. Again, aluminium contains in its composition no harmful bactericidal elements.

The addition of the safety ring (see illustration) avoids the holding of the cork and gives a more complete control over the movements of the swab, thus minimising the risk of introducing organisms other than the patient's own. In the ordinary one, as usually made, there is always the risk of the metal slipping from the cork, which is avoided by this former type. Aluminium being so light, the cost of the wire is very small. The best thickness to use is that known on the aluminium wire gauge as E 14 S. W. G. As there is no fear of 'rusting' or 'greening', the cotton-wool pleget may, if desired, be held under the running tap before swabbing the patient's throat, thus ensuring a good sample of the infected secretion, and also retarding the drying effects of transmission through the post, etc.

The throat swab is a useful item in the practitioner's armamentarium, and the aluminium wire swab holder, well made, will be found helpful in the diagnosis, prognosis and treatment of some of the diseases met with in everyday practice. We know it is practically impossible, without a bacteriological examination, to make sure whether a patient who complains of a sore throat is suffering from diphtheria, 'mixed' throat infection, Vincent's angina, follicular tonsillitis, or an infection by the *Tryponema pallidum*. Complete tests thoroughly carried out from start to finish are invaluable in speedily determining or in eliminating certain or all of these diseases and so removing the anxiety attached to an undecided clinical diagnosis. In attaining this, a hygienic, safe, clean, light and easily handled swab is an important adjunct.

Of course, whatever kind is used, it is important to take the necessary precautions to avoid its contamination. The pleget of wool for conveying the suspected material is necessarily small, and in gently rubbing the infected surface care must be used that the wool on its introduction or withdrawal does not get soaked with saliva or other oral secretions. One has also to remember that the use of antiseptic gargles prior to use may interfere with the results to be obtained from the cultural tests when the swab reaches the laboratory. It may be further mentioned that the aluminium swab can also be made longer for special uses, as, for example, in the taking of material from uterine infections.

'Aluminium and Health', letter to the editor, *Lancet*, 218:5638 (19 Sept. 1931), 662

Sir – Your leading article last week (p. 595) will be welcomed by many readers. I entirely agree with the statements made as to the harmlessness and innocuousness of this modern non-ferrous metal on the human frame. From comparative analysis it would appear that aluminium contains fewer impurities of a possibly deleterious nature than any other metal in domestic use. During the past twenty years I have had many hundreds of workers in aluminium in large factories under my care. During this time I have had no evidence whatever of any industrial disease (such as to be found in some other metal industries) resulting from the ingredients which are used in the manufacture of aluminium ingots.

The pure bauxite clay and cryolite used in the manufacture of the metal are of the highest purity. The former is carefully calcined and much of the fine aluminium dust and hot furnace fumes must be inhaled or swallowed by the workers in the factories. Yet I have never observed the slightest signs of ill-health, temporary or chronic, which could be attributed to the inhalation of alumina. Numerous workers who have spent the greater part of their working lives, some for thirty years, are in excellent health, and show no sign of nervous depression. The health of their dependents resident in the immediate vicinity is exceptionally good. Large families are the rule. For example, one busy aluminium industrial centre has a population of 1,400, including 470 thriving children.

In my own household, aluminium cooking and infusing utensils are appreciated on account of their lightness, cleanliness and easy transmission of heat. If cleaning is done by wire abrasion with a trace of soap the same articles can be kept smooth, clean, bright and spotless for years. With a cooking surface kept perfectly smooth and free from cracks, there is much less chance of particles of organic matter being left to decompose in the pans. Another helpful point in the use of aluminium vessels is that, when bringing certain foods to the boil, they are hardly ever singed.

Alumina in the shape of pure clay has of course been given in considerable quantities in certain diseases without poisonous results. As you say, aluminium appears to be mostly eliminated by the intestinal route, and does not enter the vascular channels. – I am, Sir, yours faithfully, LACHLAN GRANT, Bacteriological Laboratory, Ballachulish, Argyllshire, Sept. 14th 1931.

SECTION 6

Highland Development

An Gaidheal, 1931
A PROPOSAL TO CONVERT GLENCOE AND DISTRICT
INTO A SCOTTISH NATIONAL PARK
By Lachlan Grant

It would appear that the formation of several national public parks in the three kingdoms is now being considered.

There are municipal parks in many towns and cities, but in Scotland, with the exception of Ardgoil, there are no great national playgrounds such as they have in the United States, Canada and other countries. Such national parks would be most useful outlets for holiday makers from towns and cities and, organised for this purpose, with the nation as proprietor and caterer for the citizens, they would furnish a cheap and pleasurable means of recreation and social intercourse.

They would also enable the people to see more of their own country and come into touch with Mother Nature. And while preserving the natural aspects and health-giving qualities of our modern life, music, sport and educational activities of all kinds would be provided for. The idea is to secure for all time wide but sparsely populated tracts of nature for recreation and culture, combining as nearly as possible natural environmental conditions with modern facilities for rational enjoyment and useful change.

Now that our good friend and greatly respected Lord Strathcona has decided to part with the Glencoe estates here is a golden opportunity to secure for Scotland a national park immortal in history and in majestic grandeur unsurpassed in Europe. These historic domains, over 70,000 acres in extent, embracing part of the Moor of Rannoch, Glen Etive, and the world-famous Glencoe, could be made an ideal playground for the Scottish nation.

There are present here all the requirements for a great Scottish national recreation centre, almost everything that nature can give – mountains and glens, rivers and torrents, waterfalls, lakes, natural and artificial, with trout and salmon, moorland ground, silviculture or afforestation in all stages of development.

Wild animals such as the red deer, red foxes, roe deer, hares, rabbits, eagles, ptarmigan, grouse etc., and great wealth in wild flowers are all in this area. The Royal Forest of Dalness (Glenetive) is a natural home of deer.

The magnificence of the scenery is such that every year tourists in their thousands come from every part of the world to see it. Scope for mountaineering is almost unlimited. Range after range of towering mountains, the highest of them is the noble Ben known as Bidean nam Bian, 3,766 feet high! and the view from the summit is almost unrivalled anywhere.

Here we have the scene of that notorious episode in our history, the massacre of Glencoe, while right through the glen for miles is winding General Wade's road, now being superseded by a carefully planned and up-to-date highway. To those who are interested in our Gaelic language, its literature and music, there is the further attraction that on these historic mountains frequently roamed not only the great Gaelic bard, Duncan Ban Macintyre, but if tradition be true, the still greater genius known to the world as Ossian. On a spot almost inaccessible, high up in one of Glencoe's mighty Bens, is Ossian's cave.

In this district Scotland has almost in its centre an asset which could be made invaluable for her people. All that is required is a little of the foresight and go-ahead methods of Switzerland. Given a scenic electric railway to the top of the Bidean, visitors could thus be enabled to reach the higher altitudes, and also, if a gallery were erected for looking down the straight rugged precipice of 2,700 feet on to Loch Treachten, such would be a wonderful source of attraction. If this is done in other places, as for example, at Cape Town, why should it not be feasible in the Highlands of Scotland?

There are now good facilities of transit from the centres of population; but better and more up to date accommodation for visitors is required. In these days, when we hear such a lot about the Come to Britain movement, the opportunity to secure this magnificent National playground should not be missed.

In these glens we have scenery that is wild and majestic, a natural grandeur, amazing and inspiring, and unequalled throughout Great Britain.

There is also available a magnificent modern residence looking down Loch Leven, commanding a gorgeous view of the setting sun's reflected glories on the mountains of the West. Connected with this particular view, it may be added that travellers who have visited America and every part of Europe have frequently stated that nowhere have they found anything to surpass it.

The assets available, such as timber growing, plant cultivation, rock gardens, fishing, scope for climbing, interesting tours, walks, botanising and nature study have already been mentioned. The district is approached by two railways from Ballachulish terminus, and Bridge of Orchy stations. It is also well supplied, and the various centres linked up by charabanc and motor routes.

The idea of National Parks is a good one, and commends itself to most people.

Here is an opportunity for the Secretary for Scotland to secure for the nation a first class playground, which is in every way suitable, and in arranging for an immediate survey, the authorities will have the enthusiastic support of all those who wish to see a definite move made to secure an invaluable and inspiring national heritage. The acquiring and setting in order of such a large National Park would mean the making of suitable paths, fencings, hostels, and so on, giving work to some of the unemployed, and assisting the health of these people at the present time, as unemployment makes for degeneracy. There is only one solution of our problem of unemployment and the prevention of the monstrous evils in its train, and that is simply work, even if only at a moderate wage, while the period of depression lasts.

The National Archives, London, PRO 30/69/1518

17 Nov. 1932, Grant to MacDonald

My dear Prime Minister,

Enclosed is a little 'photo album' taken at the Mod just as you were leaving Fort William to go to London via Glencoe. I am ever so sorry I cannot share your dislike for the new road. But come up and stay with Mrs Grant and myself here, at Craig Leven, and we will explore the fastnesses adjoining the route, then perhaps you will 'melt' a little bit. You will be very welcome at any time. You wish to have a little rest and change. Enclosed also is a lecture on the 'Progress in the March in Travel', which sometime you may manage to read over. You once told me you liked these 'little efforts of mine for uplift' – hence my sending it on. It has already appeared in two Highland papers, a little homily on 'autumn' also is sent you. I underlined a sentence in it – we are all apt to 'imagine' things and so may feel the strain of life worse.

Warmest of good wishes from Mrs Grant and myself. Here's a hand clasp to you over the miles.

Ever yours
Lachlan Grant.

15 May 1933, Grant to MacDonald

Dear Prime Minister,

Thanks for your kind note telling me that the 'Heather' from here brightened your cabin in the 'Berengaria' – and that you liked the 'Bulletin' cartoon. I am so pleased to see you keep fit, and able to meet the 'big strains' now being imposed on you.

How perplexing the problems of today are! Not that they are very new. I imagine they are the very old ones in a fresh disguise. In the antique world, fire, sword and pestilence restricted the numbers of the more barbarous races and kept them within economic bounds. The more civilised communities of Egypt, Babylon, Greece and Rome adopted other measures for contracting their numbers and down they went like ninepins before the barbaric nations that had reached a high pitch of physical perfection, under the stern discipline of competition and the arrival of the more fit.

Enclosed on the 'massacre of Glencoe' is by 'Sheena' – one of our young ladies you had beside you at the last Mod. I send it on as I see she states the Macdonalds were a 'small Catholic' clan – I have never been satisfied that they were Catholics. It is a concise summary and most readable – don't trouble to return the page.

I know you must be working as you once told me 36 hours out of the 24, so don't bother to reply to this.

If ever near us and can spare the time, to 'shelter' here at any time, Mrs Grant and I will only be too pleased to see you and make you comfortable.

The 'man of the hour' deserves all the 'good terms' we can furnish. With very best wishes from us both,

Very sincerely
Lachlan Grant.

4 Mar. 1934, Grant to MacDonald

My dear Prime Minister,
I trust this finds you keeping fit and quite clear from all attacks of the prevailing catarrhal pests.

I am enclosing a few items of interest from our wonderful 'Highlands and Islands'.

One – an echo of the pleasant Fort William Mod time. 'The Photo' has again been to the fore, in the Glasgow Weekly Herald, when giving intimation of a lecture I was giving at the Highlanders Institute in Glasgow on the 23rd of last month. A copy of this address is enclosed and if you have a moment to glance at its contents you will see I deal somewhat fully with the question of 'Pauper Lunacy in the Highlands' – owing to continued depopulation resulting from emigration and migration there is a large apparent increase.

The remedies suggested are dealt with and especially the renewed efforts to deal with the existing unnatural land system – I mention <u>your own personal efforts</u> in connection with the grant of £750,000 for small holdings in Scotland, see the marked paragraphs. I know you will agree entirely with our efforts for success in endeavouring to put new life into our homeland, or, as we would say, our 'wonderful heritage.'

Reprint of 'Lecture' to the Royal Medical Society on 'eye strain and light glare' containing notes on the <u>Sun Visors</u> plan – sample pair which you tried out at Lossiemouth last autumn.

Now please excuse these personal calls but I know you are interested in one's efforts for progress.

With all good wishes from Mrs Grant and myself to you all at No. 10.

Very sincerely,
Lachlan Grant.

16 Mar. 1934, MacDonald to Grant

My dear Grant,

I have been hoping to be able to write to you myself, but the chance seems to become more and more remote, so please excuse a dictated letter. I am keeping very well I am glad to say, though a holiday would not be amiss. Short of that, the next best thing is to spend ten or fifteen minutes reading about the Highlands. I was interested in the more political papers, especially that on lunacy. I am also glad that, after a long struggle, those of us interested in land settlement have got a beginning. It is much too small for us, but it is the best that can be done and, if the expenditure is shown to be fruitful, it can easily be increased. We really must get a new life into the North, but my trouble is not to get people who agree with me, but who have got the practical means of making proposals which will produce the results. It is most disappointing to find that perhaps in a hundred letters describing wars, distresses and desirabilities there is not one which goes beyond the feeling and gets down to business.

I was especially interested to be reminded by the photograph of those delightful days at Fort William, and I wish I could have them again.

With kindest regards to Mrs Grant and all at Ballachulish, and hoping to be able to drop in and see you one day,

Yours always sincerely,
J.R.M.

11 Oct. 1934, Grant to MacDonald

My dear Prime Minister,

I am very pleased to see that you are back once again at the helm and do trust you have benefited in every way by your rest in Canada.

As you know during the last forty years I have interested myself in the life and problems of the Highlands, and as a result of many years of study, I am more than ever convinced of the urgent need for a bold and immediate effort to find some plan or means for solving our problems.

I cannot imagine one more suitable than yourself for considering this question in view of your connections, and your knowledge of the whole history, sentiment, and requirements of our Highland area. It is a long time since one of your distinguished predecessors – the Earl of Chatham – said of the Highland people: 'I looked for intelligence wherever it might be found, and I found it in the mountains of the north etc.' But in spite of this and many numerous compliments that have been paid to the Highlanders for their great services to the Empire, it is a fact that their own native problems have never been considered with the sympathy and justice that they deserve.

If, after many years of indifference and neglect you could find it possible to tackle this problem successfully, I feel sure it would go down in posterity as one of the greatest and most useful achievements of your long and distinguished career.

With a view of stimulating your interest, and in the hope that I may be in some way helpful, I am enclosing herewith a memorandum which I know will receive your most careful and sympathetic consideration.

I am,
Yours very sincerely,
Lachlan Grant.

THE HIGHLAND PROBLEM
AND SUGGESTIONS TOWARDS ITS SOLUTION

[*typescript, unpublished*]

In the Spring of this year, on the 3rd of March, I sent you a communication dealing with the Pauper Lunacy increase in the Highlands and Islands, and the depopulation question. I also pointed out the main remedies necessary for once more reviving our heritage.

On the 15th March your reply to me was sympathetic, and you agreed that 'we must try and put new life into the North.' You also mentioned that concrete proposals were necessary in order to produce tangible results.

I have no doubt that you will have many vague and impractical proposals from those who are anxious to help in reconditioning Highland life. But it is frankly impossible for any single one of us to make detailed practical proposals for reform in our Highlands without the complete and necessary data.

In this second communication I am putting forward some more suggestions of a practical nature in the sincere hope that these will assist you and your colleagues in the endeavour to put 'new life' into this large and important area of Scotland.

There is no doubt that a deliberate and calculated policy ruined the Highlands, that policy not only scattered the native people and denuded the soil, but it gave the few who remained an outlook which is quite alien to the Scottish soil, and which will require to be combated.

It is good for us here to know that you, as our Prime Minister, are sympathetic and willing to help, but the whole problem cannot be tackled, as for example, one would a small, or unimportant matter. It is well defined, but is also a very large national problem, and the first step towards its solution is a thorough survey of the whole Highland area and its varied possibilities. This work should be carried through without delay and the data forthcoming immediately considered, and duly acted upon.

Land alone will not be the only important factor in this proposed comprehensive survey. It should ascertain the potentialities of the whole Highland area, the maximum population that area can support if its resources are all fully organised and developed. Farming, fishing, tweed-making, afforestation, mineral industries and quarrying, and all the probable local industries, should be included in the survey. Particular attention should be paid to industries likely to be based on water-power, the possibilities of this have not been fully explored.

A guiding aim should be a satisfactory increase in the Highland population. This can only take place if existing industries are encouraged and new industries established, and local markets widened, and increased facilities given for the transport of produce to larger and southern markets.

I suggest that every Highland County should be sub-divided into a number of areas – say six or eight – and then ascertain the number of acres available and suitable for land settlement in each area.

Having decided the number of acres necessary for a fair economic holding, it would then be possible to estimate the number of families that could be restored to the Highland soil by a bold and comprehensive scheme of land reform.

As people cannot be settled in certain districts where the roads are bad or with no roads at all it is desirable that each area in our survey should be provided with useful roads. The statistics of the economic holding in comparable surroundings in other countries – e.g. Norway, Sweden, Denmark – should be speedily and thoroughly examined in the process of the survey. These statistics would help in indicating the type of holding that would be most advantageous.

It should not be overlooked that the size of the holdings would probably vary in some places. There are certain districts, where farming and fishing could go together, in other areas, a certain amount of land work could be undertaken in conjunction with some local industry. In all such cases the amount of land required would be less than for families depending entirely on what they produce from their own farm.

It is hardly necessary to stress the importance of ensuring that all holdings with regard to the nature of the soil, and the acreage, should be such that it would be possible for a family to get a fair living, keeping in view those districts in which income can be augmented through a local industry.

Each holding should have so many acres of arable land, where feasible also, outruns and moorland or hill pasturage, the allotments graded within limits according to the circumstances and conditions pertaining to that particular area. And here it may be added that tree-planting on what is considered good and useful arable land is in my opinion a wasteful practice and should be immediately stopped.

It is regrettable that there should be a dwindling consciousness of the importance of land in the National economy. And many of our Highlanders, like people elsewhere, have been inclined to adopt the same attitude.

To correct this it would be necessary and advisable to use all the available means of propaganda, to stimulate interest, and enlighten the people as to the possibilities as well as the National Importance of Agriculture. The Staff of the Department of Agriculture for Scotland could do very effective work by numerous lectures in various districts, a constant circulation of leaflets, and frequent broadcasts, instructing, advising, and informing people about the most modern, most economical and advantageous methods of all forms, not only of farm work but associated industries like fishing, poultry farming, wool growing and tweed-making.

The importance of restoring the fishing industry to its former prosperity by a wise expenditure on new equipment, new curing methods, reorganisation and marketing need not be emphasised, it is pleasing to note that this matter is now receiving attention.

To re-people and invigorate the Highland area some of the requirements would be –

1. To ascertain the acreage of cultivatable land in each county.
2. A division of this land into economic holdings, each capable of supporting a family in security and comfort.

3. Adequate transport facilities to open up this land and adequate grants in aid of its settlement.

4. Intensive tactful propaganda by lecture, leaflet, wireless broadcast, and other means on the best methods of cultivation to be pursued.

5. An exact understanding of how agricultural earnings could be augmented by supplementary occupations – e.g. fishing, poultry-farming and pig rearing, sylviculture, quarrying of minerals, hand-crafts, tweeds and woollen manufacture, etc. Films have a great educative value and could now be greatly used.

6. The most careful estimate of the total cost, including modernising of villages, transport by road, schools etc.

7. Schools in remote areas to be provided at public expense with up-to-date wireless sets, a special Broadcasting Station for the Highlands for broadcasting (as mentioned) lectures on the latest methods for cultivating and getting best results from the soil, on Highland and Scottish History, the history of the Gaelic language, its music and culture, and all kinds of ideas aiming at the fullest development in the economic and social life of the people.

8. In the granting of land, or any other facilities, preference should be given to the Highland people and their connections, and especially to Gaelic speaking families. In allocating holdings in each county, it would be advisable to give a preference to natives of that country. And should there be any surplus holdings in any part of the Highland area, these should be available to Highlanders from urban areas after which consideration should be given to Lowland Scots, with a knowledge of agricultural work, and overseas Highlanders who wish to return to the Mother Country. Having ascertained the approximate cost of reconditioning the whole Highland life, a grant sufficient to meet the requirements should be made. Such grants would be spread over a period of years, and should not be subject to modification or alteration by change of Government.

All these reforms will cost money, but if the Highland area can be re-populated for any sum within reason, it will be money well spent.

In my opinion it is time the British Government recognised that the service of the Highlanders to Britain and the Empire has not yet received the consideration which it is due. And if we could get one-twentieth of the value of these services in every part of the world it would be enough to ensure the re-settlement and future prosperity of the Highlands.

We appear to be entering a new era in which re-organisation is a universal slogan, and in these days of stern efforts to set the nation on its feet again, I can think of no claim more justified or more worthy of the fullest possible support, than the appeal of the Scottish Highlands and their people for the practical and sympathetic consideration of the British Government.

The Government grant of £750,000 for the purposes of land revival in Scotland is, to my mind, miserably inadequate. This grant I take it is to serve for the whole of the country, yet it is only an instalment of what would be required for the Highlands alone. You admit that the grant is, indeed, a small one, but that it is a beginning. As mentioned at the beginning of this 'memo' – it is little use trying to patch up where a wholesale overhaul is required. The object of this £750,000 grant is seemingly to settle a thousand families on the land. The Highlands alone could take 30,000 families under a wise and generous scheme. This latest grant I foresee, will be of little benefit for it is not nearly big enough.

The State must find the money to repair the damage that has been done, to re-people derelict lands and to re-equip and re-educate the people with the most up-to-date knowledge of all the potentialities of their own land. In other words the fallacies of the last two centuries must be abandoned and the Scottish Nation must go 'all out' to retain as many as possible within its own borders.

We can build ships for those who want them, we can produce cattle second to none, also Pigs, Fowls, Butter, Cheese, Eggs, Potatoes, Corn, Barley, Whisky, Fish, Timber, Tweeds, Coal and Iron, Aluminium, Slate and other building materials. We have a fair and developing tourist traffic, considerable water power, so much indeed, that it should not be impossible to have every village in the land – particularly in the Highlands – supplied with electricity.

Let those with adventurous minds roam as they will, but the soundest policy for Scotland's future is that 'every rood shall maintain its man.' Even the business man must be taught to see that the safety and welfare of the community are calling for the fullest support of home industries. The possibilities are many, but so are some of the obstacles to realisation and one of the difficulties is to see a sign of the men who are required to rouse and stimulate the nation.

I would like to suggest that some able and sympathetic person should, in association with several helpers, be entrusted with the task of rousing and maintaining renewed interest among the Highland people about the Highland soil and its undoubted possibilities.

After all, the impetus – the stimulus, to a land revival, must come from above.

It need hardly be added that a bold and comprehensive scheme of Highland re-population would materially help Scotland's unemployment problem.

For generations, Highlanders without opportunities on their own soil were compelled to flock 'Citywards' in large numbers. With a large scheme of Highland developments the numbers going to Glasgow and other Scottish cities would be considerably less, with obvious beneficial results for all concerned.

If you and your fellow statesmen get keenly interested getting things set a going, you will be the makers of a new Scotland, the creators of a bold peasantry which would be one of the mainstays of the nation both in peace and war. This is surely a noble task.

11 Oct. 1934, Grant to MacDonald

Private & Confidential

My dear Prime Minister,

The enclosed memorandum will I trust meet with your approval. I do know you will do your utmost to expedite any movement towards the establishment of a new era in the Highlands.

I do not require to indicate to you what a great natural asset, a sturdy food producing peasantry in this large area of the homeland would be, especially in the event of war. Most of us, I am sure, no one more than yourself, realise how much more difficult for us food importation will be in any future carnage, in view of the greatly increased aerial armaments. Even food carrying boats of the submarine style would be largely spotted by such enemy aircraft.

On page 10 of the memo I mention the necessity of having some able sympathetic person or persons to guide or assist in this movement. I know well one such person – one who has vision, faith and practical determination. He is a Mr Angus Clark an enthusiastic patriotic Celt resident in London. I have not mentioned this matter to Mr Clark, but perhaps sometime if you were willing I could arrange a brief, confidential, tête-à-tête, when I am sure you would find him ever so helpful.

Might I before concluding these few private lines, respectfully suggest that in some future King's Speech you might perhaps manage to touch on the Highland Problem, when it would surely be brought to the national notice. Kindly do forgive me if I appear to be carrying coals to Newcastle.

With every good wish, yours sincerely,
Lachlan Grant.

15 Oct. 1934, MacDonald to Grant

My dear Grant,

Thank you very much for your letter. You, however, enclose no memorandum. I am very much interested in the health movements that are taking place, especially for the Highlands, and anything that I can persuade my colleagues to do I shall support with great pleasure. I suppose a memorandum will explain where it is being sent and what organisation is behind it. I do not happen to know Clark. My trouble for the next week or two is to keep up all the engagements that are being thrust upon me by Ministers and Departments. They are legion, and are what I have to pay for being been away for three months but when I get your memorandum I will have it examined and, if it is not too long (my occulist is very severe on this) will read it myself.

With kindest regards to you and all your family.

Yours always sincerely,
JRM.

16 Oct. 1934

PRIME MINISTER

I attach the memorandum on the Highland problem sent to you by Dr Lachlan Grant together with a note I have made on its contents.

Dr Grant does not say that there is any organisation behind his memorandum.

Would you wish me to let the matter rest on the letter which you have already sent Dr Grant? I attach a carbon copy.

The Memorandum is a plea for a bold policy for repopulating the Highlands, but it does not purport to show how this can be done. The first step, it is urged, is 'a thorough survey of the whole Highland area and its various possibilities' to 'ascertain the maximum population that area can support if its resources (of industries old and new) are all fully organised and developed.' It is thus assumed in the Memorandum that the fishing industry, for example, can be restored to its former prosperity by a wise expenditure on new equipment, new curing methods, reorganisation and marketing, and that on the land the only problem is to discover the extent of 'the economic holding' in each district. And the general opinion, unsupported by argument, is that the Highlands can absorb 30,000 families. The recent grant of £750,000 to settle 1,000 families on the land is therefore naturally described as not nearly big enough.

The attitude and aspirations of the writer must win sympathy, but his detailed suggestions towards a solution of the problem do not seem likely to be fruitful. Indeed they are meant to be examples rather than practical proposals.

DEPARTMENT OF AGRICULTURE FOR SCOTLAND

Observations on Memorandum submitted to the Prime Minister by Dr. Lachlan Grant.

The Memorandum covers a wide scope and outlines very large proposals. The Department have carefully considered it, and they offer the following observations on the main lines of development proposed by Dr Grant.

(1) Land Settlement.
Within the limits of the funds available, land settlement has proceeded and will proceed as rapidly as circumstances allow.
During the period 1st April 1912 to 31st December 1933 the Department formed 3473 new holdings and provided for the enlargement of 1943 existing holdings. The geographical distribution of these is as follows:

	New Holdings.	Enlargements.
Crofting Counties	2017	1916
Rest of Scotland	1456	27
Total.	3473	1943

If 'Highlands and Islands' is taken in a more restricted sense as applying to the counties of Argyll, Inverness, Ross and Cromarty and Sutherland (excluding those of Caithness, Orkney and Zetland), the figures are as follows:-

	New Holdings.	Enlargements.
Four Counties	1651	1477
Rest of Scotland	1822	466
Total.	3473	1943

In addition, there must be taken into account the work carried out by the Congested Districts Board between 1897 and 1912.

These figures show clearly that the Highlands and Islands have been the object of a large proportion of the Department's activity in land settlement.

The larger resources recently made available under the Land Settlement (Scotland) Act, 1934, to which Dr Grant refers are intended, in accordance with the policy of His Majesty's Government, mainly for the formation of small holdings in the 'industrial belt' of Scotland. It does not therefore appear to be opportune at the present time to undertake a survey of the Highlands and Islands for the purpose of ascertaining what more can be or ought to be done there.

(2) Communications.

The Department have, during the last 22 years made grants amounting in all to £183,250 (an average of £8,330 per annum) to local authorities in the Congested Districts for the formation of improvement of roads, for the reconstruction of piers, for the provision or repair of minor works such as jetties, etc., and for the partial maintenance of certain telegraph and telephone services. The grant generally amounts to three-fourths of the total cost. All the County Councils concerned are well aware of the requirements of their areas, and the Department have to select for assistance, out of the various schemes proposed, those which appear most urgently needed.

The Harbours, Piers and Ferries Bill is intended to facilitate the acquisition of marine works by local authorities, which will render it possible for assistance to be given from public funds for their reconstruction where required.

(3) Agricultural Education.

The North of Scotland College of Agriculture and the West of Scotland Agricultural College are prepared, within the limits of their resources, to respond to local demand for instruction by lectures or advice. Such demand is frequently stimulated by the activity of the Scottish Women's Rural Institutes. The distribution of leaflets has little effect.

(4) Agricultural and Horticultural Development.

Ordinary crops such as oats and potatoes are grown for subsistence or for the feeding of live stock. Sheep and young cattle are the main source of the crofter's income, so far as it is derived from the use of the land and the Department's Scheme for the improvement of these classes of livestock have done much to raise the standard. Pig-keeping is almost non-existent, and there appears to be a powerful prejudice against it.

Horticulture is frequently mentioned as a possible addition to the activities of the crofter, on the ground that the winter climate of the Western Highlands and Islands is relatively mild. But the frequent heavy rain and strong wind are adverse factors, and in addition to the difficulties of production there is the problem of marketing. It is however quite feasible to develop the existing production of vegetables and fruit near such places as Oban and Fort William.

Poultry-keeping is probably capable of considerable expansion. The Scottish Agricultural Organisation Society has been at work in the Hebrides for many years and has formed a number of small co-operative societies for the sale of eggs, and the Department carry on a scheme for the improvement of poultry. Recently a scheme has been launched in Lewis, with the help of a grant from the Macaulay Trust, which may result in the establishment of a packing station under the National Mark system, and there is another scheme in Skye, which has however so far met with a large response.

(5) Rural Industries.

Tweed-making and the knitting of hosiery and other woollen goods furnish a substantial part of the income of many homes in the Highlands and Islands. Steps have been taken to protect the genuine tweed by trade-mark, and the Highland Home Industries (111 George Street, Edinburgh) is an efficient agency for the sale of woollen articles, as well as chairs etc.

Kelp-making was formerly a more profitable occupation than it is at present, but it still goes on to a considerable extent.

It has often been suggested that the Highlanders might make small fancy things for sale to tourists, as peasants do abroad.

(6) General.

Dr Grant's memorandum deals with other subjects not within the Department's sphere of action. General reference may be made to the Western Highlands and Islands Joint Council, which was formed for the purpose of considering the needs and possibilities of these districts in the widest sense, and which has an office at 23 Bream's Buildings, Chancery Lane, London, E. C. 4.

26 Nov. 1934, MacDonald to Grant

My dear Grant,

Many thanks for your letter with its enclosure and the good news of Mrs Grant.

I respond with pleasure to your request that I should send a message to be read on the occasion of a meeting at the Highlanders' Institute. The Institute serves a worthy purpose as a centre of social life for Highlanders resident in Glasgow and I wish it all success.

For generations the population of Glasgow has been recruited from the Highlands and Islands, and that great city owes an untold debt to the men and women of the glens and the isles.

But there is another side of the picture. Not only Glasgow, but England and the Dominions overseas have drawn from our Highland districts thousands upon thousands of their best people as emigrants. Too little was done in the past to make it possible for the Highlander to remain at home and to enjoy within his native shores the full opportunities of life.

We are now more fully alive to the needs of the Highlands and Islands. Much has been done by way of sharing the land more equally, helping the people to improve their houses, supplying adequate schools and medical services, and easing the difficulties of communication. But much remains yet to be done, and any well-devised scheme for the social, economic and cultural benefit of the Highlands will be received by me with the warmest sympathy.

With kindest regards,
Yours very sincerely,
J.R.M.

A New Deal for the Highlands, by Dr Lachlan Grant, JP (1935)

> O sad for me Glen Aora,
> Where I have friends no more,
> For lowly lie the rafters,
> And the lintels of the door.
> The friends are all departed,

> The hearth-stone's black and cold,
> And sturdy grows the nettle
> On the place beloved of old. – Neil Munro

WANTED, A NEW DEAL FOR THE HIGHLANDS

I propose to return once again somewhat briefly to the vexed question of the decline of our Highlands and Islands, and to bring to the attention of readers the vital necessity of re-populating the country – both Highlands and Lowlands – if we are to avoid national and racial suicide. It is the paramount duty of each of us who know the evil conditions to vindicate them unceasingly, and to advocate full and adequate reforms that will give the people a rooted interest in their country.

Individuals do what they can in their own small way, but after all the real power to move public opinion, and 'the powers that be' lies in unity and combination, and I believe that were the cottars, crofters and farmers, fishermen and agricultural workers, of the Highlands and Islands thoroughly organised like some of the great unions they would have full satisfaction from the British Legislature in a very short period. But we have difficulties of a personal and local geographical character to contend with. Outsiders and friends in the cities of Scotland who understand and sympathise can and should help in many ways. What has been robbing the country of its wealth and prosperity is depopulation and depopulation is caused principally by a wrong and unnatural land system. We all know there is plenty of good land lying uncultivated in Scotland. We also know that thousands yet remain in the country able and willing to settle thereon, and to cultivate it – not to speak of many in the towns and cities who would be only too eager to learn the first and most natural of all vocations.

INSTINCT OF THE CELTIC RACE

Here is a case in point:- A man has brought up his family of healthy sons and daughters on his small holding and the time comes when something has to be done with the grown-ups – especially the young men. Some of the bolder and more restless spirits may wish to try their luck in some other centre or country, but the other members will have the natural desire to follow in their father's footsteps and secure a holding in the land of their birth. This is surely a laudable ambition, showing good sense and healthy sentiment – and the Crofters Holdings Act of 1886 has repeatedly demonstrated how successful such settlers can be. The whole environment of the young folk specially fits them for work on the land, and from their point of view they do not see why they should not be able to make a living as well as their parents. But then the cruel fact stares them in the face – no land is available. The various raids and agitations were all indicative of the young people feeling where the shoe pinched, and in attempting to lay hands on idle land they were only following the hereditary instinct of the Celtic race. Every such family had much the same melancholy ending. Some go to the big towns and cities to swell the competing crowd of unskilled labourers and drift often into mean streets or slums, living on a pittance in unhealthy surroundings. Some are successful according to the world's standard, but that does not atone for the hard fate of their fellow clansmen. Those who persist in remaining at home under present conditions eke out too often a bare existence in overcrowded, unhealthy conditions often leading to disease and despair. It is difficult in many parts to get land for building a cottage or even land for the layout of a kitchen garden. Why should these hindrances exist? It will not do nowadays to settle the question by asserting that small holdings cannot afford a living. Those who scoff at the idea simply don't understand. Some business men make the mistake of imagining that the smallholder or crofter is a discontented mortal, because he does not make a big enough income. But my experience is that the smallholder or crofter is much more philosophical in these matters than the average commercial man. He does not pursue the middle class ideal of life in villadom with a balance at the bank. He knows he can never amass wealth, but he does know he can live contentedly, and in tolerable comfort on the land, if a reasonable chance is given him. He grasps what real happiness is and to attain it I must say his demands are modest indeed – namely, the acquirement of suitable portions of land at a fair rent with fixity of tenure, and of course other matters pertaining thereto.

BACK TO THE LAND

The land question in the Highlands stands in the forefront of the many social and economic problems that call for solution in our day. In order to be at all satisfactory this question must be settled on lines that will afford food and employment to a vastly increased population. It must be arranged so as to yield a comfortable means of livelihood to thousands of our able-bodied men and women, who are today depending on doles, public assistance relief, or casual employment which is not nowadays easily obtained at home. Surely this is a sound proposition. It sums up admirably the wisdom of the policy indicated in the phrase 'Back to the Land.' Along that road is the way to comfort and happiness that so many now seek vainly – in the crowded labour industrial centres, in the city slums, and street corners, and in listless hopelessness on the hill sides and coast lines, where casual and precarious employment too often yields nothing but a bare existence.

LOCHABER NO MORE

The land in the Highlands is not yielding its full capacity of fresh food products for the people, or for the nation. The deer forests and sheep farms invite the reforming hand to find foothold for men rather than beasts. We must not forget that the 'hardy race of Highlanders' is the stock of the Gael that largely assisted in baulking the Cuirassiors at Waterloo, that bore back the Russians at Inkerman, and crushed the Mutiny in India – yet, the stag and sheep have been the concern, not they.

The Highland clearances make a sad and damnable page (of reading) in history. 'Lochaber No More' touches one in song and story and under the hands of the artist, and it is an 'owre true tale' full of sadness and injurious consequences, too painfully obvious in these days of lackadaisical statesmanship and public unconcern.

Thus we must constantly pursue efforts for redress, and prevent these being side tracked by artifice and misrepresentation – we must make a stand for the rights of human kind and in 'the interests of the race of the brave and much wronged Scots-Gael.'

It is a great pity and a very great mistake that our own people are so short-sighted and apathetic as to neglect their national and public duties. In the Highlands, we do badly need to put 'our house in order.' There are some matters that can best be dealt with on a national scale and this question of reconstructing our whole Highlands is assuredly one of them, and that which looms largest on our horizon.

In March of last year, I sent to the Prime Minister a copy of a lecture which I delivered to the members of the Clan MacColl Society, in the Highlanders' Institute, Glasgow, dealing with the depopulation question of the Highlands and Islands of Scotland. On the 16th of March he replied sympathetically saying:- 'I was much interested in the more political papers especially those on Lunacy, and I am also glad that after a long struggle, those of us interested in the land settlement question have got a beginning. It is much too small for me and if the expenditure is shown to be fruitful it can easily be increased [. . .]' He continued, 'We really must get new life into the North, but my trouble is not to get people to agree with me, but who have got the practical sense of making proposals which will produce results.'

In consequence of the above letter, I sent him on the 10th of October, a memorandum – brief, but fairly comprehensive, containing 'Some Practical Suggestions for the Solution of our Highland Problems' [*see pages 181–186 for the original*] [. . .]

MADDENING SNAIL PACE

This communication the Prime Minister duly acknowledged along with a promise to have it carefully examined. Later I again wrote to him on the matter, and suggested the publication of the memorandum. His reply was, 'By all means publish or use the memorandum as you think fit.'

The appeal to the Prime Minister envisaged a Government with complete powers and a desire to tackle the problems, but up till now not very much has been done. I believe the first step towards remedying the position would be to form a great Highland organisation to carry on the work of enlightening our fellow countrymen, and to consider all practical proposals such as some of those set out in the memo. Unless pressure of some kind is brought to bear in the proper quarter the hope of obtaining much in the way of practical help seems to me to be very doubtful. But why should it be so? Why should a Government wait until it has to yield in the end to the clamorous cries of the people rather than be perhaps submerged by them? The way to progress in the Highlands and Islands has much too often been blocked. Important measures such as the various small Landholders Bills were often emasculated, or too long delayed by the maddening snail pace of our effete political machinery. As regards this question of land – it is long years since our landless and disinherited ones grew weary in waiting, and to this day, our great country, supposed to be full of patriots, allows its sons and daughters to leave its inhospitable shores with despair in their hearts and curses on their tongues. Is this economic harrying of our fellows to go on until the only men left in the Highlands are a few gillies, gamekeepers, hotel-keepers and a few sheep-farmers – not surely if we can help it!

What we want is a splendid assertion of Scottish rights showing up the studied neglect by all parties of our Highlands and Islands. The preservation of the life, language and culture of the Gael is calling for a great Highland rally under the ancient banner of our own land.

That our area requires reconstruction as pointed out in the appeal to the Prime Minister, is obvious to every Highlander who thinks at all about his heritage. Some of us, down the corridors of time, have been trying to waken up the Gaels in order that they may demand redress, and be further stimulated to secure much needed reforms, hence one reason for making public this memorandum. After my recent address on 'Our Highland Heritage in Danger and a Call to Action,' I received numerous letters and many queries on some of the points mooted – so I am taking this opportunity to touch briefly on some of the matters mentioned in the hope that such might prove interesting to readers, and at the same time helpful.

In the course of the address I appealed to fellow countrymen to combine together and face up boldly and support the just claims of their own homeland. I fully agree with those correspondents who suggested that it is absolutely necessary to embrace some common cause to secure justice for our country, and in common with them would like to see formed – as I have already said – a strong Highland organisation for the purposes we have in view, namely, to push the claims of the Highland people and the crying need for reconstruction. Such an organisation should be opened to Highlanders and their supporters everywhere at home and abroad. Its constitution should be a militant one aiming at nothing less than a weapon which would make itself felt to such an extent that 'the powers that be' realised once and for all, that the period of neglect and wilful disregard of Highland problems had come to an end. A feasible proposal would be to organise a mass meeting of Highlanders and their supporters in a centre such as Glasgow. This mass meeting being the nucleus of a zealous organisation. Something with spirit and flame that would genuinely fire the heather. There is no doubt that as already mentioned, organised pressure, brought forcibly to bear upon these governing powers, would prove helpful. The Glasgow Highland Societies should take the lead in these matters, for, as in the words of the Prime Minister, 'the population of Glasgow has been largely recruited from the Highlands and Islands, and that great city owes an untold debt to the men and women of the glens and isles.'

SEND ROUND THE FIERY CROSS

They – the societies – could do much good work in sending round the fiery cross – but will they? Most of their chiefs and followers seem to view the serious plight of their own country with complete equanimity and indifference. They appear to devote themselves very largely to social and musical functions – or to the somewhat futile though interesting work of the past history of their septs, etc.

I sometimes wonder if it is really possible to bring home to our people the perils which surround their homeland. It is well known that Highlanders have served the British Commonwealth and other parts of the world with much distinction, but it is also known that these distinguished services have not to any large extent benefited our own people. The homeland is still waiting for the men who will push forward and 'champion' its own cause. It has waited long and suffered much, but it cannot afford to wait much longer. Is it too much then to hope that in these days, when so much is heard about the rights of nations, that men will arise in our midst, who understand that it is true service to the world and humanity, to labour with fidelity for the long deferred rights of our own race? Much too long the Highlands have been treated as an afterthought, their possibilities have never been seriously considered, nor their potentialities explored. Therefore, I once more join issue with these correspondents everywhere to combine and face boldly, openly and earnestly, the just claims and undoubted requirements of our own land.

A NEW AND CHANGING WORLD

The second doubt raised was that of the possibility of ever getting any small holders to settle down in the country, owing to the difficulties of making their holdings pay, or on account of the lure, attractions and glitter of the towns and cities, and larger centres. It is quite impossible in the course of an article to deal completely with all points, but at the moment I just wish to present a few outstanding facts.

It is well known that there are many people willing and anxious to remain on the land and many who wish to return to it.

Such people should undoubtedly be encouraged and assisted in every possible way, and not be discouraged. We are living in a new and changing world, and this big problem will have to be approached on entirely new and different lines from that of the past. For example, holdings must be set up on good agricultural soil – and of a size large enough to enable their occupants to earn a modest and comfortable living. The holders will require instruction in the very best methods of modern farming. And again, it is not altogether so much the question of a continuous going back to the land as making it possible for those who are settled there, and their coming families, to remain there until such a time as it can be said, 'all our countryside, our glens and straths are fully populated.' Not, of course, saturated to over-flowing. No intelligent guiding government hands would ever place more people on the land than it could support.

Lloyd George, MacDougall, our own Scottish Board of Agriculture Staff, and many others have proved what can be done with arable and pasturage lands – when these are scientifically dealt with. Thus old conceptions dealing with the land problems must be scrapped and the question approached with enthusiasm in the light of modern scientific intensive agricultural knowledge, chemistry, machinery, etc.

TOWN AMENITIES

Then the town amenities are becoming more and more available for country folks – easy travel, radio, etc. This side will develop more rationally as the population increases. Radio has brought the knowledge of the everyday happenings throughout the world as much to the crofter's kitchen as to the millionaire's palace. It is urged by doubters and reactionists that the rising generation is so given up to hedonism that it wishes for nothing better than modern town and city life. This, I think, is partly a fallacy and in so far as it is true is due to the false outlook which has been to some extent developed, and is even spreading amongst our Highland people. At any rate, if given a fair living on the land – forestry, tweed-making, water power schemes, mineral and fishing industries, etc., with their reasonable monetary remunerations, the town pleasures are largely within easy reach nowadays. Wireless, as I have said, is available to all. The telephone system is extending. The postal service delivers letters to our remotest Highland glens with a minimum of loss of time in transit. The daily newspaper – the cheapest thing in the world – is now available daily. We are not like our forefathers who had frequently to wait days, weeks and months for news of important occurrences all over the world. These he can now have in the course of a few days, or a few hours; television is coming soon. Given a fair sized village there will be plenty of opportunities for all kinds of sports, recreations and cultural pursuits – vide,

Scots Community Drama. Modern transport has put our larger towns within easy reach of most of the smaller centres, so that more occasional visits are now possible. Cinemas, motors and aeroplanes are reaching an ever widening circle. The whole tendency is to increase the amenities of the countryside and approximate them more to those of the towns. The foregoing facts are apt to be forgotten. As regards housing, education, and first-class roads these are of course the responsibilities of the Government.

The real truth about the Highland land question is that our people have been passionately driven and too often encouraged to leave the land of their forefathers. Hitherto no effort, inducement or extra guidances worth much has ever been done to make life easier and worth while for crofters, cottars and small holders, and the present-day doubtings and questionings indulged in by opponents and reactionaries are always much in evidence. Unfortunately, too, such are apt to receive considerable press publicity and so intensify the vicious circle. It is also well known that in all walks of life there is to be found the 'black sheep,' small holders are no exception to the rule. Nevertheless, the whole cannot be condemned on account of a few unsuccessful ones, who, perhaps, have failed to make a success of their holdings. All these matters and conditions will have to be met and combated.

As the Highlands have been sacrificed on the altars of the British Empire for two centuries, common justice demands that a substantial grant be made over a period of years to re-construct and re-people the homeland of the Gael, and this should be done now before it is too late. To secure this we must have a new spirit and determined leaders – what kind of leaders? Men who will count the fallacies of the past in which they have been taught to believe in – as what – as nothing in comparison with the re-awakening, restoration and proper re-education of their own people.

A TASK OF GREAT MAGNITUDE

These are a few of the reasons why I agree with some writers that the task is not a small one. It is one of considerable magnitude – but that nothing else will suffice, I am quite convinced. It is a problem which can only be met and tackled by sincere and determined patriots armed with considerable powers and of course a money grant. Our Highlands require leadership, guidance, education and tuition in modern scientific advances in so far as they affect life and happiness.

All such must also be called on to create the new spirit and a new outlook.

Another point – a third one – which must be considered, is that of our language. 'If Gaelic is dying out, why bother about its upkeep?' There is little doubt as Mr Angus Clark has said, that 'The loss of Scots independence is the chief cause of the decline of our Gaelic heritage, and that language and nationality cannot be divorced. Language is an invincible bulwark of nationality, hence the main reason why the conquerors impose their language on the conquered people in Europe. The preservation of our Gaelic tradition is therefore of great importance if we are to remain a nation.' If it dies there is very little left to distinguish us from any other English-speaking people. In every land struggling for freedom, the preservation of their language is always considered of sublime importance. If then the Gaelic tradition dies and Scotland remains completely under London, then, truly, will the Scot become a northern Englishman.

The present efforts of the Mod and language movements are all very interesting and to some extent helpful. But though most educated Highlanders see the truth, they do not appear to have any great wish to help towards a big revival. I am afraid that most of our Scottish Parliamentary representatives care very little once they get to Westminster. Scotland and its Gaelic language might be in, or pertain to, Basutoland, for all they seem to care. Nothing can save the things An Comunn Gaidhealach stands for, unless someone comes along and changes the mentality and outlook of our people. This, I fear, will never be done by any party or organisation at present in the public or political areas. Who then is more capable of dealing with this vital Highland question than the Gaels themselves? Would that they would move.

I am convinced it is a delusion to think that the salvation of our Highlands and Islands can come through putting all our trust in any of the present parties. The bulk of the present-day politicians seem to me to have no desire to see that justice is done to the Highlands of Scotland. In fact, so far as our problems are concerned, there is a complete lack of interest, due, no doubt, to our comparatively poor voting strength, and as a consequence the political parties and their representatives 'pass by on the other side.'

INTERNATIONALISM

Many of our countrymen are also suffering from an exotic disease – internationalism. For Scots to talk about Internationalism is absurd, especially seeing their own country is not recognised at all in the international scheme of things. Some time ago in a little Highland hotel, a distinguished Scottish Nationalist met three long-haired self-styled 'Internationalists.' They were Scot Trade Unionists from the south. In the course of conversation they largely pooh-poohed his strong Scottish Nationalist bent, and with a superior air told him that they were not Nationalists but Internationalists, and that they had no time at all for such paltry and insignificant matters as Scottish Nationalism. He promptly addressed them in several European languages including Gaelic, none of which they could understand. With a look of contempt he speedily told them not to make d----- fools of themselves, and to try and do something for the one country – the nation they knew and understood, and to which they belonged.

During a recent election an eminent leader of the Labour Party most truly stated again and again that 'Internationalism pre-supposes Nationalism, and unless you are a good strong Nationalist you cannot be an Internationalist.'

There is no doubt all the great political parties have failed to face the bedrock evils of which we Highlanders complain, and instead of serious endeavours to prevent further decay of our homeland, to remove hardships and render justice, we have been met by political chicane and emasculating promises.

We require and must have great developments in the Highlands, in regard to agriculture, afforestation, quarrying, farming, dairying, fishing and various important industries, and also in public health, housing, education and telephone services, and secure increased facilities for transit by road, motor, trams, steamers, with the linking up of outlying sections of the country. These are the days of rapid organisation and scientific precision, so there is no reason why we too should not formulate a healthy comprehensive programme of essentials for the rejuvenation of our Highlands, and thus add a further quota to the National assets of the country. With reference to the housing question in the Highlands, I wish, in passing, to voice my protest against the tenement erections which are being dumped and clumped in many parts. Such are not at all in keeping with our beautiful countryside. As I stated a short time ago, 'Where does Scotland stand in Internationalism or any other scheme of things?' The answer is, 'Nowhere.' In a world where every other nation from China to Peru, are determined to rule and decide their own national affairs, why should anyone, least of all a Scotsman, be so ridiculous to think that Scotland should not have similar powers? The Scottish people can never express their own mind unless they have the sovereign freedom to which they are fully entitled as a distinct nation. All this is quite in line with their being good Internationalists, and why should Scotland be left out at Geneva when even Abyssinia and Afghanistan are represented there. Are the Scots not allowed their lawful status which among other things would give them the power to help forward all good world causes? Unless Self Government is a good thing for nations spiritually, as well as racially and economically, why is every other country, large and small, determined to preserve its rights? And unless every nation rules itself, who, in God's name has the right to do it, or even the knowledge, or the interest? All this Internationalism coming from Scots makes one despair of them.

START IN THE LAND OF THE GAEL

If we Scots are going to try to put the world right we must start at the City of Jerusalem which to every intelligent Scot, must in their case be Scotland, including, of course, our own Highlands and Islands – the land of the Gael. The preservation of everything Celtic and National worth preserving then depends on our freedom to control and manage our own affairs as we think best.

The situation is not altogether hopeless, but the Scots, on the whole, appear to find it much more difficult to be true to, and honest to their own country than most races. The chief reason is probably that the Scots for two centuries have been born and bred in an environment of subserviency foreign to their marrow, and have to some extent, although I blush to admit it, acquired the 'inferiority complex.' We have lost our functioning capital, and the lack of self Government has damaged Scottish interest, and has been a source of vexation and discontent to the patriot.

In many parts of our country there is often too much sectional division and stand offishness on the part of many Highlanders who could make themselves useful in the community. Whatever differences there may be regarding party, position or sect, we should, however, all be willing to meet as Highlanders, clansmen and citizens. A united people makes a nation invincible to all the powers of evil – external and internal. Even although we are struggling with this depopulation question, with poverty and adverse economic conditions and their necessary detachment of mind and absence of surplus energy, depression and indifferentism, let us all try to win those victories in civilisation that bring prosperity and happiness in their train. As mentioned, the whole of Scotland needs drastic changing and this can only be managed by some grim and determined Scotsmen who hold a new outlook.

THE NEW GAELDOM

If a new Scotland including our new Gaeldom should ever arise in the near future, then its true greatness in the world, the brilliance of its beacon light among the nations, the weight of its influence by example and in council, the happiness of its people and the strength of real Scottish and Highland character can never reach their maximum unless the power and freedom to administer and develop the potentialities and resources of our own land are in the hands of our own people.

Here is the secret of our deserted Highland glens and straths, the dispersion of the Gael and the decline of Scotland's position in every way. And while I believe this larger task must be faced by the Scots people, my present mission is to appeal to Highlanders to rally into one great organisation determined to leave no stone unturned to secure for our own race, every possible opportunity which our own land can afford. Unless we undertake this work ourselves and see it carried to a successful issue, it will forever remain undone. We can no longer afford the apathy and indifference which have been characteristic of the past. Inaction will ensure a continuation of the sacrifice of the interests and future of the Highlands. Therefore, I appeal with confidence for a united and enthusiastic rally of Highlanders in support of the just claims of our homeland, and the formation of a vigorous organisation aimed at nothing less than the wholesale reconstruction of our Highland areas as the one and only way that can save our glorious heritage and ensure its vigorous preservation down the ages.

Oban Times, 1 June, 1935

HIGHLANDS AND HEBRIDES
STATE POLICY LACKING DIFFERENT CONDITIONS
REQUIRE DIFFERENT TREATMENT

If there be doubt that the Highlands and Islands require special consideration and different treatment from that of other British areas, let one
look at the map.

What is found? A gathering of islands, some near, some distant from
the mainland, extending from North to South at least two hundred miles,
and stretching as far as 60 miles West from the compacted mainland.
And on the latter there is a coastline with innumerable openings, while
bordering inland are long fresh water lochs. With the indentations of the
sea the County of Argyll has itself a coastline measuring 2,000 miles –
the distance between the two capitals, Edinburgh and London, is only
400 miles.

Therefore one will at once gather from a mere glance at the map that
water, with all its dangers and inconveniences, form the main roadways
instead of solid earth.

Does this fact not require a different attitude on the part of Government to the Western Highlands and Islands?

Further, these physical differences have a contracting effect upon
industry and trade, in so far that the natives of these areas do not enjoy,
automatically as it were, the benefit of speedy intercourse with their
neighbours. To maintain living at the standard of the present day is but
an easy affair for the inhabitants of the mainland, with all their facilities
of communication and exchange of labour, while for the natives of the
Highlands and Islands it is a continuous struggle.

But one may say that the Highland area has received special treatment. There is the Crofters' Act, the Land Court, the Department of
Agriculture, a subsidy for Medical Services, a considerable sum for Mail
Transport, which in turn reduces the cost of general transport, and
various other payments.

Admitted that these benefits have been given, but the contention is that
they have been grudgingly and in piecemeal fashion. There has been no
policy behind them.

The Department of Agriculture is the biggest landlord now in the
Highlands, but it fails as a co-operating landlord. It is looked upon as

a machine to draw rents, and to receive the interest on loans. It may provide bulls and rams, at a price, but that desired beneficial relation of landlord to tenant does not agree with its constitution. It may not be the fault of the executive, housed in York Place, Edinburgh, though it stands against them that, if they are aware of the shortcomings of their Department, they have not been informative or combative enough with the Treasury and Secretary of State. The permanent official can have great power behind the scenes.

WANT OF A STUDIED POLICY

The want of a studied policy by the Government is the main cause of the plight into which the Highlands and Islands have fallen, in comparison with other areas of the Kingdom. The neglect spells depopulation.

The means of communication in the Highlands and Islands are not worthy of a great and wealthy nation. The soil is deteriorating, its useable extent is pitiably shrinking through the inroads of bracken, the resident population is diminishing.

It is not charity that is wanted.

Recognising it as the duty of the State to equalise public benefits among its subjects, the inhabitants of the Highlands and Islands regard themselves as omitted from the general dispensation.

The Government insists upon the same standard of public duty as in other parts of the Kingdom – education is an instance. It works out that a school has to be provided for even three pupils!

The Government is promoting a Housing Scheme which may be all very well for the better-off areas of the Kingdom, but which, if applied with similar provisions to the Highlands and Islands, will add an intolerable burden on the ratepayers. By a recent decision of the Valuation Appeal Court in Edinburgh, extension of a smallholder's dwelling will take it out of the former free category.

It is the post office subsidy which allows transport of goods and stock to be practicable – if not particularly profitable – to senders. With the adoption of sending the mails by air will the subsidy be withdrawn? What then? This may be mentioned to show the uncertainty of conditions which is corroding the enterprise of the people.

DEFINITE ALL-EMBRACING POLICY WANTED

A definite policy of subsidising the means of communication in the Highlands and Islands, which must needs include steamers, piers, harbours and jetties, and the roads, requires to be established.

The Department of Agriculture must assume the responsibilities such as the best type of landlord carries.

There is a big road fund available, and the Ministry of Transport should be allowed to translate 'road-way' into 'sea-way', and required to make more generous grants to the ordinary roads in the areas, because it is beyond the means of the inhabitants to maintain them at standard.

If left with their present deficiencies the Highlands and Islands might prove a vulnerable area to our cost. Home defence holds the mind of Parliament at present, and no Statesman can ignore this particular weakness.

From consideration of national interest and public policy therefore, measures for the levelling up of the public conditions in the Highlands and Islands, which should be progressive and fit into each other, are due by Parliament. Discontent among the native population is being shown by further depopulation.

There is no reflection upon the Members of Parliament of Highland constituencies. Mr Macquisten, Sir Murdoch MacDonald, Mr Wilson Ramsay and Sir Ian Macpherson lose no opportunity of pressing the demands of their constituents. But the levers of the Parliamentary machine are worked by Ministers, and it requires someone of the Cabinet to be the saviour of the Highlands and Islands.

The measures for the amelioration of the Highlands and Islands must be far-reaching and flexible. The assistance to the public services must be granted after taking the broadest and longest view of the situation. The ordinary frontiers of Government assistance must not be the limits. And above all, the measures must possess the spirit which will fire the imagination of the people and animate them to the certainty of prosperity in the land of their fathers.

Oban Times, 20 July, 1935

HIGHLANDS AND HEBRIDES
A STUDIED, CONTINUOUS POLICY WANTED.
TOO MANY ISOLATED MEASURES

Tigh a thubhadh gun a shiomaineachadh, sasthair dhiomhain.
Thatching a house without roping it is vain labour

The recent discussion in the House of Commons on Scottish agricultural affairs, particularly those affecting the Highlands and Islands, was again disappointing. The misfortune is that Parliament has never formulated or followed a concrete policy for the Highlands and Islands. Isolated measures have been squeezed out of the Ministry, and each of the concessions to public demand has included some counteracting restriction or excluded the essential accessory. Here are some examples.

UNSUPPORTED SMALLHOLDINGS

Smallholdings were demanded and granted, but the properties acquired were often not of the quality required. Luskentyre is an example.

ESSENTIAL ERROR

The government made advances (on bonds) to smallholders for them to take over the sheep stock on certain big sheep farms, which the Board of Agriculture had purchased. The price of the stock acquired at the time was abnormally high. The value, at once, commenced to fall, and has now sunk to a figure which spells bankruptcy to the smallholder. There was one revision, with qualifications, of the conditions in the bonds, sanctioned and carried through by the Land Court, but that was twelve years ago. The Department of Agriculture, if things are allowed to go on as they are, will have got out of an uneconomic bargain in the purchase they made, at the expense of the smallholders. The contract for the repayment of the loans might be also looked upon as a contract which should be reduced owing to 'essential error'. There was land hunger at the time and the applicants trusted in a Government engagement.

GOVERNMENT AS LANDLORD

The Government owns 134 estates, aggregating over 400,000 acres principally in the Highlands and Islands. The Department of Agriculture are really the factors. The Government have disclaimed their responsibilities as proprietors. They are even worse than the old type of absentee landlord. Having settled the smallholders on the estates, was not their well-being the primary consideration, and it may be asked – was it honest to burden the simple smallholder with an inflated cost of sheep stock on a falling market, and fix him with a bond?

Grants have been made to the Forestry Commission, the reason advanced for the public interest being, that the nation must not be wholly dependent upon foreign countries for timber supplies. But at the same time, as the Government, through their Commission, are covering areas – some of the best pastoral land, too – with tree cultivation, they are allowing thousands of acres to be put out of beneficial use through the spread of bracken.

TRANSPORT NEGLECTED

After an irresistible agitation, a bigger subsidy was granted for transport, particularly to the new company, MacBraynes (1928) Ltd. Some better steamers were provided, but little else, because the subsidy was insufficient. No new routes have been provided, and reduction of 10 per cent on freights was all that could be conceded. Such may be stated as another example of cramping a benefit.

Fishing on the Western seas and lochs has been a mainstay industry of the Island population. Trawlers were allowed, through want of punitive regulation until recently, to despoil the fishing grounds, but the main reason for the decline in this industry is the want of regular transport to the mainland from the different ports. MacCallum, Orme and Co.'s vessels courageously cover the outer boundaries of the Hebrides, as far as commercial enterprise will permit, but the subsidy they receive is inadequate for extension or for a substantial reduction of freight.

The re-making of the main roads in the Highlands – the Islands being practically ignored – has been subsidised, but the maintenance of these highways, which has thus become much more expensive, is a load on the already overburdened ratepayers. The Road Ministry might have learned a lesson from the same sort of omission in the Highland Roads and Bridges Act of 1803, which gave the first Government subsidy to road construction in the Highlands, apart from the military roads perpetuated by General Wade. The Bill provided for the repair of the new roads, but this was struck out of the Act, and Highland roads were never first-class.

It may be well to recall the words of Telford, on whose survey and recommendations the Bill was brought into Parliament:

It is incalculable the loss which the public have sustained, and are about to suffer from the want of roads in this country.

These examples show how the benefits have been neutralised, and why the measures have failed to accomplish their purpose. All that has been done for the Highlands and Islands is a series of unrelated measures, each of which could not gain its objects, because it was incomplete or left out the necessary auxiliary.

There is ample evidence now, upon which to act without further enquiry through a Commission. The Ministry have the Land Court at call. No advice less unerring could be obtained than from this impartial and experienced body. And if the Government require an executive, they have only to revise the personnel, change the locus and enlarge the activities of the Department of Agriculture. But above all the power behind must believe without misgiving in the policy to be undertaken.

The official mind must be Hebridised.

POSTSCRIPT

Through the public spirited action of a Highland Association, and the generosity of its members and friends, funds were provided to publish and distribute a first edition of 5,000 copies of this brochure. Copies will be sent to Highland and Scottish Associations, and to individuals generally, so as to ensure that in every Scottish Constituency there will be broadcast a knowledge of existing conditions in the Highlands and Islands, and the remedies proposed to make good the errors of the past.

The new deal for the Highlands is a call for the economic regeneration of our people. Economics are a necessary condition of life. No intellectual and spiritual life, NO ideology are thinkable without an economic basis, and only in our economic and social regeneration will come the recovery of true life values: in regaining these Celtic culture will again shine a beacon and inspiration to all men of goodwill.

As suggested by Dr Grant a meeting of Highlanders and their supporters will be held in Glasgow later in the year for the purpose of forming an organisation to ensure that the remedies proposed in the new deal, and the studied continuing policy for the Highlands and Islands advocated by *The Oban Times*, are made part of the National development scheme. The good will and practical help of all our Highland and

Scottish Societies are needed, and called for, as well as the co-operation and assistance from Gaels and friends within the Highland area: given these the new deal and all it implies can be accomplished.

Notice of the meeting hereafter to be called will be advertised in the Highland and Glasgow press.

September, 1935.

'Modern Highland Problems', *British Medical Journal*, 2 (9 Dec. 1905), 999

In a lecture recently delivered before the Glasgow High School Gaelic class, Dr Lachlan Grant of Ballachulish said that at the opening of the twentieth century every country in the world found itself confronted with social and economic problems of the deepest import, and the Highlands had their share of burning questions awaiting solution to enable the people to live that large and rounded life demanded by true civilisation. The first problem to be solved was 'freeing the land.' Land nationalisation simply meant that the nation took over the land at a fair valuation, and the purchase money was crystallised in the form of Consols. There would be a central land office with departments and branches, whose business it would be to develop the natural resources of the country and probably agriculture would require to be a State industry. Afforestation would be an important branch in itself. Whatever plans might be suggested to solve the land problem, emigration certainly was not one of them. Emigration simply meant exporting the best bone and muscle of the population, which ought to be considered a portion of the real wealth of the country, thus leaving more and more of the physically degenerated population at home. No one could believe that emigration was good for the Highlands during the clearances or since, and he thought they would also agree that what was wanted was a vast increase in the population of the straths and hills that at one time furnished homes for many thousands of sturdy Highlanders. Instead of spending £300,000 to take 15,000 families to Australia, as recently proposed by General Booth, it would be more sensible to adopt the plan of Mr Fels to spend that sum in settling the people at home. Neither exporting people nor limiting families would solve any of the bread and butter problems. They must get to the root of the evils and discover how to extract the greatest amount of sustenance from the land with the least possible expenditure.

Sanitation was another important matter requiring the earnest attention of all local authorities in the Highlands as well as Parliament. Some districts, especially in the Western Highlands, were notoriously insanitary. The Local Government Board Inspectors, Dr Dittmar and Dr Miller, recently reported on the state of things in the Lews and other parts, and the state of things revealed was something incredible. They talked about the awful insanitary places not fit for cattle, and that many of the houses were uninhabitable and a disgrace to civilisation. From personal experience he could confirm these sad details made public. The housing problem was as acute in the remote Highlands as in our towns. Something would have to be done to put in operation the provisions of the law condemning insanitary houses or overcrowding in houses in the country. The law, as it stood, was quite sufficient to operate in condemning many dwellings, but the difficulty seemed to be in the lack of administrative adherence to the law, and he understood that many medical officers found their work much hampered by unprogressive County Councils and certain influences at work to prevent any action that might lead to an increase in the rates. There were, no doubt, parts of the country that were rated and taxed to the utmost already, but if more money was required to enable the people in those parts to live decent lives, then grants of money must be got from the national exchequer to make up any deficiency; that applied also to the Poor Law administration and educational matters.

The movement throughout the country for feeding school children and attention to the general health of boys and girls must also come into operation in the Highlands. Many schools in scattered districts were attended by children who walked as far as five or six miles, and in all such cases, provision should be made for supplying suitable meals and conveyance to their homes, and in some needy cases, even to supply them with their boots, shoes and overcoats. All children should be medically examined in schools periodically, and defective eye sight, bad hearing, infectious skin diseases etc, should be treated without delay.

The whole question of medical service required the attention of legislators, and in the Highlands every family should be entitled to medical attendance as a simple right of citizenship. This would be properly carried out only if the commercial system of fee-paying doctors were done away with, and instead a system of State medicine was established on a similar basis to the rate-supported fever isolation hospitals or asylums. The efficiency should not depend on the wealth or poverty of a district; it was a question of general efficiency throughout the country. For instance, they knew that the Government run scores of post-offices at a loss simply to meet the requirements and convenience of a district. And so with medical service, the well-to-do sections of the country should pay for the poorer parts. Good medical men could then be had to attend the more remote parts of the Highlands without any risk of leading a starving existence. On the one hand, they found many districts were quite neglected for want of doctors and capable, trustworthy nurses; while, on the other hand, scores of qualified medical men were vainly seeking employment of eking out a miserable pittance until they found a more lucrative post. Many doctors in poorer districts did a vast deal of work for no remuneration whatever.

More local industries were required in the Highlands. County councils might have their own farms and dairies, and supply the people with milk, butter, cheese and eggs, under best conditions. It was rather strange that milk should be scarce in the very districts where it was produced, and he knew from experience how difficult it was in some parts of the Highlands to get an adequate supply of good milk for the children. The Councils might even have their own sheep farms and weave cloth for the people, who would no longer require to import the shoddy rubbish now being used. All this might seem to them like the dreams from some Utopia, but many of them, knowing the trend of the times, saw that the awakening consciousness of the people would insist on the establishment of publicly-owned organisations to deal with the wants of the public.

Northern Times, 10 Oct. 1937

JUSTICE FOR THE HOMELAND

Big United Effort Wanted to Save Gaeldom
'Restore to them the Land of their Ancestors'
Stirring Address by Dr L. Grant, J.P.

A great gathering under the auspices of the Gaelic League of Scotland was held in the Christian Institute, Glasgow, on Tuesday evening, 5th October. The chief speaker was Dr Lachlan Grant, J.P., chairman of the Highland Development League. In the same hall Dr Grant addressed a meeting of Highlanders as far back as 11th November 1905, and he favoured the audience with an abstract from the forceful effort of those days [...]

After introductory remarks in Gaelic, Dr Grant continued:- I have often felt that social political endeavour is not the province of a medical man, but in the course of the life's work in the Highlands I have been so appalled by the continued physical and racial decline that I considered it my duty to sound the alarm, indicate basic causes and suggest remedies for its arrest. I thank you for inviting me to address you this evening. Now I thought you might like to hear something about an organisation whose aims and policy are along the same lines although perhaps different channels to those of the Gaelic League of Scotland. I refer to the Highland Development League. The League is almost two years old, and I consider that this time – during the autumn months when propaganda effort is inclined to lag a bit – is quite an opportune time for analysis, in so far as it spurs us on to further effort.

'The Highland Problem'

We have at least focused considerable attention on 'The Highland Problem'. More speeches have been made on it, and, as you are aware, further committees are inquiring into it; but are we any nearer a solution? We must remember that during the last hundred years a multitude of speeches, a score or so of committees and several officially appointed Government commissions have left our problem still unsolved, because there has been a lack of determined united effort on the part of the Highland people themselves to demand, enforce and uphold their rights. Our problem has been created and has remained unsolved largely because of our own lack of intelligent action and it will never be solved till the Highland and Scots people prove by their attitude that the solution is to them the first and most important question. It is really a Scottish National question. Socially, culturally and economically the Highland structure is approaching collapse. Half-hearted efforts cannot save it. The crash is inevitable unless we can have an united front of Gaeldom which alone can prevent it. We must have a complete re-awakening of racial consciousness, engendered rather by a material rather than a sentimental conception of our national worth. Given this new spirit and a combined front we would certainly be on the right road towards achieving a 'New Deal for the Highlands' in the shape of a complete re-organisation and reconstruction of the various aspects of our national economy. Half measures will not suffice. The same militancy and arrogance which characterised the forces which have drawn Gaeldom to its present low level must characterise any effort to revive it and the whole of Gaeldom, along with their friends and supporters must be the force behind this militant arrogance. These are ugly words, but friends, we are in an ugly position.

Injustice and Neglect

Our League owes its genesis not only to the alarm at the depletion of the Highland population, but to the firm conviction that justice will never be done to Highlanders unless a strong organisation takes the matter up with grim determination. Depopulation is chiefly due to the prolonged injustice and neglect by successive British Governments and unless Highlanders show more fight and spirit no effectual redress is ever likely to be forthcoming.

In connection with the lack of organisation of our Highland race, my attention has been drawn to the large number of Clan and Territorial societies devoted to its continuance. I agree that there are many such societies all over the world, but I submit that their record in the fight for Highland reconstruction and the saving of our glorious heritage is altogether an unenviable one. Neither singly nor collectively have the societies come fully into the open and supported the renaissance movement which, as you know, was set a-going in Glasgow, the chief centre of the Highland societies. At this stage I would like to say that the Clan MacColl Society there – a very young society – did give me a 'preliminary' platform for a lecture and discussion on 'Our Highland Heritage in danger – a call to action'. But the result of this effort was disappointing. Of the 70,000 Gaels and their relations in the City of Glasgow, only a mere handful appeared to be interested. Then I gave out to the Press 'A New Deal for the Highlands' which caught the eye of a well-known London Scot, Colonel Campbell Galbraith, who was responsible, with the assistance of some friends, for its publication. The brochure included a 'forcible' forward by Mr William Power. After this had appeared the committee of the Gaelic League of Scotland invited me to the Caledonian Night in St Andrew's Hall, where a short address on the 'New Highland Movement' was given. About this time the intensive propaganda undoubtedly gave a fillip to the movement and I addressed a meeting convened by the Highland Society of Carlisle. Then the Scottish Group in the Forum Club, London, asked for an address on the

Highlands and Islands problem. These were all interesting and, I think, helpful nights, in so much as they ventilated the Gaels' biggest problem.

Now, the excuse for not taking up this question is generally that the Societies wish to avoid political issues. Politics or no politics, their attitude is indefensible, and I feel pretty certain that an examination of most of their constitutions would rather justify Highland Development League affiliation than otherwise.

We are aware, of course, that such bodies are numerous furth of Scotland, in London and other English towns, also in every part of the Commonwealth overseas, but, in spite of annual spates of sentimental oratory and social functions galore, they have as yet given very little practical help to the efforts made for their rehabilitation of the homeland of their race.

Most disappointing of all so far is the lack of response in the great city of Glasgow, with its legion of Highland Societies and its multitude of Gaels and their descendants.

Out of Touch with the People

As a result of their indifference, most of the members appear to be quite out of touch with the people and conditions at home, and those who profess to know something about the actual situation are mostly apathetic and at times even unsympathetic, finding it easier to shut their eyes to the true position.

Let us consider for a moment the procedure at a so-called 'annual gathering'. The chairman, surrounded by a large platform party, is usually a prominent and successful Highlander, and I take it that his presence on a Highland platform signifies his interest in his country and its race. Yet how many chairmen ever refer to the Highland problem, or make one practical suggestion for its solution? I refuse to believe that most of these ladies and gentlemen do not know of its existence, and I submit that ignoring it does not contribute towards any solution – rather the reverse. Social and economic affairs in these materialistic days are often of much more importance to the Highlander than the eulogies of scenery, language, music, Jacobitism, kilts and Tir nam Og, which are the hardy annuals which we have come to expect. Gaeldom looks to the Highland Societies, as already organised units of Highland opinion, for a lead towards economic and social redress, but 'The hungry sheep look up and are not fed.'

A Major Issue for the Race

The unhelpful attitude of An Comunn Gaidhealach to our Highland problem has already been frequently referred to. It will always remain a mystery, in view of the steady decline of our race and the decay of our glorious heritage, how An Comunn in view of its objects can justify its refusal to give its support to an organised effort to secure reconstruction of our homeland. Many of the Highland Societies are affiliated to this organisation and I have no doubt a strong lead from the parent body would have been sufficient to ensure their following, but that lead was not forthcoming. Such an attitude to Highland development is very difficult to understand. An Comunn has no policy of its own in what should be to it, what is certainly a major issue for our race and the Gaelic language, and it is making no effort to support a kindred body, on the success of whose policy depends very largely the future of all An Comunn stands for. It would appear that the interminable singing which engages so much of its time, as well as that of the Highland Societies, is to be the death knell of Gaeldom. None of the songs you will notice incite us to arise and demand redress. The spirit of the race is largely broken. We are just on a par with the crooners who sing of our 'Misty Islands'. To be enthusiastic about Gaelic music and culture without a parallel enthusiasm for Highland development and reconstruction seems to me to be altogether illogical. People professing cultural enthusiasm should be in the forefront of the economic fight for the rehabilitation of the Highlands. The fact that culture and economic freedom and security go hand in hand in unequivocal. (Applause).

Church Leaders Waking Up

In a recent editorial in a leading Highland newspaper, it was stated when commenting on the Church of Scotland Moderator's able address at this year's General Assembly that 'a land which offers no reward to industry and no opportunity to enterprise, is a land where spiritual interests must soon wither and decay.' This is true. It is interesting to see our Church leaders waking up. Why not other Scottish leaders as well?

I have already suggested that the spirit of the race seems to be broken. Evidence of this is the lack of energy, initiative and enterprise which is often so characteristic of Highland life. Proof of this lack of 'push' is to be found in the apathy and indifference of most of our people to the serious plight of their homeland. I submit that this decline of racial consciousness is a result rather than a cause of our social decline. And I sometimes wonder if we can blame our own people altogether for this weak and hesitating attitude, as there is no doubt that a deliberate and calculated policy ruined Scotland. What I refer to is obvious. First you have the uncalled for brutalities following the '45, the chief object being to smash the race. And all along you have policies, or the lack of them, which compelled the Highland people to clear out, in fact, they were driven out, and in the clearances special attention was given to make sure of the Gaelic speaking people, so that they would not escape. Again, there was no other section of people in Europe at that time who were so completely broken and driven out, and this in spite of the fact that Highlanders on the whole were a God-fearing type of people. In fact, the whole thing is so damnable that it will forever remain a mystery why they did not form secret societies and turn on their persecutors. (Applause).

I think it can be stated that the origin of Highland decay and decline dates from the risings of 1715 and especially of 1745. Into the rights or otherwise of these causes it is not necessary for me to enter further tonight but I think that whatever has been said to the contrary, the fundamental reason for the '45 was not so much the glamour of Prince Charlie as smouldering resentment against the closure of the Scottish Parliament and the loss of our status as an independent nation. Up to this time the chiefs and clans had a tolerable existence and a comparative degree of security in the land of their forefathers. To their descendants they bequeathed a reputation, language and culture of which we should be proud, but which we as a race are apparently unable to maintain, as without doubt all the things which constitute our national heritage are threatened with extinction.

A Poisonous Fallacy

The spirit of the present generation of the race, then, is still much too frequently the expression of hopelessness. Neglect, misrule, cruel oppression and forced emigration have taken their toll. The best brain and muscle of the Highlands has been too often compelled to leave the homeland, and our more enviable racial attributes have gone with them. Emigration and the misrule which gave rise to it have intensified our poverty, culturally and materially, and have depressed our people. Someone has summarised as follows: 'Emigration has but one result – an impoverished nation. It never solves a nation's problems, nor cures its ills.

It is a poisonous fallacy which none but Scotland's enemies will support, a policy of despair which every friend of Scotland will oppose.'

If emigration had been a cure we would now be at the 'peak' of prosperity. What have we for it? An area now largely derelict and fallow which several generations ago was the homeland of a hardy and much respected race which lived in comparative security.

Friends, as has been pointed out, 'The true greatness of a race is determined not by the number of its exiles toiling to develop foreign lands, nor by its deserted countrysides and silent straths and glens, but by a country fully populated by a strong and virile people, confident and secure in the prosperity which, can and must derive from the fullest development of our own natural resources.' (Applause).

Lack of Change

Now regarding self-decimation in the race, the chief offenders are the so-called successful exiles, emigrants or immigrants, who have usually made good in the Colonies or in the larger English or southern cities. And they should really be the men to whom we should look for all possible support in our renaissance movement. But I fear support shall not come from that quarter. For example, how many Highlanders have risen to positions of eminence, even to Cabinet rank, and not one has made the slightest effort to help the Highlands or Highlanders. Why is it too that the average businessman, while professing sympathy, is so very reluctant to give us any practical help, and why in so many cases are they even hostile or apathetic? If these men lack merely courage to embrace our cause then let them help in other ways, e.g. financially.

Resources Needed for Development

The New Deal for the Highlands organisation aims at enlisting Highlanders and those who support our aims from everywhere, and, as its principal object is to apply pressure on the 'powers that be' it is necessary for the League to have as you will see, widespread membership. Sinews of war are also required in the shape of cash in order to run the Highland Development League. I read lately in the Press about some unknown friend handing over in 'trust' to Earl Baldwin a sum of a quarter of a million pounds to be used for strengthening further the 'ties' of Empire. Would, friends, that some kind and even anonymous Celt or Scot give or do something in the way of furthering and strengthening our League's resources, in order that we might be in a better position to help our 'beloved Highlands.'

Potentialities of the Highlands

Mr Wm Murray Morrison, a London Gael, conferred an undoubted benefit on the Highlands and Islands when he established the thriving aluminium industry in the central Highlands. Here is an example which other successful Highlanders might emulate: a few such actions would be more valuable for the future of the Highlands than a century of high sounding but empty oratory, to which we are accustomed at Highland gatherings in Glasgow and elsewhere. I think there is little doubt about the potentialities of the Highlands, if only we could get talk superseded by action. I believe that the Highlands of Scotland could be made comparatively prosperous, were the Government immediately compelled to take the matter earnestly in hand. All members of Highland Societies could and should do something according to their status and talents and try and rehabilitate this wonderful half of Scotland, and I believe the energetic branch of the Highland Development League in Glasgow this winter intends approaching all the societies to 'pull their weights' collectively. As Captain D. Munro, C.M.G, R.N., an enthusiastic member of our Association, wrote recently: 'Go where you will, Highlanders will be found occupying responsible positions and leaders of men and affairs. They have been distinguished in art, literature, exploration and war, and it is the proud boast of thousands throughout the world that their fathers, mothers, grandmothers or other distant ancestor was of Highland origin. Is the race which has done this worth preserving? I leave the answer to my readers.'

A Sound Land System

I have consistently stressed the great necessity for any successful scheme of Highland reconstruction to have as its basis a sound 'land' system.

We are all agreed that 'back to the land' is a pressing need of the times, and one of the essential steps in combating physical degeneration. Naturally all men cannot work on the land, but there are thousands suited for agricultural pursuits who are only too eager to return to country life, if reasonable facilities be given, and thousands more who are compelled to leave the country would I think, gladly remain if encouraged to do so. With plenty of idle men and thousands of idle acres, both in the Highlands and the Lowlands of Scotland, it should not be an insoluble problem to bring the two together for the people's well being and national prosperity. Otherwise, if depopulation of rural districts continues, and if waste of town life be not fully made up, we are bound to go under as a great nation, and especially if our sturdy emigrants continue going forth to feed foreign countries and rising colonies. A large robust population in the British Isles is absolutely necessary to grow more food and make us more self-supporting, to provide a healthy stock as the nation's backbone, and to make good the inevitable wastage going on under urban conditions. Our population problem all over presents many different aspects. 'It is indeed one of the most important problems that now confronts the whole British people.' Co-operation in farming, more land holdings, increased attention to scientific agriculture are all hopeful signs of the times.

The 'Sanctuary of the Stag'

The true welfare of the Scottish state in common with others, demands a higher population on the soil and considerably more production of fresh home products, including various kinds of fruits and vegetables. (Applause).

The truth about the Highland Land system is that the people have too often been relegated to the wind-swept, barren, rocky, unproductive parts, or have been driven off or encouraged to leave the land. Take even the recent 'rating decisions' on crofters' houses, which apparently do involve great hardship on many of the poorer crofters and have been justly receiving great criticism in the Press. No offer or any inducement worth while has been made to make life easier for smallholders, crofters and cottars. And many of the present day questionings and doubtings by some hostile people are indulged in by these opponents and reactionaries, and especially by those who would perhaps rather see the land in the Highlands still the 'sanctuary of the stag' and preserved for sport than full of thriving, busy, though small towns.

Sad Hearts and Broken Lives

May I briefly mention here that in this very building on the 11th November 1905, whilst addressing the Glasgow High School Gaelic Class ceilidh, I made the following remarks – the title of the address was that of 'Modern Highland Problems':- 'Whatever plans may be suggested to solve the land question, emigration is certainly not one of them. Emigration simply means exporting the best bone and muscle of our population which ought to be considered a portion of the real wealth of the country, thus leaving more and more of the physically degenerated at home.' No one can believe that emigration was good for the Highlands during the clearances or since and I think you will also agree that what we want is a vast increase in the population of the straths and hills that at one time furnished homes for many thousand sturdy Highlanders. Perhaps I may be allowed to give an illustration of what I say, drawn from Loch Awe side, the facts of which may be known to some of you here. The usual wealthy gentleman bought up so many square miles there, and immediately notice was given to all the people on the ground to clear out with their stock, bag and baggage. The consequence is, that particular neighbourhood is practically depopulated, and doubtless, among the scattered residents there have been many sad hearts and broken lives. Amongst them were three poor old women who had lived all their days on their little crofts, and I am informed that one of them took her expulsion so much to heart that she passed to the Land of True Freedom before the limit of the legal notice had expired. Now, in the name of common humanity, are there any conceivable rights of property that can justify such ante-social, cruel and unpatriotic action towards helpless people? Is this not a case where Government action is urgently demanded? Are the Scottish Highlands to be nothing better than the sporting ground of the world's plutocrats, and is our beautiful country to be largely turned into a huge playground, at the mercy of those who have the dollars? Are there not some things that money should never be able to buy? Why should people be compelled to leave the land of their forefathers to make room for sheep and deer? If some say it is the law of the land, then the sooner the law is amended in the interests of the people at large the better for our country's future. I quite admit there are some cases where extermination and capacity are not the leading characteristics of landowners and where consideration is extended to the vested rights of the crofters, farmers and others, sons and daughters of the soil following in the footsteps of their forefathers, and we also know there are some deer forests that are quite natural to the configuration of the country. Let the deer roam through them by all means. (Applause).

It is, of course, a difficult problem, and can only be met by sincere and determined practical, sympathetic patriots, armed with considerable powers, and financial and technical assistance.

Agricultural Workers

Now, one important point which must be recognised in this question of the land is the disrepute into which agriculture has fallen in the Highlands and Islands, and, of course, elsewhere as well. This is largely due to the condition under which the agricultural workers are compelled to work and live. Small wonder at the reluctance of men and women to follow the oldest and most natural of all occupations. Wages, working conditions and social amenities for all types of workers, especially in the big centres, have been improved vastly during the last fifty years, but agriculture has lagged behind. Agricultural workers' wages and conditions are in many cases deplorable in comparison with the returns of industrial and municipal workers. What has all this done? It has tended to create a false impression that agriculture is one of the unskilled and less important occupations. But it must be realised that land work is absolutely essential for national continuance, and those embracing it must be given status and returns commensurate with their contribution to the national well-being. At the inauguration of the Fort William branch of the Highland Development League last winter, I said that a largely industrialised country such as ours which is so much dependent on import trade for food, is especially so in an international crisis. Despite adverse climate conditions, and with the resources of modern scientific agriculture, a considerable area of Gaeldom now lying derelict could be made to produce many of the urgent necessities. Meanwhile the Highlands and Islands, a great potential source of agricultural produce, has been permitted to continue in decline. It is indeed a sad commentary on the myopia of our statesmen and Governments. It even savours of lack of common sense. Again, in a recent article by Mr James Leatham, he states that 'Germany's land is over 90% in use. With it she withstood a siege (1914–18) but a beleaguered Britain would be starving in a few weeks.'

The Tourist Industry

Let me now touch on another subject. You know that recently we have heard much of the possibilities of the tourist industry in the Highlands. The fact that such irresponsible talk has been let loose about the possibilities of the so-called tourist industry is proof that the question has never been seriously considered.

Within reasonable proportions a tourist industry is quite all right and helpful in its own way – I am not condemning it in total – but as a staple industry it is impossible. In fact, it is ridiculous to refer to it as an industry which at best would not maintain more than a fraction of our people for a very few months each year, at a kind of work which is largely alien to the whole tradition of our race. After making the fullest allowances for the business, it is obvious to those who know the Highlands and the Highlanders that the greatly boosted possibilities of the tourist industry is merely an empty shell.

The hotel and boarding house business has undoubtedly its own most useful place in the scheme of things, but to put it forward as a serious proposition in Highland development is almost bordering on absurdity. The sort of flunkying work which is associated with this industry is largely alien and objectionable to Highlanders. This is certainly work for which the Highlander is unsuited. One does not object to our visitors, the temporary presence of the increased transit services. Indeed, we feel highly honoured and pleased that visitors should deem our beauty spots worth sharing with us. We appreciate too the part Messers David MacBrayne and other tourist concerns are playing in the development of the tourist industry. Their finely appointed modern steamers and buses laden with happy holiday makers are 'bright spots' during the short summer season. This firm is aware of the Highland problem. In its broader aspects, and its chairman Sir Alfred Read, has supported the Highland Development League in a most practical manner [sic]. Would, as already mentioned, that some others of the business fraternity would show the same foresight and sympathy. (Applause).

But, friends, making the question of catering to holiday visitors a steady, staple industry is so ridiculous as to not merit serious discussion. With the tourist industry as the main flank in a Highland reconstruction programme, I would safely forecast the disappearance of the Gael and his language and tradition in one or two generations. At its best the tourist industry can never be more than a useful and important side-line, and can never be accepted as a complete solution for the fullest development of our native resources. No nation can thrive or flourish if its roots are to be entirely nurtured and if its existence to depend on the amount of cash it can extract from visitors, and I am just a little bit surprised that the Rt. Hon. Mr Tom Johnston, M.P. should have – apparently from one of the Press reports of his speech at one of the Highland Development League meetings in Glasgow – so energetically stressed this plan.

Hikers, the caravaners and sportsmen must to a large extent take a back seat when considering the question of Highland development.

You will, I feel sure, then agree that the tourist industry cannot alone be the salvation of the Highlands, perhaps it may be that I rate its usefulness too low. As it is worked at present it seems to me to lack organisation, good sense and the economic bond with agriculture and local industry, all of which I understand it has in Norway, where it is definitely in its right place.

Prosperity on their own Soil

The guiding principle of all true reformers must be to secure every possible opportunity, as well as the highest standards of prosperity for all Highlanders on their own soil and all other interests should be very largely subordinated.

We League members believe the possibilities connected with land settlement, fisheries in all its branches, the development and the use of the immense shores of water power, mineral development, tweed making, poultry rearing, and the tourist and many other industries are very considerable, and with efficient and up to date transport facilities on land and water, we are confident that the Highlands and Islands can be restored to a state of great prosperity. We wish to see ensured to the Highland area every available opportunity to renew its life and establish it on a permanent basis that will endure through the generations to come. (Applause).

Many years of misgovernment and neglect have drained the Highlands of their best stock, and practically dried up its natural capital resources, and left it without the finance necessary even for moderate development.

The greatest service, therefore, that Scotsmen – Highlanders and Lowlanders – can render to their native country and the British Commonwealth is to combine with enthusiasm to ensure the fullest reconstruction of the Highlands until it can be said with confidence that every possible rood is maintaining its man.

Reconstruct the Homeland

As the Highlands and their people have been sacrificed on the altars of causes not their own for 200 years, common justice demands that a substantial financial grant should be made for a period of years to reconstruct and re-people the homeland of the Gael.

The important factor, however, to remember is that neither grants nor anything else will be considered, unless an atmosphere can be created, which will convince our rulers that procrastination and evasion have just gone too far. As I mentioned in a previous lecture, 'some people fail to realise or take into account that the idea of securing these grants is to restore life to a seriously ill, almost moribund patient, and that after putting him on his feet again, he will be expected, and should too, I believe, be able to live without outside assistance, the normal, vigorous life of a self-supporting individual.'

Our problems are indeed big ones, and we do want people who will think them out to their very roots.

The initiative, energy and brain power of the Scot, and particularly the Highlander, has been largely devoted to the service and development of the Empire, with the inevitable moral, spiritual and economic loss to their own land and race.

Afforestation

Let me now draw your attention for the moment to the important question of afforestation. Some believe that this is a good thing – a suitable industry for the Highlands. I agree, but with reservations. Afforestation should never be permitted on arable land, or on land fit for farm grazing and stock rearing. You might think that that goes without saying, but you would be very much surprised if you knew the part that afforestation has played and is still playing in the vast diminution of stock in the Highlands. It might be pertinent to examine possible Highland industries and note the reservations which must be placed in their establishment or development, but I do not propose to do so tonight. But if health and opportunity permit I hope to say something later on in the year.

Now, the time allotted for my talk is wearing on, and before I stop I would just like to refer to one or two sentences which appeared in the 'New Deal' brochure.

One of them is the following: 'That the strength of the real Scottish and Highland character can never reach their maximum unless the power and freedom to administer and develop the potentialities and resources of our own land are in the hands of our own people.' And another sentence which follows is this: 'Here is the secret of our deserted Highland glens and straths, the dispersion of the Gael, and the decline of Scotland's position in every way.'

A National Cure Wanted

I still believe the foregoing to be ever so true. We want, then, to see our own Parliament in session and at work at our problems in Edinburgh, the capital of our nation.

May I quote again briefly in support of these views the following: 'The position as regards all those things for which the Gael stands is exceedingly grave; the tendency of the Gaelic-speaking population is downwards. If the cause is to succeed the rising generation must be imbibed through their early training with true Scottish spirit. Men with Scottish minds must apply themselves to Scottish problems; the opportunities for our own people must be increased to the maximum on our own soil. Then, and not till then, can be established those things for which the supporters of the Gaelic movement profess to stand.' So wrote that patriotic Scot, Mr Angus Clark, a former President of the Gaelic Society of London.

I agree with him entirely – a national defect requires a national remedy, a national disease, a national cure. Any Government of a nation must be in the most intimate relationship with all the activities of the people.

We all know that in its language, the soul of the race is enshrined, but, as is to be expected, the decrease of population has produced a rapid decline in the Gaelic language and, despite the efforts made for its preservation by your goodselves and others, it is obvious that unless you save the people you cannot save the tongue. It is unfortunate that in spite of all these serious aspects, the apathy and indifference of many Highlanders is a very serious hindrance to reforms. This despairing indifference – in spite of numerous glowing orations at Highland Gatherings – is strange.

Broadcasting Programmes
In Scotland too, we are suffering from not having full control of our own broadcasting programmes. Without doubt much good work could be done through the wireless to enlighten and interest the Highland and Scots people about their problems and how best to solve them. Whatever opinions we may hold regarding the need of Scottish autonomy, I am convinced that, as regards broadcasting, the sooner we are free from any form of London control, the better it will be for our Scottish land and country. Everything should be given from the Scottish standpoint. No country can be properly served by this great invention unless it has the power to give free and full expression to its own views. The Highlands then wants more use of its own 'station', e.g. we must have incessant pro-Highland propaganda of all kinds, drawing attention to our plight and the 'powers that be' to the clamorous intensity of our demands. We want a constant series of lectures on the latest methods of cultivating and getting the best results from the soil, Highland and Scottish history,

the history of the Gaelic language, the music and culture since Malcolm Canmore, and all kinds of ideas aiming at the fullest development in the economic and social life of the people. Further developments should be discussed and our gaze concentrated as much as possible on homeland opportunities. The future rulers of Scotland must put Scotland and the Scots first and foremost and consign to the scrapheap the humbugs and cant about pioneers and big positions outside Scotland. Let those with adventurous minds roam as they will, but Scotland's policy should be every rood shall maintain its man.

At the moment, however, I am more concerned about activating the British Government, whose craven duty it is to re-organise Gaeldom. I am, however, very sceptical of the results. We have trusted the Government for the last one hundred years and what has our trust brought in? Behold the result! Nothing. And we can go on trusting them for another hundred years, and the answer will still be the same, unless we can by our strong and vigorous action impress our rulers that the indifference of the past will no longer be tolerated.

It cannot be pointed out too often, or too strongly, that no depressed or distressed area can show a greater claim on the attention of the Government than the Highlands. This area reconstructed and revived would become Scotland's most valuable asset, impregnable in war and prosperous in peace.

The Rights of the Highlands
Our League, then, must be made strong enough to compel any party in power to take up seriously the rights of the Highlands. This all parties have hitherto failed to do, and it is not likely that any party will ever do it unless there is some Scottish organisation strong enough to goad them into action. Perhaps I am wrong, I hope so, but in the meantime let us be up and doing – so come along and help.

Any Highlander you meet will admit that our race is not organised, but unfortunately, as I have so often said to you this evening, the majority don't seem to worry about it. They may do so when it is too late; and after all, if the Gaels themselves and their friends do not move in the matter who else will ever do so?

Intense Propaganda
Any movement for a complete cure of the Highlands and Islands' conditions must be preceded by intense propaganda for the education of the

Gaels themselves to the extreme urgency and great importance of the new Highland movement.

If you will pardon the reiteration, let me insist once more on the dire necessity of organising the Scottish race and to bring this consciousness of disorganisation properly and seriously home to them, so that it would be omnipresent in the minds of all Highland, all Lowland, London and other Scots, and act as a spur to achieve that unity of purpose and combination which alone is so essential to our task.

New Day of Hope and Opportunity

We members of the Highland Development League, its Council and its able Secretary, Mr Donald MacKay, wish to see an organisation which will have the fullest regard to all Gaelic interests – a real forum of Gaeldom. In it we aim at shoulder to shoulder action on behalf of our Highlands and Islands. In this connection all the Highland societies could do a great deal to help. They could continue their useful cultural activities and entertainments as before – perhaps even more so – but they would affiliate to and help on the work of the Highland Development League. Our League is a collective organisation and is not out for idle or ornamental purposes. We are really skirmishers trying to clear the way, doing spade work for the fullest reconstruction of our Motherland. We wish to bring into our ranks men and women especially of the rising generation. For this we require the driving force and sustained enthusiasm that comes from strong faith in a great national movement, and surely the regeneration and rehabilitation of Gaeldom is a great cause.

Let us convince, then, our fellow countrymen of the justice and extreme urgency of our movement and let us proceed with the enthusiasm and strength which unity begets. If our country is to be made the happy home of a peaceful and prosperous people this can only be achieved by the giving of more and more attention to those things which concern ourselves, and the giving of less attention to those extraneous matters which have so little bearing on our Scottish national life.

Let the 'powers that be' see that they have to face 'Clana na gaidheil re gualibh a-cheille.' Such, along with unflinching determination, and we shall have taken the first steps which will lead us to a new day of hope and opportunity. (Loud applause).

Index